Science HWK: Work on Posterbo[ard]
Due on 10th: outline or rough draft / brainstorm

Volcano project due February 21st

On the 14th:

ONE WEEK TIL
VOLCANO PROJECT

Render Packet
Due on 3...

16th or 17th
Bibliography Check

X X

I like scoth. Scothy, schotchy
Scotch! Here goes down.
Down into my belly

Scotch

Kirsten's B-day on the 17th.
Hola. Me llamo Margarita
Como et llamas?

17

Page 88.
"Discover"
Activity

Read & Answer
Review
Questions for
S-1 and bring
in Geodes

PRENTICE HALL

SCIENCE EXPLORER

Inside Earth

Prentice
Hall

Needham, Massachusetts
Upper Saddle River, New Jersey
Glenview, Illinois

Inside Earth

Book-Specific Resources

Student Edition
Annotated Teacher's Edition
Teaching Resources with Color Transparencies
Consumable and Nonconsumable Materials Kits
Guided Reading Audio CDs
Guided Reading Audiotapes
Guided Reading and Study Workbook
Guided Reading and Study Workbook, Teacher's Edition
Lab Activity Videotapes
Science Explorer Videotapes
Science Explorer Web Site at **www.phschool.com**

Program-Wide Resources

Computer Test Bank Book with CD-ROM
How to Assess Student Work
How to Manage Instruction in the Block
Inquiry Skills Activity Book
Integrated Science Laboratory Manual
Integrated Science Laboratory Manual, Teacher's Edition
Interactive Student Tutorial CD-ROM
Prentice Hall Interdisciplinary Explorations
Probeware Lab Manual
Product Testing Activities by Consumer Reports™
Program Planning Guide
Reading in the Content Area with Literature Connections
Resource Pro® CD-ROM (Teaching Resources on CD-ROM)
Science Explorer Videodiscs
Standardized Test Preparation Book
Student-Centered Science Activity Books
Teacher's ELL Handbook: Strategies for English Language Learners

Spanish Resources

Spanish Student Edition
Spanish Guided Reading Audio CDs with Section Summaries
Spanish Guided Reading Audiotapes with Section Summaries
Spanish Science Explorer Videotapes

Science Explorer Student Editions

From Bacteria to Plants

Animals

Cells and Heredity

Human Biology and Health

Environmental Science

Inside Earth

Earth's Changing Surface

Earth's Waters

Weather and Climate

Astronomy

Chemical Building Blocks

Chemical Interactions

Motion, Forces, and Energy

Electricity and Magnetism

Sound and Light

Cover: Lava flows down a mountainside on the Big Island of Hawaii.

Acknowledgments ••••••••••••••••••••••••••••••••

Activity on pages 108-109 is from *Exploring Planets in the Classroom*. Copyright by Hawaii Space Grant Consortium, based on experiments done by R. Fisk and D. Jackson, U.S. Geological Survey.

ISBN 0-13-054075-7
6 7 8 9 10   05 04 03

Program Authors

Michael J. Padilla, Ph.D.
Professor
Department of Science Education
University of Georgia
Athens, Georgia

Michael Padilla is a leader in middle school science education. He has served as an editor and elected officer for the National Science Teachers Association. He has been principal investigator of several National Science Foundation and Eisenhower grants and served as a writer of the National Science Education Standards.

As lead author of *Science Explorer,* Mike has inspired the team in developing a program that meets the needs of middle grades students, promotes science inquiry, and is aligned with the National Science Education Standards.

Ioannis Miaoulis, Ph.D.
Dean of Engineering
College of Engineering
Tufts University
Medford, Massachusetts

Martha Cyr, Ph.D.
Director, Engineering
   Educational Outreach
College of Engineering
Tufts University
Medford, Massachusetts

Science Explorer was created in collaboration with the College of Engineering at Tufts University. Tufts has an extensive engineering outreach program that uses engineering design and construction to excite and motivate students and teachers in science and technology education.

Faculty from Tufts University participated in the development of *Science Explorer* chapter projects, reviewed the student books for content accuracy, and helped coordinate field testing.

CHAPTER PROJECT

Book Author

Carole Garbuny Vogel
Science Writer
Lexington, Massachusetts

Contributing Writers

Holly Estes
Science Instructor
Hale Middle School
Stow, Massachusetts

Greg Hutton
Science and Health
   Curriculum Coordinator
School Board of
   Sarasota County
Sarasota, Florida

Lauren Magruder
Science Instructor
St. Michael's Country
   Day School
Newport, Rhode Island

Sharon M. Stroud
Science Instructor
Widefield High School
Colorado Springs,
   Colorado

Thomas R. Wellnitz
Science Instructor
The Paideia School
Atlanta, Georgia

Reading Consultant

Bonnie B. Armbruster, Ph.D.
Department of Curriculum
   and Instruction
University of Illinois
Champaign, Illinois

Interdisciplinary Consultant

Heidi Hayes Jacobs, Ed.D.
Teacher's College
Columbia University
New York, New York

Safety Consultants

W. H. Breazeale, Ph.D.
Department of Chemistry
College of Charleston
Charleston, South Carolina

Ruth Hathaway, Ph.D.
Hathaway Consulting
Cape Girardeau, Missouri

Tufts University Program Reviewers

Content Reviewers

Teacher Reviewers

Stephanie Anderson
Sierra Vista Junior
    High School
Canyon Country, California

John W. Anson
Mesa Intermediate School
Palmdale, California

Pamela Arline
Lake Taylor Middle School
Norfolk, Virginia

Lynn Beason
College Station Jr. High School
College Station, Texas

Richard Bothmer
Hollis School District
Hollis, New Hampshire

Jeffrey C. Callister
Newburgh Free Academy
Newburgh, New York

Judy D'Albert
Harvard Day School
Corona Del Mar, California

Betty Scott Dean
Guilford County Schools
McLeansville, North Carolina

Sarah C. Duff
Baltimore City Public Schools
Baltimore, Maryland

Melody Law Ewey
Holmes Junior High School
Davis, California

Sherry L. Fisher
Lake Zurich Middle
    School North
Lake Zurich, Illinois

Melissa Gibbons
Fort Worth ISD
Fort Worth, Texas

Debra J. Goodding
Kraemer Middle School
Placentia, California

Jack Grande
Weber Middle School
Port Washington, New York

Steve Hills
Riverside Middle School
Grand Rapids, Michigan

Carol Ann Lionello
Kraemer Middle School
Placentia, California

Jaime A. Morales
Henry T. Gage Middle School
Huntington Park, California

Patsy Partin
Cameron Middle School
Nashville, Tennessee

Deedra H. Robinson
Newport News Public Schools
Newport News, Virginia

Bonnie Scott
Clack Middle School
Abilene, Texas

Charles M. Sears
Belzer Middle School
Indianapolis, Indiana

Barbara M. Strange
Ferndale Middle School
High Point, North Carolina

Jackie Louise Ulfig
Ford Middle School
Allen, Texas

Kathy Usina
Belzer Middle School
Indianapolis, Indiana

Heidi M. von Oetinger
L'Anse Creuse Public School
Harrison Township, Michigan

Pam Watson
Hill Country Middle School
Austin, Texas

Activity Field Testers

Nicki Bibbo
Russell Street School
Littleton, Massachusetts

Connie Boone
Fletcher Middle School
Jacksonville Beach, Florida

Rose-Marie Botting
Broward County
    School District
Fort Lauderdale, Florida

Colleen Campos
Laredo Middle School
Aurora, Colorado

Elizabeth Chait
W. L. Chenery Middle School
Belmont, Massachusetts

Holly Estes
Hale Middle School
Stow, Massachusetts

Laura Hapgood
Plymouth Community
    Intermediate School
Plymouth, Massachusetts

Sandra M. Harris
Winman Junior High School
Warwick, Rhode Island

Jason Ho
Walter Reed Middle School
Los Angeles, California

Joanne Jackson
Winman Junior High School
Warwick, Rhode Island

Mary F. Lavin
Plymouth Community
    Intermediate School
Plymouth, Massachusetts

James MacNeil, Ph.D.
Concord Public Schools
Concord, Massachusetts

Lauren Magruder
St. Michael's Country
    Day School
Newport, Rhode Island

Jeanne Maurand
Glen Urquhart School
Beverly Farms, Massachusetts

Warren Phillips
Plymouth Community
    Intermediate School
Plymouth, Massachusetts

Carol Pirtle
Hale Middle School
Stow, Massachusetts

Kathleen M. Poe
Kirby-Smith Middle School
Jacksonville, Florida

Cynthia B. Pope
Ruffner Middle School
Norfolk, Virginia

Anne Scammell
Geneva Middle School
Geneva, New York

Karen Riley Sievers
Callanan Middle School
Des Moines, Iowa

David M. Smith
Howard A. Eyer Middle School
Macungie, Pennsylvania

Derek Strohschneider
Plymouth Community
    Intermediate School
Plymouth, Massachusetts

Sallie Teames
Rosemont Middle School
Fort Worth, Texas

Gene Vitale
Parkland Middle School
McHenry, Illinois

Zenovia Young
Meyer Levin Junior
    High School (IS 285)
Brooklyn, New York

Contents

Inside Earth

Activities

Interdisciplinary Activities

FOCUS ON FAULTS

"When I was about fourteen, my family was living in Taiwan," Geologist Carol Prentice recalls. "One day I was playing pinball, and a little earthquake happened. It tilted my pinball machine."

Unlike most people experiencing their first quake, her reaction was not fright but fascination. *What in the world is that?* I wondered. That was the first time I consciously remember thinking that earthquakes were something interesting." Later, she recalls, "When I was teaching earth science in high school, I realized that my favorite section to teach was on earthquakes and faults."

During an earthquake, forces from inside Earth fracture, or break, Earth's crust, producing a powerful jolt called an earthquake. As Earth's crust moves and breaks, it forms cracks called faults. Over the centuries, the faults may move again and again.

Geologist Carol Prentice climbs into these faults to study the soil and rocks. She hunts for clues about the history of a fault and estimates the risk of a serious earthquake in the future.

Carol Prentice studied geology at Humboldt State University and the California Institute of Technology. She is currently a Research Geologist for the United States Geological Survey in Menlo Park, California.

Finding Clues to Ancient Earthquakes

Today, Dr. Prentice is an expert in the field of paleoseismology. *Paleo* means "ancient" and *seismology* is "the study of earthquakes." So it's the study of ancient earthquakes. "Paleoseismologists search for evidence of earthquakes that happened hundreds or thousands of years ago," explains Dr. Prentice.

There are written records about earthquakes that happened years ago. But the real story of a quake is written in the rocks and soil. Years after an earthquake, wind, rain, and flowing water can wear the fault lines away from Earth's surface. Then the evidence of the quake is buried under layers of sediment. But the fault is still there.

The cracks of recent earthquakes, such as the Gobi-Altay fault shown here, are sometimes visible for hundreds of kilometers. Because this quake happened in the Mongolian desert, it is especially easy to see.

Choosing a Site

How do you pick a site to research? "First we study aerial photographs, geological maps, and satellite images of the fault line," Dr. Prentice explains. "We will have some sites in mind. Then, we go out and look at the sites and do some digging with a shovel to get samples."

"We look for places where sediments, such as sand and gravel, have been building up. If sediments have been depositing there for many thousands of years, you're likely to have a good record of prehistoric earthquakes at that site. When you dig, you're likely to see not only the most recent earthquake buried and preserved in the sediments, but also earlier earthquakes. That's a really good site." Once the site is established, the geological team begins digging a trench across the fault.

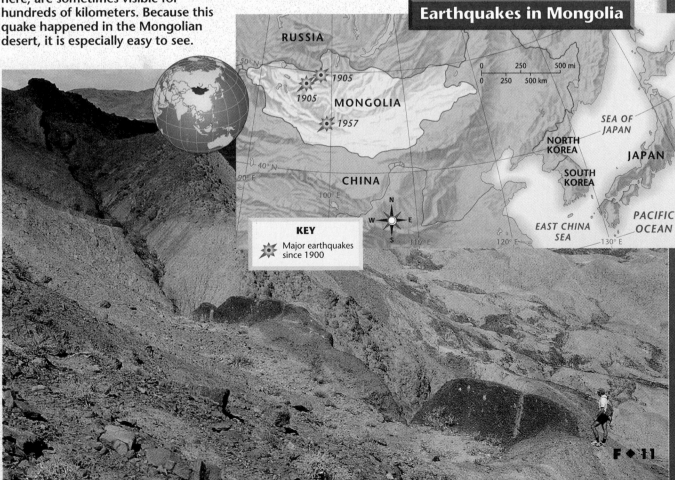

Earthquakes in Mongolia

RUSSIA

1905
1905 MONGOLIA
1957

CHINA

NORTH KOREA
SOUTH KOREA

SEA OF JAPAN

JAPAN

EAST CHINA SEA

PACIFIC OCEAN

0   250   500 mi
0   250   500 km

KEY

Major earthquakes since 1900

Working in the Trenches

What's it like to work in a spot where Earth's surface ruptured? Does Carol Prentice ever think that an earthquake might occur when she is digging in the fault? "It's always in the back of your mind when you are working in the trench," she admits.

But, she says, "The trenches are dangerous, not so much because there might be an earthquake while you are working there but because the trench can cave in. If a trench is 4 to 5 meters deep, or just over your head, it needs shores—braces and supports— or it might cave in. When sediments are soft, and the trench is deep, it's more likely to cave in. That could happen in a place like Mongolia."

Carol (in back) and another geologist in a deep trench.

In Mongolia, in northeast Asia, it's difficult for geologists to find the right materials to support a deep trench. It could cave in while someone is in it. "That would be very frightening," she says.

Looking at the Gobi-Altay Quake

Carol Prentice travels to earthquake sites around the world—Dominican Republic, Thailand, Mongolia—as well as to the San Andreas fault in California. One of Dr. Prentice's most recent research expeditions was to the site of the monster Gobi-Altay earthquake of 1957 in the Mongolian desert. In earthquakes like this one, the faults are easy to see. "We're taking a look at this Gobi Altay earthquake and seeing whether the next-to-last earthquake had the same pattern," Dr. Prentice says.

The faults of the Gobi-Altay earthquake are similar in some ways to the San Andreas fault and to the faults of other earthquakes in the United States. That's one of the reasons the Gobi-Altay is so interesting to geologists.

Interpreting the Data

When Dr. Prentice finds evidence of several earthquakes in one spot, she takes measurements that tell her when the layers of rocks, sand, and gravel were deposited and when they split. From that she knows when and how frequently earthquakes have occurred there.

She also determines how fast the opposite sides of the fault are slipping past each other. "Those two pieces of information— the dates of prehistoric earthquakes and the slip rate—are very, very important in trying to

String grid lines are used to map out sections of the trench.

Shores support the trench walls.

An earthquake is caused by movement on a fault deep beneath Earth's surface. If this movement is large enough, it can cause cracks in the ground surface. Over the years, layers of sediment are deposited on top of the crack. The next earthquake causes a new crack in the surface, and new sediments are deposited. By studying evidence of the cracks in these layers of sediment, geologists learn about past earthquakes along the fault.

figure out how dangerous a particular fault is," Dr. Prentice explains.

Since faults don't move every year, but over thousands of years, you can figure out the average slip per year and make some predictions. The faster the fault is moving, the greater the danger. "We can look at the landforms around a fault.

> ❝ . . . the real story of a quake is written in the rocks and soil. ❞

We can look at what our instruments record, and say: This is an active fault. Someday it might produce a big earthquake, but what we really want to know is when. Is that earthquake likely to happen in the next fifty years, in the next hundred years, or is it going to be a thousand years before the next big earthquake?"

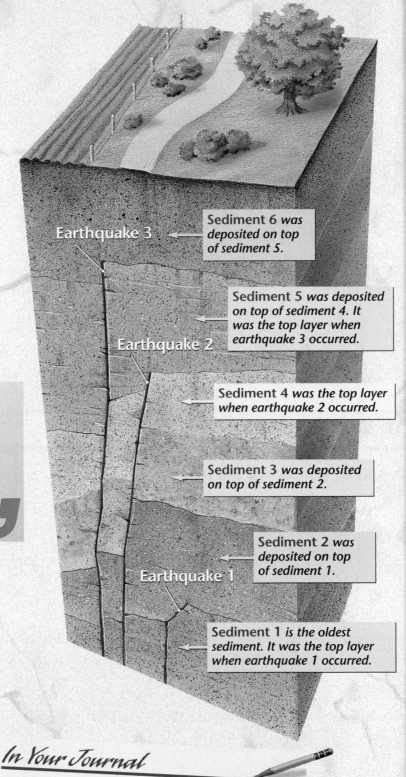

Earthquake 3

Sediment 6 *was deposited on top of sediment 5.*

Sediment 5 *was deposited on top of sediment 4. It was the top layer when earthquake 3 occurred.*

Earthquake 2

Sediment 4 *was the top layer when earthquake 2 occurred.*

Sediment 3 *was deposited on top of sediment 2.*

Sediment 2 *was deposited on top of sediment 1.*

Earthquake 1

Sediment 1 *is the oldest sediment. It was the top layer when earthquake 1 occurred.*

In Your Journal

Carol Prentice relies on close observation and making inferences in her study of earthquakes. Write a paragraph describing some of the other skills that Dr. Prentice needs to do her work as a paleoseismologist.

This is a satellite image of the San Francisco Bay area. The row of lakes below marks the line of the San Andreas fault, a crack in Earth's crust.

www.phschool.com

PROJECT 1

Cut-Away Earth

Along the San Andreas fault in California, two vast pieces of Earth's crust slowly slide past each other. In this chapter, you will learn how movements deep within Earth cause movements on the surface. These movements help to create mountains and other surface features. You will build a model that shows Earth's interior and how the interior affects the planet's surface.

Your Goal To build a three-dimensional model that shows Earth's surface features as well as a cutaway view of Earth's interior.

To complete this project, you must

◆ build a scale model of the layers of Earth's interior
◆ include at least three of the plates that form Earth's surface, as well as two landmasses or continents
◆ show how the plates push together, pull apart, or slide past each other and indicate their direction of movement
◆ label all physical features clearly
◆ follow the safety guidelines in Appendix A

Get Started Begin now by previewing the chapter to learn about Earth's interior. Brainstorm a list of the kinds of materials that could be used to make a three-dimensional model. Start a project folder in which you will keep your sketches, ideas, and any information needed to design and build your model.

Check Your Progress You will be designing and building your model as you study this chapter. To keep your project on track, look for Check Your Progress boxes at the following points.

Section 1 Review, page 24: Begin sketching and designing your model.
Section 4 Review, page 39: Revise your design and start building the base of your model.
Section 5 Review, page 47: Complete the final construction of your model.

Wrap Up At the end of the chapter (page 51), you will present your completed model to the class and discuss the features you included.

 SECTION 4 **Sea-Floor Spreading**

Discover **What Is the Effect of a Change in Density?**
Try This **Reversing Poles**
Skills Lab **Making Models: Modeling Sea-Floor Spreading**

 SECTION 5 **The Theory of Plate Tectonics**

Discover **How Well Do the Continents Fit Together?**
Sharpen Your Skills **Predicting**
Skills Lab **Observing: Hot Plates**

1 Earth's Interior

How Do Scientists Determine What's Inside Earth?

1. Your teacher will provide you with three closed film canisters. Each canister contains a different material. Your goal is to determine what is inside each canister—even though you can't directly observe what it contains.

2. Stick a label made from a piece of tape on each canister.

3. To gather evidence about the contents of the canisters, you may tap, roll, shake, or weigh them. Record your observations.

4. What differences do you notice between the canisters? Apart from their appearance on the outside, are the canisters similar in any way? How did you obtain this evidence?

Think It Over

Inferring Based on your observations, what can you infer about the contents of the canisters? How do you think scientists gather evidence about Earth's interior?

GUIDE FOR READING

◆ What does a geologist do?

◆ What are the characteristics of Earth's crust, mantle, and core?

Reading Tip Before you read, rewrite the headings in the section as what, how, or why questions. As you read, look for answers to these questions.

In November 1963, the people of Iceland got to see how the world begins in fire. With no warning, the waters south of Iceland began to hiss and bubble. Soon there was a fiery volcanic eruption from beneath the ocean. Steam and ash belched into the sky. Molten rock from inside Earth spurted above the ocean's surface and hardened into a small island. Within the next several years, the new volcano added 2.5 square kilometers of new, raw land to Earth's surface. The Icelanders named the island "Surtsey." In Icelandic mythology, Surtsey is the god of fire.

Figure 1 The island of Surtsey formed in the Atlantic Ocean.

The Science of Geology

Newspapers reported the story of Surtsey's fiery birth. But much of what is known about volcanoes like Surtsey comes from the work of geologists. **Geologists** are scientists who study the forces that make and shape planet Earth. Geologists study the chemical and physical characteristics of **rock,** the material that forms Earth's hard surface. They map where different types of rock are found on and beneath the surface. Geologists describe landforms, the features formed in rock and soil by water, wind, and waves. **Geologists study the processes that create Earth's features and search for clues about Earth's history.**

The modern science of **geology,** the study of planet Earth, began in the late 1700s. Geologists of that time studied the rocks on the surface. These geologists concluded that Earth's landforms are the work of natural forces that slowly build up and wear down the land.

Studying Surface Changes Forces beneath the surface are constantly changing Earth's appearance. Throughout our planet's long history, its surface has been lifted up, pushed down, bent, and broken. Thus Earth looks different today from the way it did millions of years ago.

Today, geologists divide the forces that change the surface into two groups: constructive forces and destructive forces. **Constructive forces** shape the surface by building up mountains and landmasses. **Destructive forces** are those that slowly wear away mountains and, eventually, every other feature on the surface. The formation of the island of Surtsey is an example of constructive forces at work. The ocean waves that wear away Surtsey's shoreline are an example of destructive forces.

Two hundred years ago, the science of geology was young. Then, geologists knew only a few facts about Earth's surface. They knew that Earth is a sphere with a radius at the equator of more than 6,000 kilometers. They knew that there are seven great landmasses, called **continents,** surrounded by oceans. They knew that the continents are made up of layers of rock.

Figure 2 The work of geologists often takes them outdoors—from mountainsides to caves beneath the surface. *Observing What are the geologists in each picture doing?*

Figure 3 This cave in Georgia may seem deep. But even a deep cave is only a small nick in Earth's surface.

These layers can sometimes be seen on the walls of canyons and the sides of valleys. However, many riddles remained: How old is Earth? How has Earth's surface changed over time? Why are there oceans, and how did they form? For 200 years, geologists have tried to answer these and other questions about the planet.

Finding Indirect Evidence One of the most difficult questions that geologists have tried to answer is, What's inside Earth? Much as geologists might like to, they cannot dig a hole to the center of Earth. The extreme conditions in Earth's interior prevent exploration far below the surface. The deepest mine in the world, a gold mine in South Africa, reaches a depth of 3.8 kilometers. But it only scratches the surface. You would have to travel more than 1,600 times that distance—over 6,000 kilometers—to reach Earth's center.

Geologists cannot observe Earth's interior directly. Instead, they must rely on indirect methods of observation. Have you ever hung a heavy picture on a wall? If you have, you know that you can knock on the wall to locate the wooden beam underneath the plaster that will support the picture. When you knock on the wall, you listen carefully for a change in the sound.

When geologists want to study Earth's interior, they also use an indirect method. But instead of knocking on walls, they use seismic waves. When earthquakes occur, they produce **seismic waves** (SYZ mik). Geologists record the seismic waves and study how they travel through Earth. The speed of these seismic waves and the paths they take reveal how the planet is put together. Using data from seismic waves, geologists have learned that Earth's interior is made up of several layers. Each layer surrounds the layers beneath it, much like the layers of an onion.

Checkpoint *What kind of indirect evidence do geologists use to study the structure of Earth?*

A Journey to the Center of the Earth

If you really could travel through these layers to the center of Earth, what would your trip be like? To begin, you will need a vehicle that can travel through solid rock. The vehicle will carry scientific instruments to record changes in temperature and pressure as you descend.

Temperature As you start to tunnel beneath the surface, you might expect the rock around you to be cool. At first, the surrounding rock is cool. Then at about 20 meters down your instruments report that the surrounding rock is getting warmer. For every 40 meters that you descend from that point, the temperature rises 1 Celsius degree. This rapid rise in temperature continues for several kilometers. After that, the temperature increases more slowly, but steadily.

Pressure During your journey to the center of Earth, your instruments also record an increase in pressure in the surrounding rock. The deeper you go, the greater the pressure. **Pressure** is the force pushing on a surface or area. Because of the weight of the rock above, pressure inside Earth increases as you go deeper.

As you go toward the center of Earth, you travel through several different layers. **Three main layers make up Earth's interior: the crust, the mantle, and the core. Each layer has its own conditions and materials.** You can see these layers in *Exploring Earth's Interior* on pages 22–23.

Language Arts
CONNECTION

Imagine taking a trip to the center of Earth. That's what happens in a novel written by Jules Verne in 1864. At that time, scientists knew almost nothing about Earth's interior. Was it solid or hollow? Hot or cold? People speculated wildly. Verne's novel, called *Journey to the Center of the Earth*, describes the adventures of a scientific expedition to explore a hollow Earth. On the way, the explorers follow caves and tunnels down to a strange sea lit by a miniature sun.

In Your Journal

Write a paragraph that describes the most exciting part of your own imaginary journey to Earth's center.

Pressure Increases

Depth
0
.5m
1m
1.5m
2m

Figure 4 The deeper this swimmer goes, the greater the pressure from the surrounding water. *Comparing and Contrasting* How is the water in the swimming pool similar to Earth's interior? How is it different?

The Crust

Your journey to the center of Earth begins in the crust. The **crust** is a layer of rock that forms Earth's outer skin. On the crust you find rocks and mountains. But the crust also includes the soil and water that cover large parts of Earth's surface.

This outer rind of rock is much thinner than what lies beneath it. In fact, you can think of Earth's crust as being similar to the paper-thin skin of an onion. The crust includes both the dry land and the ocean floor. It is thinnest beneath the ocean and thickest under high mountains. The crust ranges from 5 to 40 kilometers thick.

The crust beneath the ocean is called oceanic crust. Oceanic crust consists mostly of dense rocks such as basalt. **Basalt** (buh SAWLT) is dark, dense rock with a fine texture. Continental crust, the crust that forms the continents, consists mainly of less dense rocks such as granite. **Granite** is a rock that has larger crystals than basalt and is not as dense. It usually is a light color.

Figure 5 Two of the most common rocks in the crust are basalt and granite. **A.** The dark rock is basalt, which makes up much of the oceanic crust. **B.** The light rock is granite, which makes up much of the continental crust.

The Mantle

Your journey downward continues. At a depth of between 5 and 40 kilometers beneath the surface, you cross a boundary. Above this boundary are the basalt and granite rocks of the crust. Below the boundary is the solid material of the **mantle,** a layer of hot rock.

The crust and the uppermost part of the mantle are very similar. The uppermost part of the mantle and the crust together form a rigid layer called the **lithosphere** (LITH uh sfeer). In Greek, *lithos* means "stone." The lithosphere averages about 100 kilometers thick.

Figure 6 At the surface, Earth's crust forms peaks like these in the Rocky Mountains of Colorado. Soil and plants cover much of the crust.

Next you travel farther into the mantle below the lithosphere. There your vehicle encounters material that is hotter and under increasing pressure. In general, temperature and pressure in the mantle increase with depth. The heat and pressure make the part of the mantle just beneath the lithosphere less rigid than the rock above. Like road tar softened by the heat of the sun, the material that forms this part of the mantle is somewhat soft—it can bend like plastic.

This soft layer is called the **asthenosphere** (as THEHN uh sfeer). In Greek, *asthenes* means "weak." Just because *asthenes* means weak, you can't assume this layer is actually weak. But the asthenosphere is soft. The material in this layer can flow slowly.

The lithosphere floats on top of the asthenosphere. Beneath the asthenosphere, solid mantle material extends all the way to Earth's core. The mantle is nearly 3,000 kilometers thick.

✓ *Checkpoint* *How does the material of the asthenosphere differ from the material of the lithosphere?*

The Core

After traveling through the mantle, you reach the core. Earth's core consists of two parts—a liquid outer core and a solid inner core. The metals iron and nickel make up both parts of the core. The **outer core** is a layer of molten metal that surrounds the inner core. In spite of enormous pressure, the outer core behaves like a thick liquid. The **inner core** is a dense ball of solid metal. In the inner core, extreme pressure squeezes the atoms of iron and nickel so much that they cannot spread out and become liquid.

The outer and inner cores make up about one third of Earth's mass, but only 15 percent of its volume. The inner and outer cores together are just slightly smaller than the moon.

Sharpen your Skills

Creating Data Tables

ACTIVITY

Imagine that you have invented a super-strong vehicle that can resist extremely high pressure as it bores a tunnel deep into Earth's interior. You stop several times on your trip to collect data using devices located on your vehicle's outer hull. To see what conditions you would find at various depths on your journey, refer to *Exploring Earth's Interior* on pages 22–23. Copy the table and complete it.

Depth	Name of Layer	What Layer Is Made Of
20 km	Crust	Rocky water
150 km	Mantle	Silicon, iron oxygen, magnesium
2,000 km		
4,000 km		
6,000 km		

EXPLORING Earth's Interior

Earth's interior is divided into layers: the crust, mantle, outer core, and inner core. Although Earth's crust seems stable, the extreme heat of Earth's interior causes changes that slowly reshape the surface.

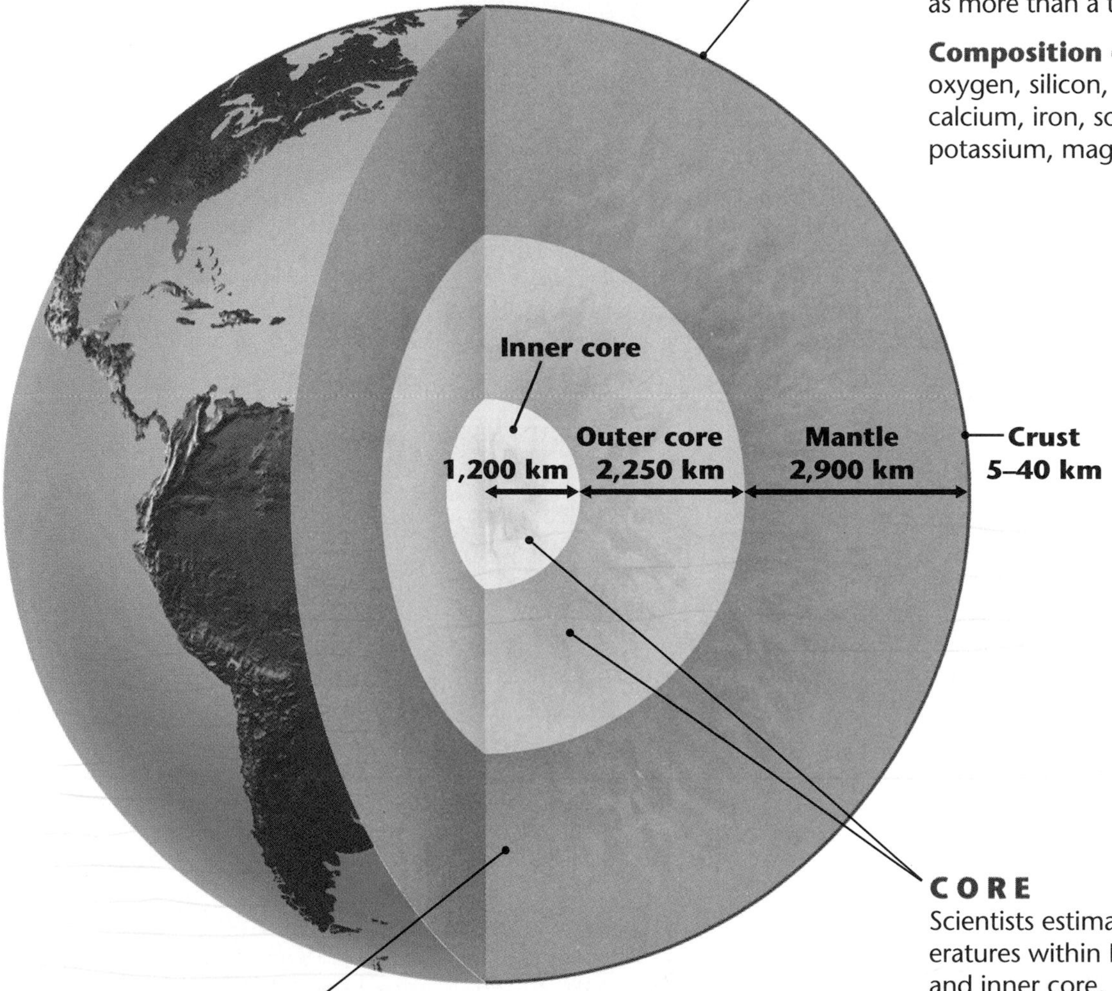

CRUST

The crust is Earth's solid and rocky outer layer, including both the land surface and the ocean floor. The crust averages 32 km thick. At the scale of this drawing, the crust is too thin to show up as more than a thin line.

Composition of crust:
oxygen, silicon, aluminum, calcium, iron, sodium, potassium, magnesium

Inner core

Outer core 2,250 km   **Mantle** 2,900 km   Crust 5–40 km

1,200 km

MANTLE

A trip through Earth's mantle goes almost halfway to the center of Earth. The chemical composition of the mantle does not change much from one part of the mantle to another. However, physical conditions in the mantle change because pressure and temperature increase with depth.

Composition of mantle:
silicon, oxygen, iron, magnesium

CORE

Scientists estimate that temperatures within Earth's outer core and inner core, both made of iron and nickel, range from about 2,000°C to 5,000°C. If these estimates are correct, then Earth's center may be as hot as the sun's surface.

Composition of core:
iron, nickel

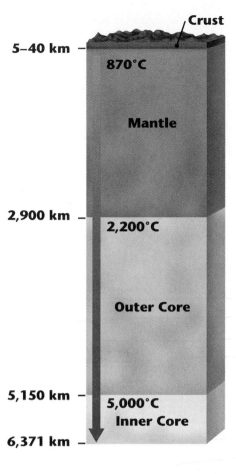

5–40 km —
870°C
Crust
Mantle

2,900 km —
2,200°C
Outer Core

5,150 km —
5,000°C
Inner Core

6,371 km —

◄ CROSS-SECTION FROM SURFACE TO CENTER

From Earth's surface to its center, the layers of Earth's interior differ in their composition, temperature, and pressure. Notice how temperature increases toward the inner core.

CRUST-TO-MANTLE

The rigid crust and lithosphere float on the hot, plastic material of the asthenosphere. Notice that continental crust, made mostly of granite, is several times thicker than oceanic crust, made mostly of basalt. ▼

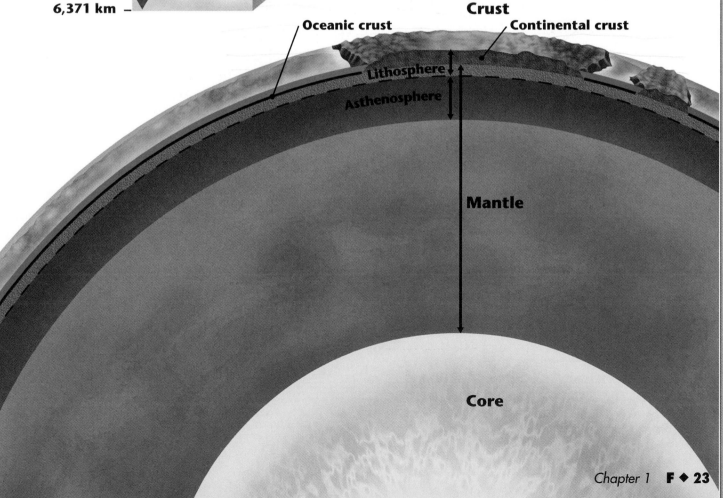

Oceanic crust

Crust

Continental crust

Lithosphere

Asthenosphere

Mantle

Core

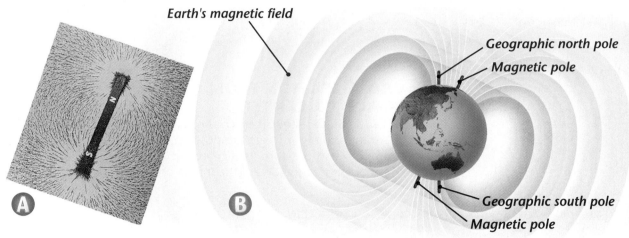

Earth's magnetic field

Geographic north pole

Magnetic pole

Geographic south pole

Magnetic pole

A

B

Figure 7 **A.** The pattern of iron filings was made by sprinkling them on paper placed over a bar magnet. **B.** Like a magnet, Earth's magnetic field has north and south poles. *Relating Cause and Effect If you shifted the magnet beneath the paper, what would happen to the iron filings?*

Earth's Magnetic Field

 INTEGRATING PHYSICS Currents in the liquid outer core force the solid inner core to spin at a slightly faster rate than the rest of the planet. These currents in the outer core create Earth's magnetic field, which causes the planet to act like a giant bar magnet. As you can see in Figure 7, the magnetic field affects the whole Earth. When you use a compass, the compass needle aligns with the lines of force in Earth's magnetic field. The north-seeking end of the compass needle points to Earth's magnetic north pole.

Consider an ordinary bar magnet. If you place it beneath a piece of paper and sprinkle iron filings on the paper, the iron filings line up with the bar's magnetic field. If you could cover the entire planet with iron filings, they would form a similar pattern.

Section 1 Review

1. What are two things that geologists study about Earth?
2. What are the layers that make up Earth? Write a sentence about each one.
3. What happens in Earth's interior to produce Earth's magnetic field? Describe the layers of the interior where the magnetic field is produced.
4. **Thinking Critically Comparing and Contrasting** What are some of the differences and similarities between the mantle and the core? Explain.

Check Your Progress

CHAPTER PROJECT 1

Begin by drawing a sketch of your three-dimensional model. Think about how you will show the thicknesses of Earth's different layers at the correct scale. How can you show Earth's interior as well as its surface features? What materials can you use for building your model? Experiment with materials that might work well for showing Earth's layers.

SECTION 2 Convection Currents and the Mantle

DISCOVER ···ACTIVITY···

How Can Heat Cause Motion in a Liquid?

1. ⚠ Carefully pour some hot water into a small, shallow pan. Fill a clear, plastic cup about half full with cold water. Place the cup in the pan.

2. Allow the water to stand for two minutes until all motion stops.

3. Fill a plastic dropper with some food coloring. Then, holding the dropper under the water surface and slightly away from the edge of the cup, gently squeeze a small droplet of the food coloring into the water.

4. Observe the water for one minute.

5. Add another droplet at the water surface in the middle of the cup and observe again.

Think It Over

Inferring How do you explain what happened to the droplets of food coloring? Why do you think the second droplet moved in a way that was different from the way the first droplet moved?

Earth's molten outer core is nearly as hot as the surface of the sun. To explain how heat from the core affects the mantle, you need to know how heat is transferred in solids and liquids. If you have ever touched a hot pot accidentally, you have discovered for yourself (in a painful way) that heat moves. In this case, it moved from the hot pot to your hand. The movement of energy from a warmer object to a cooler object is called **heat transfer**.

Heat is always transferred from a warmer substance to a cooler substance. For example, holding an ice cube will make your hand begin to feel cold in a few seconds. But is the coldness in the ice cube moving to your hand? Since cold is the absence of heat, it's the heat in your hand that moves to the ice cube! **There are three types of heat transfer: radiation, conduction, and convection.**

Radiation

The transfer of energy through empty space is called **radiation.** Sunlight is radiation that warms Earth's surface. Heat transfer by radiation takes place with no direct contact between a heat source and an object. Radiation enables sunlight to warm Earth's surface. Other familiar forms of radiation include the heat you feel around a flame or open fire.

GUIDE FOR READING

◆ How is heat transferred?

◆ What causes convection currents?

Reading Tip As you read, draw a concept map of the three types of heat transfer. Include supporting ideas about convection.

Figure 8 In conduction, the heated particles of a substance transfer heat to other particles through direct contact. That's how the spoon and the pot itself heat up.

Conduction

Heat transfer by direct contact of particles of matter is called **conduction.** What happens as a spoon heats up in a pot of soup? Heat is transferred from the hot soup and the pot to the particles that make up the spoon. The particles near the bottom of the spoon vibrate faster as they are heated, so they bump into other particles and heat them, too. Gradually the entire spoon heats up. When your hand touches the spoon, conduction transfers heat from the spoon directly to your skin. Then you feel the heat. Look at Figure 8 to see how conduction takes place.

Convection

Conduction heats the spoon, but how does the soup inside the pot heat up? Heat transfer involving the movement of fluids— liquids and gases—is called convection. **Convection** is heat transfer by the movement of a heated fluid. During convection, heated particles of fluid begin to flow, transferring heat energy from one part of the fluid to another.

Heat transfer by convection is caused by differences of temperature and density within a fluid. **Density** is a measure of how much mass there is in a volume of a substance. For example, rock is more dense than water because a given volume of rock has more mass than the same volume of water.

When a liquid or gas is heated, the particles move faster. As the particles move faster, they spread apart. Because the particles of the heated fluid are farther apart, they occupy more space. The density decreases. But when a fluid cools, its particles move more slowly and settle together more closely. As the fluid becomes cooler, its density increases.

If you look at Figure 9, you can see how convection occurs when you heat soup on a stove. As the soup at the bottom of the pot gets hot, it expands and therefore becomes less dense. The warm, less dense soup moves upward and floats over the cooler, denser soup. At the surface, the warm soup spreads out and cools, becoming denser. Then, gravity pulls this cooler, denser soup back down to the bottom of the pot, where it is heated again.

Figure 9 In this pot, the soup close to the heat source is hotter and less dense than the soup near the surface. These differences in temperature and density cause convection currents.

A constant flow begins as the cooler soup continually sinks to the bottom of the pot and the warmer soup rises. A **convection current** is the flow that transfers heat within a fluid.

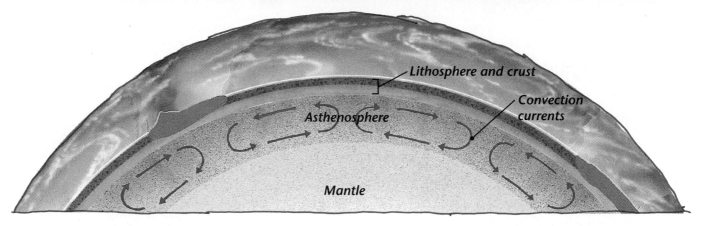

Lithosphere and crust

Asthenosphere

Convection currents

Mantle

The heating and cooling of the fluid, changes in the fluid's density, and the force of gravity combine to set convection currents in motion. Convection currents continue as long as heat is added. What happens after the heat source is removed? Without heat, the convection currents will eventually stop when all of the material has reached the same temperature.

☑ *Checkpoint* What is convection?

Convection in Earth's Mantle

Like soup simmering in a pot, Earth's mantle responds to heat. Notice in Figure 10 how convection currents flow in the asthenosphere. The heat source for these currents is heat from Earth's core and from the mantle itself. Hot columns of mantle material rise slowly through the asthenosphere. At the top of the asthenosphere, the hot material spreads out and pushes the cooler material out of the way. This cooler material sinks back into the asthenosphere. Over and over, the cycle of rising and sinking takes place. Convection currents like these have been moving inside Earth for more than four billion years!

Figure 10 Heat from Earth's mantle and core causes convection currents to form in the asthenosphere. Some geologists think convection currents extend throughout the mantle. *Applying Concepts What part of Earth's interior is like the soup in the pot? What part is like the burner on the stove?*

Section 2 Review

1. What are the three types of heat transfer?
2. Describe how convection currents form.
3. In general, what happens to the density of a fluid when it becomes hotter?
4. What happens to convection currents when a fluid reaches a constant temperature?
5. **Thinking Critically Predicting** What will happen to the flow of hot rock in Earth's mantle if the planet's core eventually cools down? Explain your answer.

Science at Home

Convection currents may keep the air inside your home at a comfortable temperature. Air is made up of gases, so it is a fluid. Regardless of the type of home heating system, heated air circulates through a room by convection. You may have tried to adjust the flow of air in a stuffy room by opening a window. When you did so, you were making use of convection currents. With an adult family member, study how your home is heated. Look for evidence of convection currents.

SECTION
3 Drifting Continents

DISCOVER ●●●●●●●●●●●●●●●●●●●●●●●●●●●●●● ACTIVITY ●●●●

How Are Earth's Continents Linked Together?

1. Find the oceans and the seven continents on a globe showing Earth's physical features.

2. How much of the globe is occupied by the Pacific Ocean? Does most of Earth's "dry" land lie in the Northern or Southern hemisphere?

3. Find the points or areas where most of the continents are connected. Find the points at which several of the continents almost touch, but are not connected.

4. Examine the globe more closely. Find the great belt of mountains running from north to south along the western side of North and South America. Can you find another great belt of mountains on the globe?

Think It Over

Posing Questions What questions can you pose about how oceans, continents, and mountains are distributed on Earth's surface?

GUIDE FOR READING

◆ What is continental drift?

◆ Why was Alfred Wegener's theory rejected by most scientists of his day?

Reading Tip As you read, look for evidence that supports the theory of continental drift.

Five hundred years ago, the sea voyages of Columbus and other explorers changed the map of the world. The continents of Europe, Asia, and Africa were already known to mapmakers. Soon mapmakers were also showing the outlines of the continents of North and South America. Looking at these world maps, many people wondered why the coasts of several continents matched so neatly.

Look at the modern world map in Figure 11. Notice how the coasts of Africa and South America look as if they could fit together like jigsaw-puzzle pieces. Could the continents have once been a single landmass? In the 1700s, the first geologists thought that the continents had remained fixed in their positions throughout Earth's history. Early in the 1900s, however, one scientist began to think in a new way about this riddle of the continents. His theory changed the way people look at the map of the world.

World map drawn by Juan Vespucci in 1526. ▶

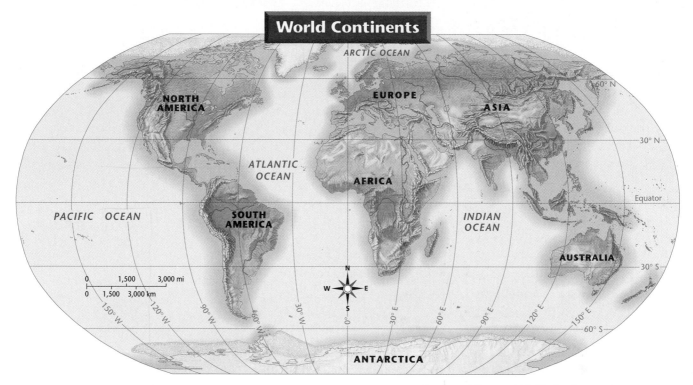

World Continents

Figure 11 Today's continents provide clues about Earth's history. *Observing Which coastlines of continents seem to match up like jigsaw-puzzle pieces?*

The Theory of Continental Drift

In 1910, a young German scientist named Alfred Wegener (VAY guh nur) became curious about the relationship of the continents. He formed a hypothesis that Earth's continents had moved! **Wegener's hypothesis was that all the continents had once been joined together in a single landmass and have since drifted apart.**

Wegener named this supercontinent **Pangaea** (pan JEE uh), meaning "all lands." According to Wegener, Pangaea existed about 300 million years ago. This was the time when reptiles and winged insects first appeared. Great tropical forests, which later formed coal deposits, covered large parts of Earth's surface.

Over tens of millions of years, Pangaea began to break apart. The pieces of Pangaea slowly moved toward their present-day locations, becoming the continents as they are today. Wegener's idea that the continents slowly moved over Earth's surface became known as **continental drift**.

Have you ever tried to persuade a friend to accept a new idea? Your friend's opinion probably won't change unless you provide some convincing evidence. Wegener gathered evidence from different scientific fields to support his ideas about continental drift. In particular, he studied landforms, fossils, and evidence that showed how Earth's climate had changed over many millions of years. Wegener published all his evidence for continental drift in a book called *The Origin of Continents and Oceans*, first published in 1915.

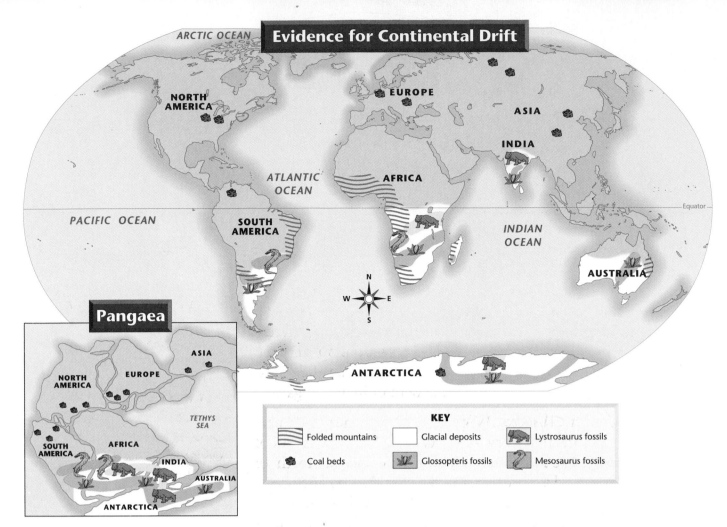

Evidence for Continental Drift

ARCTIC OCEAN

NORTH AMERICA

EUROPE

ASIA

INDIA

ATLANTIC OCEAN

AFRICA

PACIFIC OCEAN

SOUTH AMERICA

INDIAN OCEAN

Equator

AUSTRALIA

ANTARCTICA

Pangaea

ASIA

NORTH AMERICA

EUROPE

TETHYS SEA

SOUTH AMERICA

AFRICA

INDIA

AUSTRALIA

ANTARCTICA

KEY

Folded mountains	Glacial deposits	Lystrosaurus fossils
Coal beds	Glossopteris fossils	Mesosaurus fossils

Figure 12 Wegener used several types of evidence to support his idea that the continents were once joined in a single landmass called Pangaea. *Inferring According to Wegener's theory, what does the presence of similar mountain ranges in Africa and South America indicate?*

Figure 13 Fossils of the freshwater reptile *Mesosaurus* found in Africa and South America provide evidence of continental drift.

Evidence from Landforms Mountain ranges and other features on the continents provided evidence for continental drift. When Wegener pieced together maps of Africa and South America, he noticed that a mountain range in South Africa lines up with a mountain range in Argentina. European coal fields match up with similar coal fields in North America. Wegener compared matching these features to reassembling a torn-up newspaper. If the pieces could be put back together, the "words" would match.

Evidence From Fossils Wegener also used fossils to support his argument for continental drift. A **fossil** is any trace of an ancient organism that has been preserved in rock. For example, fossils of the reptiles *Mesosaurus* and *Lystrosaurus* have been found in places now separated by oceans. Neither reptile could have swum great distances across salt water. It is therefore likely that these reptiles lived on a single landmass that has since split apart. Another example is *Glossopteris* (glaw SAHP tuh ris), a fernlike plant that lived 250 million years ago. *Glossopteris* fossils have been found in rocks in Africa, South America, Australia, India, and Antarctica. The occurrence of *Glossopteris* on these widely separated landmasses convinced Wegener that the continents had once been united.

Figure 14 Fossils of *Glossopteris* are found on continents in the Southern Hemisphere and in India.

INTEGRATING LIFE SCIENCE The seedlike structures of *Glossopteris* could not have traveled the great distances that separate the continents today. The "seeds" were too large to have been carried by the wind and too fragile to have survived a trip by ocean waves. How did *Glossopteris* develop on such widely separated continents? Wegener inferred that the continents at that time were joined as the supercontinent Pangaea.

Evidence From Climate Wegener used evidence of climate change to support his theory—for example, from the island of Spitsbergen. Spitsbergen lies in the Arctic Ocean north of Norway. This island is ice-covered and has a harsh polar climate. But fossils of tropical plants are found on Spitsbergen. When these plants lived about 300 million years ago, the island must have had a warm and mild climate. According to Wegener, Spitsbergen must have been located closer to the equator.

Thousands of kilometers to the south, geologists found evidence that at the same time it was warm in Spitsbergen, the climate was much colder in South Africa. Deep scratches in rocks showed that continental glaciers once covered South Africa. Continental glaciers are thick layers of ice that cover hundreds of thousands of square kilometers. But the climate of South Africa is too mild today for continental glaciers to form. Wegener concluded that, when Pangaea existed, South Africa was much closer to the South Pole.

According to Wegener, the climates of Spitsbergen and South Africa changed because the positions of these places on Earth's surface changed. As a continent moves toward the equator, its climate becomes warmer. As a continent moves toward the poles, its climate becomes colder. But the continent carries with it the fossils and rocks that formed at its previous location. These clues provide evidence that continental drift really happened.

Checkpoint *What were the three types of evidence Wegener used to support his theory of continental drift?*

Figure 15 Although scientists rejected his theory, Wegener continued to collect evidence on continental drift and to update his book. He died in 1930 on an expedition to explore Greenland's continental glacier.

Scientists Reject Wegener's Theory

Wegener did more than provide a theory to answer the riddle of continental drift. He attempted to explain how drift took place. He even offered a new explanation for how mountains form. Wegener thought that when drifting continents collide, their edges crumple and fold. The folding continents slowly push up huge chunks of rock to form great mountains.

Unfortunately, Wegener could not provide a satisfactory explanation for the force that pushes or pulls the continents. Because Wegener could not identify the cause of continental drift, most geologists rejected his idea. In addition, for geologists to accept Wegener's idea, they would need new explanations of what caused continents and mountains to form.

Many geologists in the early 1900s thought that Earth was slowly cooling and shrinking. According to this theory, mountains formed when the crust wrinkled like the skin of a dried-up apple. Wegener said that if the apple theory were correct, then mountains should be found all over Earth's surface. But mountains usually occur in narrow bands along the edges of continents. Wegener thought that his own theory better explained where mountains occur and how they form.

For nearly half a century, from the 1920s to the 1960s, most scientists paid little attention to the idea of continental drift. Then new evidence about Earth's structure led scientists to reconsider Wegener's bold theory.

Section 3 Review

1. What was Wegener's theory of continental drift?
2. How did Wegener use evidence based on fossils to support his theory that the continents had moved?
3. What was the main reason scientists rejected Wegener's theory of continental drift?
4. **Thinking Critically Inferring** Coal deposits have also been found beneath the ice of Antarctica. But coal only forms in warm swamps. Use Wegener's theory to explain how coal could be found so near the poles.

Science at Home

You can demonstrate Wegener's idea of continental drift. Use the map of the world in Figure 11. On a sheet of tracing paper, trace the outlines of the continents bordering the Atlantic Ocean. Label the continents. Then use scissors to carefully cut the map along the eastern edge of South America, North America, and Greenland. Next, cut along the western edge of Africa and Europe (including the British Isles). Throw away the Atlantic Ocean. Place the two cut-out pieces on a dark surface and ask family members to try to fit the two halves together. Explain to them about the supercontinent Pangaea and its history.

SECTION
4 Sea-Floor Spreading

DISCOVER • ACTIVITY • • •

What Is the Effect of a Change in Density?

1. Partially fill a sink or dishpan with water.

2. Open up a dry washcloth in your hand. Does the washcloth feel light or heavy?

3. Moisten one edge of the washcloth in the water. Then gently place the washcloth so that it floats on the water's surface. Observe the washcloth carefully (especially at its edges) as it starts to sink.

4. Remove the washcloth from the water and open it up in your hand. Is the mass of the washcloth the same as, less than, or greater than when it was dry?

Think It Over

Observing How did the washcloth's density change? What effect did this change in density have on the washcloth?

Deep in the ocean, the temperature is near freezing. There is no light, and living things are generally scarce. Yet some areas of the deep-ocean floor are teeming with life. One of these areas is the East Pacific Rise, a region of the Pacific Ocean floor off the coasts of Mexico and South America. Here, ocean water sinks through cracks, or vents, in the crust. The water is heated by contact with hot material from the mantle and then spurts back into the ocean.

Around these hot-water vents live some of the most bizarre creatures ever discovered. Giant, red-tipped tube worms sway in the water. Nearby sit giant clams nearly a meter across. Strange spiderlike crabs scuttle by. Surprisingly, the geological features of this strange environment provided scientists with some of the best evidence for Wegener's theory of continental drift.

GUIDE FOR READING

◆ What is the process of sea-floor spreading?

◆ What happens to the ocean floor at deep ocean trenches?

Reading Tip Before you read, preview the art and captions looking for new terms. As you read, find the meanings of these terms.

Figure 16 Tube worms cluster near hot water vents in the ocean floor.

Figure 17 Scientists use sonar to map the ocean floor.

Mapping the Mid-Ocean Ridge

The East Pacific Rise is just one part of the **mid-ocean ridge,** the longest chain of mountains in the world. In the mid-1900s, scientists mapped the mid-ocean ridge using sonar. **Sonar** is a device that bounces sound waves off underwater objects and then records the echoes of these sound waves. The time it takes for the echo to arrive indicates the distance to the object.

The mid-ocean ridge curves like the seam of a baseball along the sea floor, extending into all of Earth's oceans. Most of the mountains in the mid-ocean ridge lie hidden under hundreds of meters of water. However, there are places where the ridge pokes above the surface. For example, the island of Iceland is a part of the mid-ocean ridge that rises above the surface in the North Atlantic Ocean. A steep-sided valley splits the top of the mid-ocean ridge for most of its length. The valley is almost twice as deep as the Grand Canyon. The mapping of the mid-ocean ridge made scientists curious to know what the ridge was and how it got there.

✓ *Checkpoint* *What device is used to map the ocean floor?*

Figure 18 The mid-ocean ridge is more than 50,000 kilometers long.

Earth's Ocean Floor

ASIA

NORTH AMERICA

EUROPE

ASIA

ATLANTIC OCEAN

AFRICA

PACIFIC OCEAN

SOUTH AMERICA

INDIAN OCEAN

AUSTRALIA

ANTARCTICA

KEY
— Mid-ocean ridge
— Deep-ocean trench

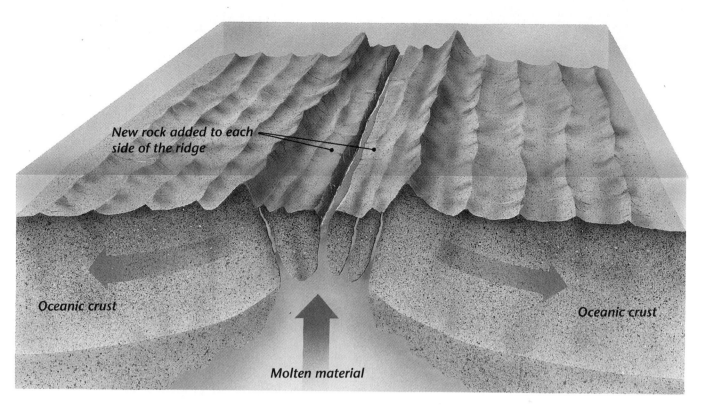

New rock added to each side of the ridge

Oceanic crust

Oceanic crust

Molten material

Evidence for Sea-Floor Spreading

Harry Hess, an American geologist, was one of the scientists who studied the mid-ocean ridge. Hess carefully examined maps of the mid-ocean ridge. Then he began to think about the ocean floor in relation to the problem of continental drift. Finally, he reconsidered an idea that he previously had thought impossible: Maybe Wegener was right! Perhaps the continents do move.

In 1960, Hess proposed a radical idea. He suggested that the ocean floors move like conveyor belts, carrying the continents along with them. This movement begins at the mid-ocean ridge. The mid-ocean ridge forms along a crack in the oceanic crust. **At the mid-ocean ridge, molten material rises from the mantle and erupts. The molten material then spreads out, pushing older rock to both sides of the ridge.** As the molten material cools, it forms a strip of solid rock in the center of the ridge. Then more molten material flows into the crack. This material splits apart the strip of solid rock that formed before, pushing it aside.

Hess called the process that continually adds new material to the ocean floor **sea-floor spreading.** He realized that the sea floor spreads apart along both sides of the mid-ocean ridge as new crust is added. Look at Figure 19 to see the process of sea-floor spreading.

Several types of evidence from the oceans supported Hess's theory of sea-floor spreading—evidence from molten material, magnetic stripes, and drilling samples. This evidence also led scientists to look again at Wegener's theory of continental drift.

Figure 19 Molten material erupts though the valley that runs along the center of the mid-ocean ridge. This material hardens to form the rock of the ocean floor. *Applying Concepts* What happens to the rock along the ridge when new molten material erupts?

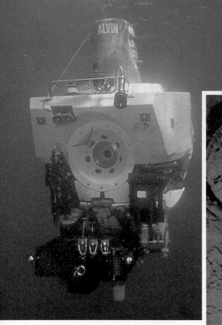

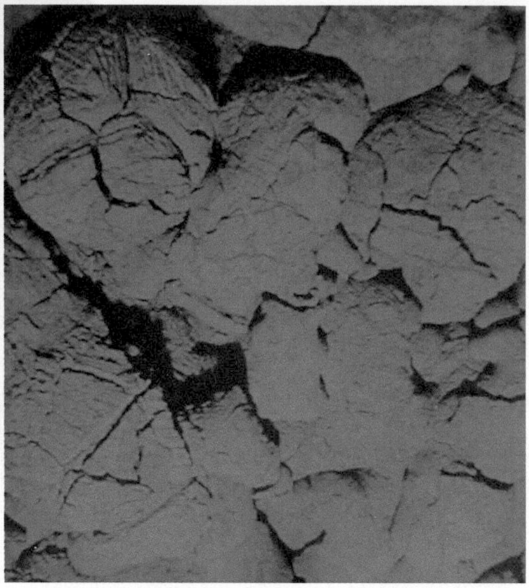

Figure 20 The submersible *Alvin* photographed pillow lava along the mid-ocean ridge. These "pillows" form under water when cold ocean water causes a crust to form on erupting molten material. Each pillow expands until it bursts, allowing molten material to flow out and form the next pillow.

Evidence From Molten Material In the 1960s, scientists found evidence that new material is indeed erupting along the mid-ocean ridge. The scientists dived to the ocean floor in *Alvin*, a small submersible built to withstand the crushing pressures four kilometers down in the ocean. In the central valley of the mid-ocean ridge, *Alvin's* crew found strange rocks shaped like pillows or like toothpaste squeezed from a tube. Such rocks can form only when molten material hardens quickly after erupting under water. The presence of these rocks showed that molten material has erupted again and again from cracks along the central valley of the mid-ocean ridge.

Evidence From Magnetic Stripes When scientists studied patterns in the rocks of the ocean floor, they found more support for sea-floor spreading. In Section 1 you read that Earth behaves like a giant magnet, with a north pole and a south pole. Evidence shows that Earth's magnetic poles have reversed themselves. This last happened 780,000 years ago. If the magnetic poles suddenly reversed themselves today, you would find that your compass needle pointed south. Scientists discovered that the rock that makes up the ocean floor lies in a pattern of magnetized "stripes." These stripes hold a record of reversals in Earth's magnetic field.

INTEGRATING PHYSICS

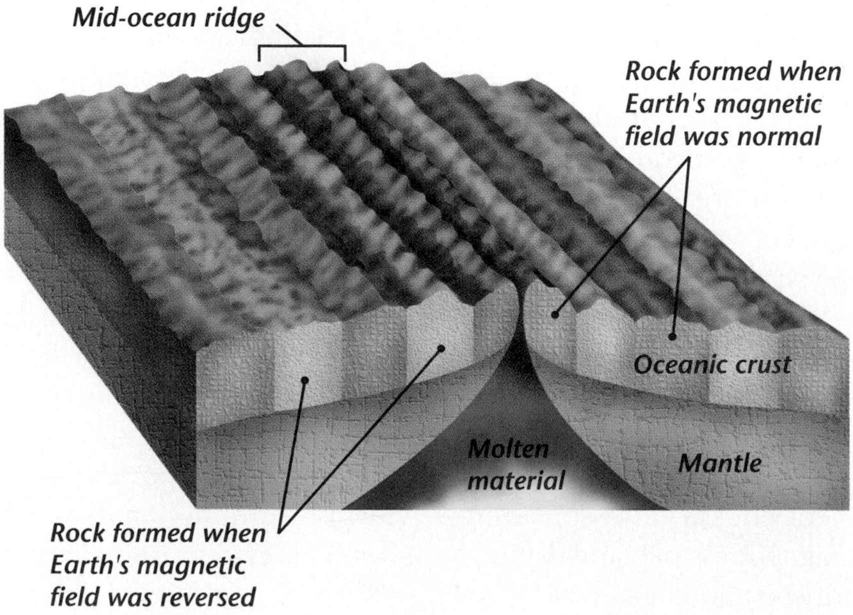

Figure 21 Magnetic stripes in the rock of the ocean floor show the direction of Earth's magnetic field at the time the rock hardened. *Interpreting Diagrams How are these matching stripes evidence of sea-floor spreading?*

Mid-ocean ridge

Rock formed when Earth's magnetic field was normal

Oceanic crust

Molten material

Mantle

Rock formed when Earth's magnetic field was reversed

The rock of the ocean floor, which contains iron, began as molten material. As the molten material cooled, the iron bits inside lined up in the direction of Earth's magnetic poles. When the rock hardened completely, it locked the iron bits in place, giving the rocks a permanent "magnetic memory." You can think of it as setting thousands of tiny compass needles in cement.

Using sensitive instruments, scientists recorded the magnetic memory of rocks on both sides of the mid-ocean ridge. They found that a stripe of rock that shows when Earth's magnetic field pointed north is followed by a parallel stripe of rock that shows when the magnetic field pointed south. As you can see in Figure 21, the pattern is the same on both sides of the ridge. Rock that hardens at the same time has the same magnetic memory.

Evidence From Drilling Samples The final proof of sea-floor spreading came from rock samples obtained by drilling into the ocean floor. The *Glomar Challenger*, a drilling ship built in 1968, gathered the samples. The *Glomar Challenger* sent drilling pipes through water six kilometers deep to drill holes in the ocean floor. This feat has been compared to using a sharp-ended wire to dig a hole into a sidewalk from the top of the Empire State Building.

Samples from the sea floor were brought up through the pipes. Then the scientists determined the age of the rocks in the samples. They found that the farther away from the ridge the samples were taken, the older the rocks were. The youngest rocks were always in the center of the ridges. This showed that sea-floor spreading really has taken place.

☑ *Checkpoint* *What evidence did scientists find for sea-floor spreading?*

Figure 22 The *Glomar Challenger* was the first research ship designed to drill samples of rock from the deep-ocean floor.

Reversing Poles

1. Cut six short pieces, each about 2.5 cm long, from a length of audiotape.
2. Tape one end of each piece of audiotape to a flat surface. The pieces should be spaced 1 cm apart and line up lengthwise in a single line.
3. Touch a bar magnet's north pole to the first piece of audiotape. Then reverse the magnet and touch its south pole to the next piece.
4. Repeat Step 3 until you have applied the magnet to each piece of audiotape.
5. Sweep one end of the magnet about 1 cm above the line of audiotape pieces. Observe what happens.

Making Models What characteristic of the ocean floor did you observe as you swept the magnet along the line of audiotape pieces?

Subduction at Deep-Ocean Trenches

How can the ocean floor keep getting wider and wider? The answer is that the ocean floor generally does not just keep spreading. Instead, the ocean floor plunges into deep underwater canyons called **deep-ocean trenches.** A deep-ocean trench forms where the oceanic crust bends downward.

Where there are deep-ocean trenches, subduction takes place. **Subduction** (sub DUK shun) is the process by which the ocean floor sinks beneath a deep-ocean trench and back into the mantle. Convection currents under the lithosphere push new crust that forms at the mid-ocean ridge away from the ridge and toward a deep-ocean trench.

New oceanic crust is hot. But as it moves away from the mid-ocean ridge, it cools and becomes more dense. Eventually, as shown in Figure 23, gravity pulls this older, denser oceanic crust down beneath the trench. The sinking crust is like the washcloth in the Discover activity at the beginning of this section. As the dry washcloth floating on the water gets wet, its density increases and it begins to sink.

At deep-ocean trenches, subduction allows part of the ocean floor to sink back into the mantle, over tens of millions of years. You can think of sea-floor spreading and subduction together as if the ocean floor were moving out from the mid-ocean ridge on a giant conveyor belt.

Figure 23 Oceanic crust created along the mid-ocean ridge is destroyed at a deep-ocean trench. In the process of subduction, oceanic crust sinks down beneath the trench into the mantle. *Drawing Conclusions Where would denser oceanic crust be found?*

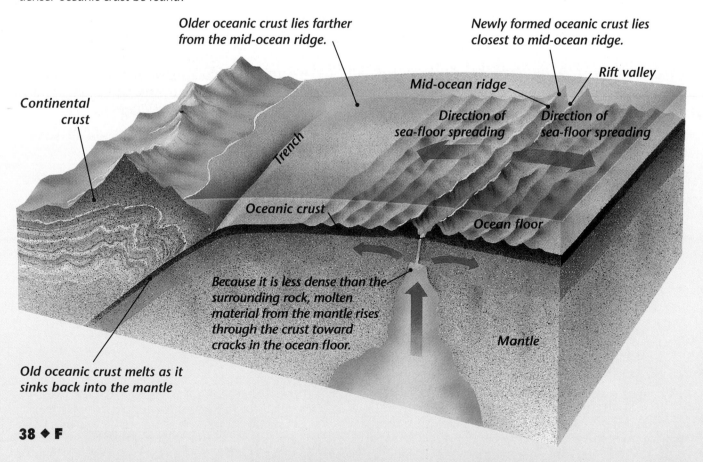

Older oceanic crust lies farther from the mid-ocean ridge.

Newly formed oceanic crust lies closest to mid-ocean ridge.

Rift valley

Mid-ocean ridge

Continental crust

Trench

Direction of sea-floor spreading

Direction of sea-floor spreading

Oceanic crust

Ocean floor

Because it is less dense than the surrounding rock, molten material from the mantle rises through the crust toward cracks in the ocean floor.

Mantle

Old oceanic crust melts as it sinks back into the mantle

Subduction and Earth's Oceans

The processes of subduction and sea-floor spreading can change the size and shape of the oceans. Because of these processes, the ocean floor is renewed about every 200 million years. That is the time it takes for new rock to form at the mid-ocean ridge, move across the ocean, and sink into a trench.

Subduction in the Pacific Ocean The vast Pacific Ocean covers almost one third of the planet. And yet it is shrinking. How could that be? Sometimes a deep ocean trench swallows more oceanic crust than the mid-ocean ridge can produce. Then, if the ridge does not add new crust fast enough, the width of the ocean will shrink. This is happening to the Pacific Ocean, which is ringed by many trenches.

Subduction in the Atlantic Ocean The Atlantic Ocean, on the other hand, is expanding. Unlike the Pacific Ocean, the Atlantic Ocean has only a few short trenches. As a result, the spreading ocean floor has virtually nowhere to go. In most places, the oceanic crust of the Atlantic Ocean floor is attached to the continental crust of the continents around the ocean. So as the Atlantic's ocean floor spreads, the continents along its edges also move. Over time, the whole ocean gets wider. The spreading floor of the North Atlantic Ocean and the continent of North America move together like two giant barges pushed by the same tugboat.

Figure 24 It is cold and dark in the deep ocean trenches where subduction occurs. But even here, scientists have found living things, such as this angler fish.

Section 4 Review

1. What is the role of the mid-ocean ridge in sea-floor spreading?
2. What is the evidence for sea-floor spreading?
3. Describe the process of subduction at a deep-ocean trench.
4. **Thinking Critically Relating Cause and Effect** Where would you expect to find the oldest rock on the ocean floor? Explain your answer.
5. **Thinking Critically Predicting** As you can see in Figure 18, the mid-ocean ridge extends into the Red Sea between Africa and Asia. What do you think will happen to the Red Sea in the future? Explain your answer.

Check Your Progress
CHAPTER PROJECT 1
Now that you have learned about sea-floor spreading, draw a revised sketch of your model. Include examples of sea-floor spreading and subduction on your sketch. Show the features that form as a result of these processes. How will you show what happens beneath the crust? Improve your original ideas and add new ideas. Revise your list of materials if necessary. Begin building your model.

MODELING SEA-FLOOR SPREADING

Along the entire length of Earth's mid-ocean ridge, the sea floor is spreading. Although this process takes place constantly, it is difficult to observe directly. You can build a model to help understand this process.

Problem

How does sea-floor spreading add material to the ocean floor?

Materials

scissors
metric ruler
2 sheets of unlined paper
colored marker

Procedure

1. Draw stripes across one sheet of paper, parallel to the short sides of the paper. The stripes should vary in spacing and thickness.
2. Fold the paper in half lengthwise and write the word "Start" at the top of both halves of the paper. Using the scissors, carefully cut the paper in half along the fold line to form two strips.
3. Lightly fold the second sheet of paper into eighths. Then unfold it, leaving creases in the paper. Fold this sheet in half lengthwise.

4. Starting at the fold, draw lines 5.5 cm long on the middle crease and the two creases closest to the ends of the paper.

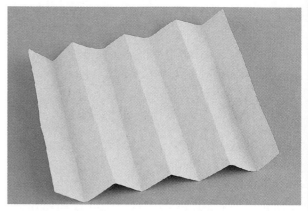

5. Now carefully cut along the lines you drew. Unfold the paper. There should be three slits in the center of the paper.

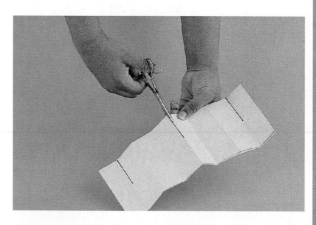

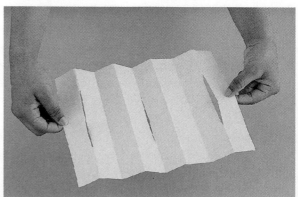

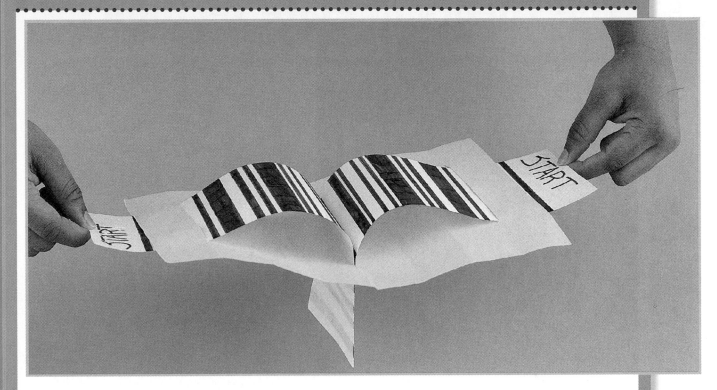

6. Put the two striped strips of paper together so their Start labels touch one another. Insert the Start ends of the strips up through the center slit and then pull them toward the side slits.

7. Insert the ends of the strips into the side slits. Pull the ends of the strips and watch what happens at the center slit.

8. Practice pulling the strips through the slits until you can make the two strips come up and go down at the same time.

Analyze and Conclude

1. What feature of the ocean floor does the center slit stand for? What prominent feature of the ocean floor is missing from the model at this point?

2. What do the side slits stand for? What does the space under the paper stand for?

3. How does the ocean floor as shown by the part of a strip close to the center slit differ from the ocean floor as shown by the part near a side slit? How does this difference affect the depth of the ocean?

4. What do the stripes on the strips stand for? Why is it important that your model have an identical pattern of stripes on both sides of the center slit?

5. Explain how differences in density and temperature provide some of the force needed to cause sea-floor spreading and subduction.

6. **Think About It** Use your own words to describe the process of ocean-floor spreading. What parts of the process were not shown by your model?

More to Explore

Imagine that so much molten rock erupted from the mid-ocean ridge that an island formed there. How could you modify your model to show this island? How could you show what would happen to it over a long period of time?

The Theory of Plate Tectonics

How Well Do the Continents Fit Together?

1. Using a world map in an atlas, trace the shape of each continent and Madagascar on a sheet of paper. Also trace the shape of India and the Arabian Peninsula.

2. ✂ Carefully cut apart the landmasses, leaving Asia and Europe as one piece. Separate India and the Arabian Peninsula from Asia.

3. Piece together the continents as they may have looked before the breakup of Pangaea. Then attach your reconstruction of Pangaea to a sheet of paper.

Think It Over

Drawing Conclusions How well did the pieces of your continents fit together? Do your observations support the idea that today's landmasses were once joined together? Explain.

GUIDE FOR READING

◆ What is the theory of plate tectonics?

◆ What are the three types of plate boundaries?

Reading Tip Before you read, preview *Exploring Plate Tectonics* on pages 46–47. Write a list of any questions you have about plate tectonics. Look for answers as you read.

Have you ever dropped a hard-boiled egg? If so, you may have noticed that the eggshell cracked in an irregular pattern of broken pieces. Earth's lithosphere, its solid outer shell, is not one unbroken layer. It is more like that cracked eggshell. It's broken into pieces separated by jagged cracks.

A Canadian scientist, J. Tuzo Wilson, observed that there are cracks in the continents similar to those on the ocean floor. In 1965, Wilson proposed a new way of looking at these cracks. According to Wilson, the lithosphere is broken into separate sections called **plates.** The plates fit closely together along cracks in the lithosphere. As shown in Figure 26, the plates carry the continents or parts of the ocean floor, or both.

Figure 25 The Great Rift Valley in east Africa is a crack in Earth's crust where two pieces of crust are pulling apart.

A Theory of Plate Motion

Wilson combined what geologists knew about sea-floor spreading, Earth's plates, and continental drift into a single theory—the theory of plate tectonics (tek TAHN iks). A **scientific theory** is a well-tested concept that explains a wide range of observations. **Plate tectonics** is the geological theory that states that pieces of Earth's lithosphere are in constant, slow motion, driven by convection currents in the mantle. **The theory of plate tectonics explains the formation, movement, and subduction of Earth's plates.**

How can Earth's plates move? The plates of the lithosphere float on top of the asthenosphere. Convection currents rise in the asthenosphere and spread out beneath the lithosphere. Most geologists think that the flow of these currents causes the movement of Earth's plates.

No plate can budge without affecting the other plates surrounding it. As the plates move, they collide, pull apart, or grind past each other, producing spectacular changes in Earth's surface. These changes include volcanoes, mountain ranges, and deep-sea trenches.

Sharpen your Skills

Predicting

ACTIVITY

Study the map of Earth's plates in Figure 26. Notice the arrows that show the direction of plate movement. Now find the Nazca plate on the map. Which direction is it moving? Find the South American plate and describe its movement. What do you think will happen as these plates continue to move?

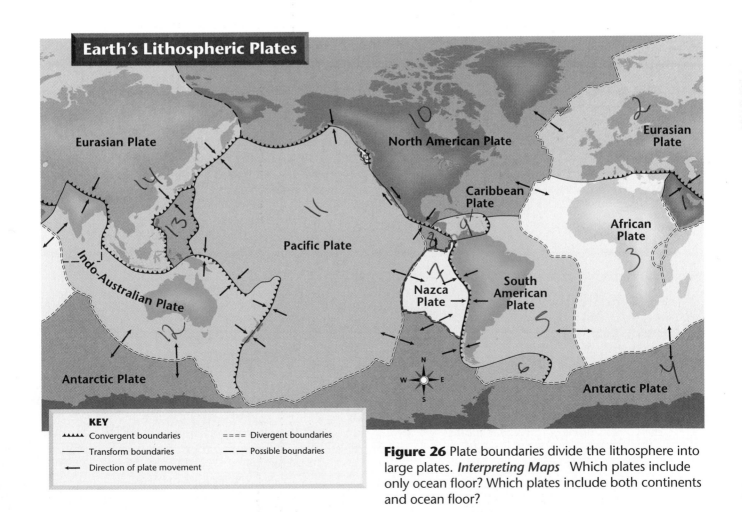

Earth's Lithospheric Plates

KEY
- ˄˄˄˄ Convergent boundaries
- ——— Transform boundaries
- ⟵ Direction of plate movement
- ==== Divergent boundaries
- – – Possible boundaries

Figure 26 Plate boundaries divide the lithosphere into large plates. *Interpreting Maps* Which plates include only ocean floor? Which plates include both continents and ocean floor?

Plate Boundaries

The edges of different pieces of the lithosphere—Earth's rigid shell—meet at lines called plate boundaries. Plate boundaries extend deep into the lithosphere. **Faults**—breaks in Earth's crust where rocks have slipped past each other—form along these boundaries. There are three kinds of plate boundaries: transform boundaries, divergent boundaries, and convergent boundaries. For each type of boundary, there is a different type of plate movement.

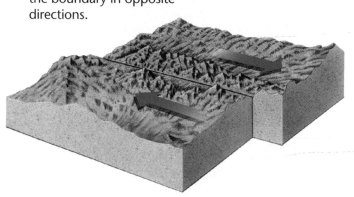

Figure 27 At a transform boundary, two plates move along the boundary in opposite directions.

Transform Boundaries Along transform boundaries, crust is neither created nor destroyed. A **transform boundary** is a place where two plates slip past each other, moving in opposite directions. Earthquakes occur frequently along these boundaries. Look at Figure 27 to see the type of plate movement that occurs along a transform boundary.

EXPLORING *Plate Tectonics*

Plate movements have built many of the features of Earth's land surfaces and ocean floors.

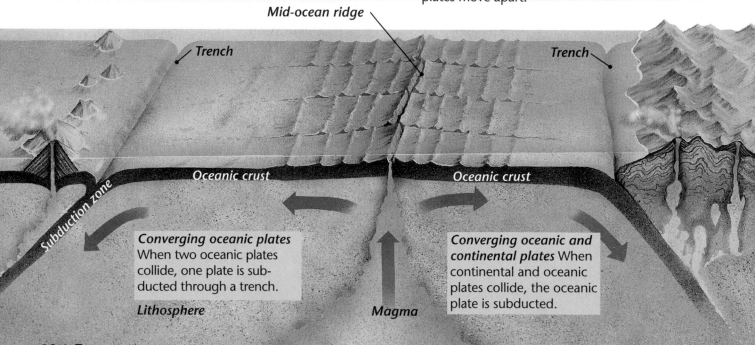

Diverging oceanic plates
The mid-ocean ridge marks a divergent boundary where plates move apart.

Mid-ocean ridge

Trench

Trench

Subduction zone

Oceanic crust

Oceanic crust

Converging oceanic plates
When two oceanic plates collide, one plate is subducted through a trench.

Lithosphere

Converging oceanic and continental plates When continental and oceanic plates collide, the oceanic plate is subducted.

Magma

Divergent Boundaries The place where two plates move apart, or diverge, is called a **divergent boundary** (dy VUR junt). Most divergent boundaries occur at the mid-ocean ridge. In Section 4, you learned how oceanic crust forms along the mid-ocean ridge as sea-floor spreading occurs.

Divergent boundaries also occur on land. When a divergent boundary develops on land, two of Earth's plates slide apart. A deep valley called a **rift valley** forms along the divergent boundary. For example, the Great Rift Valley in east Africa marks a deep crack in the African continent that runs for about 3,000 kilometers. Along this crack, a divergent plate boundary is slowly spreading apart. The rift may someday split the eastern part of Africa away from the rest of the continent. As a rift valley widens, its floor drops. Eventually, the floor may drop enough for the sea to fill the widening gap.

☑ *Checkpoint* *What is a rift valley? How are rift valleys formed?*

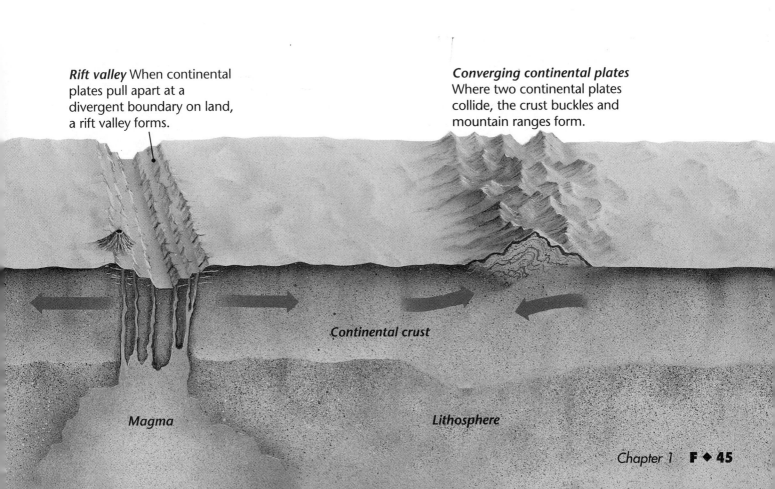

Rift valley When continental plates pull apart at a divergent boundary on land, a rift valley forms.

Converging continental plates Where two continental plates collide, the crust buckles and mountain ranges form.

Continental crust

Magma

Lithosphere

225 million years ago
All Earth's major landmasses were joined in the supercontinent Pangaea before plate movements began to split it apart.

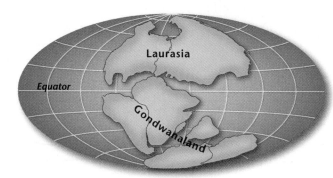

180–200 million years ago
Pangaea continued to split apart, opening narrow seas that later became oceans.

Figure 29 It has taken about 225 million years for the continents to move to their present locations. *Posing Questions* What questions would you need to answer in order to predict where the continents will be in 50 million years?

Convergent Boundaries The place where two plates come together, or converge, is called a **convergent boundary** (kun VUR junt). When two plates converge, the result is called a collision. Collisions may bring together oceanic crust and oceanic crust, oceanic crust and continental crust, or continental crust and continental crust.

When two plates collide, the density of the plates determines which one comes out on top. Oceanic crust, which is made mostly of basalt, is more dense than continental crust, which is made mostly of granite. And oceanic crust becomes cooler and denser as it spreads away from the mid-ocean ridge.

Where two plates carrying oceanic crust meet at a trench, the plate that is more dense dives under the other plate and returns to the mantle. This is the process of subduction that you learned about in Section 4.

Sometimes a plate carrying oceanic crust collides with a plate carrying continental crust. The less dense continental crust can't sink under the more dense oceanic crust. Instead, the oceanic plate begins to sink and plunges beneath the continental plate.

When two plates carrying continental crust collide, subduction does not take place. Both continental plates are mostly low-density granite rock. Therefore, neither plate is dense enough to sink into the mantle. Instead, the plates crash head-on. The collision squeezes the crust into mighty mountain ranges.

☑ *Checkpoint* *What types of plate movement occur at plate boundaries?*

Figure 28 A collision between two continental plates produced the majestic Himalayas. The collision began 50 million years ago, when the plate that carries India slammed into Asia.

135 million years ago Gradually, the landmasses that became today's continents began to drift apart.

Earth today
Note how far to the north India has drifted—farther than any other major landmass.

65 million years ago
India was still a separate continent, charging toward Asia, while Australia remained attached to Antarctica.

The Continents' Slow Dance

The plates move at amazingly slow rates: from about one to ten centimeters per year. The North American and Eurasian plates are floating apart at a rate of 2.5 centimeters per year—that's about as fast as your fingernails grow. This may not seem like much, but these plates have been moving for tens of millions of years.

About 260 million years ago, the continents were joined together in the supercontinent that Wegener called Pangaea. Then, about 225 million years ago, Pangaea began to break apart. Figure 29 shows how Earth's continents and other landmasses have moved since the break-up of Pangaea.

Section 5 Review

1. What is the theory of plate tectonics?
2. What are the different types of boundaries found along the edges of Earth's plates?
3. What major event in Earth's history began about 225 million years ago? Explain.
4. **Thinking Critically Predicting** Look at Figure 26 on page 43 and find the divergent boundary that runs through the African plate. Predict what could eventually happen along this boundary.

Check Your Progress
CHAPTER PROJECT 1

Now that you have learned about plate tectonics, add examples of plate boundaries to your model. If possible, include a transform boundary, a convergent boundary, and a divergent boundary. Complete the construction of your model by adding all the required surface features. Be sure to label the features on your model. Include arrows that indicate the direction of plate movement.

HOT PLATES

In this lab, you will observe a model of convection currents in Earth's mantle.

Problem

How do convection currents affect Earth's plates?

Materials

1 aluminum roasting pan
2 candles, about 10 cm long
clay to hold the candles up
6 bricks
2 medium-sized kitchen sponges
10 map pins
2 L water

Procedure

1. Stick ten pins about halfway into a long side of one of the sponges.
2. Place an aluminum pan on top of two stacks of bricks. **CAUTION:** *Position the bricks so that they fully support both ends of the pan.*
3. Fill the pan with water to a depth of 4 cm.
4. Moisten both sponges with water and float them in the pan.
5. Slowy nudge the two sponges together with the row of map pins between them. (The pins will keep the sponges from sticking together.)
6. Carefully let go of the sponges. If they drift apart, gently move them back together again.
7. Once the sponges stay close together, place the candles under opposite ends of the pan. Use clay to hold up the candles.
8. Draw a diagram of the pan, showing the starting position of the sponges.
9. Carefully light the candles. Observe the two sponges as the water heats up.

10. Draw diagrams showing the position of the sponges 1 minute and 2 minutes after placing the candles under the pan.

Analyze and Conclude

1. What happens to the sponges as the water heats up?
2. What can you infer is causing the changes you observed?
3. What material represents the mantle in this activity? What represents Earth's plates?
4. What would be the effect of adding several more candles under the pan?
5. **Think About It** How well did this activity model the movement of Earth's plates? What type of plate movement did you observe in the pan? How could you modify the activity to model plate movement more closely?

More to Explore

You can observe directly the movement of the water in the pan. To do this, squeeze a single drop of food coloring into the pan. After the drop of coloring has sunk to the bottom, place a lit candle under the pan near the colored water. How does the food coloring move in the water? How does this movement compare with convection currents in the mantle?

SECTION 1 Earth's Interior

Key Ideas
◆ Earth's interior is divided into the crust, the mantle, the outer core, and the inner core.
◆ The lithosphere includes the crust and the rigid upper layer of the mantle; beneath the lithosphere lies the asthenosphere.

Key Terms
geologist   seismic wave   lithosphere
rock   pressure   asthenospere
geology   crust   outer core
constructive force basalt   inner core
destructive force granite
continent   mantle

 ## SECTION 2 Convection Currents and the Mantle
INTEGRATING PHYSICS

Key Ideas
◆ Heat can be transferred in three ways: radiation, conduction, and convection.
◆ Differences of temperature and density within a fluid cause convection currents.

Key Terms
heat transfer   convection
radiation   density
conduction   convection current

 ## SECTION 3 Drifting Continents

Key Ideas
◆ Alfred Wegener developed the idea that the continents were once joined and have since drifted apart.
◆ Most scientists rejected Wegener's theory because he could not identify a force that could move the continents.

Key Terms
Pangaea
continental drift
fossil

 ## SECTION 4 Sea-Floor Spreading

Key Ideas
◆ In sea-floor spreading, molten material forms new rock along the mid-ocean ridge.
◆ In subduction, the ocean floor sinks back to the mantle beneath deep ocean trenches.

Key Terms
mid-ocean ridge   deep-ocean trench
sonar   subduction
sea-floor spreading

SECTION 5 The Theory of Plate Tectonics

Key Ideas
◆ The theory of plate tectonics explains plate movements and how they cause continental drift.
◆ Plates slip past each other at transform boundaries, move apart at divergent boundaries, and come together at convergent boundaries.

Key Terms
plate   transform boundary
scientific theory   divergent boundary
plate tectonics   rift valley
fault   convergent boundary

Organizing Information

Cycle Diagram To show the processes that link a trench and the mid-ocean ridge, copy the cycle diagram into your notebook and fill in the blanks.

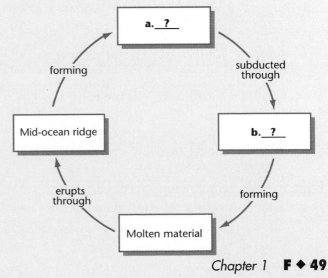

CHAPTER 1 ASSESSMENT

Reviewing Content

 For more review of key concepts, see the Interactive Student Tutorial CD-ROM.

Multiple Choice
Choose the letter of the answer that best completes each statement.

1. The layer of the upper mantle that can flow is the
   a. asthenosphere.
   b. lithosphere.
   c. inner core.
   d. continental crust.
2. Most scientists rejected Wegener's theory of continental drift because the theory failed to explain
   a. coal deposits in Antarctica.
   b. formation of mountains.
   c. climate changes.
   d. how the continents move.
3. Subduction of the ocean floor takes place at
   a. the lower mantle.
   b. mid-ocean ridges.
   c. rift valleys.
   d. trenches.
4. The process that powers plate tectonics is
   a. radiation.   b. convection.
   c. conduction.   d. subduction
5. Two plates collide with each other at
   a. a divergent boundary
   b. a convergent boundary
   c. the boundary between the mantle and the crust.
   d. a transform boundary.

True or False
If the statement is true, write true. If it is false, change the underlined word or words to make the statement true.

6. The Earth's <u>outer core</u> is made of basalt and granite.
7. The spinning of the <u>asthenosphere</u>, made of iron and nickel, explains why Earth has a magnetic field.
8. <u>Convection currents</u> form because of differences of temperature and density in a fluid.
9. <u>Magnetic stripes</u> on the ocean floor are places where oceanic crust sinks back to the mantle.
10. When two continental plates <u>converge</u>, a rift valley forms.

Checking Concepts

11. How is the inner core different from the outer core?
12. Why are there convection currents in the mantle? Explain.
13. What evidence of Earth's climate in the past supports the theory of continental drift?
14. What was the importance of the discovery that molten rock was coming out of cracks along the mid-ocean ridge?
15. How do magnetic stripes form on the ocean floor? Why are these stripes significant?
16. What happens when a plate of oceanic crust collides with a plate of continental crust? Why?
17. **Writing to Learn** Imagine that Alfred Wegener is alive today to defend his theory of continental drift. Write a short interview that Wegener might have on a daytime talk show. You may use humor.

Thinking Critically

18. **Classifying** Classify these layers of Earth's crust as liquid, solid, or solid but able to flow slowly: crust, lithosphere, asthenosphere, outer core, inner core.
19. **Comparing and Contrasting** How are oceanic and continental crust alike? How do they differ?
20. **Relating Cause and Effect** What do many geologists think is the driving force of plate tectonics? Explain.
21. **Making Generalizations** State in one sentence the most significant discovery that geologists established through their study of plate tectonics.

Applying Skills

Geologists think that a new plate boundary is forming in the Indian Ocean. The part of the plate carrying Australia is twisting away from the part of the plate carrying India.

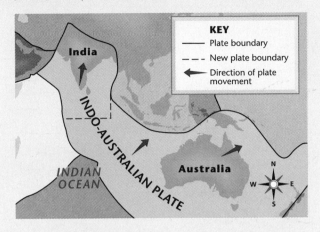

22. Interpreting Maps Look at the arrows showing the direction of plate motion. In what direction is the part of the plate carrying Australia moving? In what direction is the part carrying India moving?

23. Predicting As India and Australia move in different directions, what type of plate boundary will form between them?

24. Inferring On the map you can see that the northern part of the Indo-Australian plate is moving north and colliding with the Eurasian plate. What features would occur where these plates meet? Explain.

Performance ▼ CHAPTER PROJECT 1 Assessment

Project Wrap Up Present your model to the class. Point out the types of plate boundaries on the model. Discuss the plate motions and landforms that result in these areas. What similarities and differences exist between your model and those of your classmates?

Reflect and Record In your journal, write an evaluation of your project. What materials would you change? How could you improve your model?

Test Preparation

Use these questions to prepare for standardized tests.

Use the diagram to answer Questions 25–28.

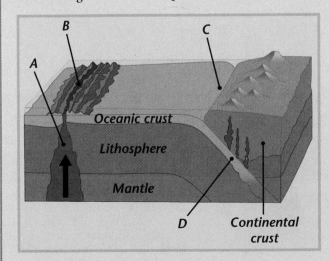

25. The arrow at A represents
a. a transform boundary.
b. continental crust.
c. a subduction zone.
d. molten magma rising from the mantle.

26. What is occurring at the feature labeled B?
a. New rock is being added to the oceanic plate.
b. The ocean floor is sinking.
c. Subduction is occurring.
d. Two plates are colliding.

27. As sea-floor spreading occurs, the oceanic plate
a. does not move.
b. moves from C toward B.
c. moves from B toward C.
d. floats higher on the mantle.

28. What is occurring at D?
a. New material is rising from the mantle.
b. The oceanic plate is melting as it sinks into the mantle.
c. Sedimentary rock is being added to the plate.
d. The oceanic plate is pushing the continental plate into the mantle.

CHAPTER
2 Earthquakes

Nearly 2,000 years ago, the ancient Chinese invented this instrument to detect earthquakes.

WEB ACTIVITY www.phschool.com

SECTION 1 Earth's Crust in Motion

Discover **How Does Stress Affect Earth's Crust?**
Try This **It's a Stretch**
Sharpen Your Skills **Measuring**
Skills Lab **Modeling Movement Along Faults**

SECTION 2 Measuring Earthquakes

Discover **How Do Seismic Waves Travel Through Earth?**
Try This **Recording Seismic Waves**
Real-World Lab **Locating an Epicenter**

SECTION 3 Earthquake Hazards and Safety

Discover **Can Bracing Prevent Building Collapse?**
Sharpen Your Skills **Calculating**

Shake, Rattle, and Roll

The ground shakes ever so slightly. A bronze dragon drops a ball into the mouth of the frog below. Nearly 2,000 years ago in China, that's how an instrument like this one would have detected a distant earthquake. Earthquakes are proof that our planet is subject to great forces from within. Earthquakes remind us that we live on the moving pieces of Earth's crust. In this chapter, you will design a structure that will withstand earthquakes.

Your Goal To design, build, and test a model structure that is earthquake resistant.

Your model should
♦ be made of materials that are approved by your teacher
♦ be built to specifications agreed on by your class
♦ be able to withstand several simulated earthquakes of increasing intensity
♦ be built following the safety guidelines in Appendix A

Get Started Before you design your model, find out how earthquakes cause damage to structures such as homes, office buildings, and highway overpasses. Preview the chapter to find out how engineers design structures to withstand earthquakes.

Check Your Progress You will be working on this project as you study this chapter. To keep your project on track, look for Check Your Progress boxes at the following points.

Section 1 Review, page 61: Design your model.
Section 2 Review, page 69: Construct, improve, and test your model.
Section 4 Review, page 81: Test your model again, and then repair and improve it.

Wrap Up At the end of the chapter (page 85), you will demonstrate how well your model can withstand the effects of a simulated earthquake and predict whether a building that followed your design could withstand a real earthquake.

SECTION 4

Integrating Technology

Monitoring Faults

Discover Can Stress Be Measured?

1 Earth's Crust in Motion

How Does Stress Affect Earth's Crust?

1. Put on your goggles.

2. Holding a popsicle stick at both ends, slowly bend it into an arch.

3. Release the pressure on the popsicle stick and observe what happens.

4. Repeat Steps 1 and 2. This time, however, keep bending the ends of the popsicle stick toward each other. What happens to the wood?

Think It Over
Predicting Think of the popsicle stick as a model for part of Earth's crust. What do you think might eventually happen as the forces of plate movement bend the crust?

GUIDE FOR READING

◆ How do stress forces affect rock?

◆ Why do faults form and where do they occur?

◆ How does movement along faults change Earth's surface?

Reading Tip Before you read, use the headings to make an outline about stress in the crust, faults, and mountain building.

You are sitting at the kitchen table eating breakfast. Suddenly you notice a slight vibration, as if a heavy truck were rumbling by. At the same time, your glass of orange juice jiggles. Dishes rattle in the cupboards. After a few seconds, the rattling stops. Later, when you listen to the news on the radio, you learn that your region experienced a small earthquake. Earthquakes are a reminder that Earth's crust can move.

Stress in the Crust

An **earthquake** is the shaking and trembling that results from the movement of rock beneath Earth's surface. The movement of Earth's plates creates powerful forces that squeeze or pull the rock in the crust. These forces are examples of **stress,** a force that acts on rock to change its shape or volume. (Volume is the amount of space an object takes up.) Because stress is a force, it adds energy to the rock. The energy is stored in the rock until the rock either breaks or changes shape.

Figure 1 Stress in the crust folded this rock like a sheet of ribbon candy.

Types of Stress

Three different kinds of stress occur in the crust—shearing, tension, and compression. **Shearing, tension, and compression work over millions of years to change the shape and volume of rock.** These forces cause some rocks to become brittle and snap. Other rocks tend to bend slowly like road tar softened by the heat of the sun.

Stress that pushes a mass of rock in two opposite directions is called **shearing**. Shearing can cause rock to break and slip apart or to change its shape.

The stress force called **tension** pulls on the crust, stretching rock so that it becomes thinner in the middle. The effect of tension on rock is somewhat like pulling apart a piece of warm bubble gum. Tension occurs where two plates are moving apart.

The stress force called **compression** squeezes rock until it folds or breaks. One plate pushing against another can compress rock like a giant trash compactor.

Any change in the volume or shape of Earth's crust is called **deformation**. Most changes in the crust occur so slowly that they cannot be observed directly. But if you could speed up time so a billion years passed by in minutes, you could see the deformation of the crust. The crust would bend, stretch, break, tilt, fold, and slide. The slow shift of Earth's plates causes this deformation.

✓ *Checkpoint* *How does deformation change Earth's surface?*

Figure 2 Deformation pushes, pulls, or twists the rocks in Earth's crust. *Relating Cause and Effect Which type of deformation tends to shorten part of the crust?*

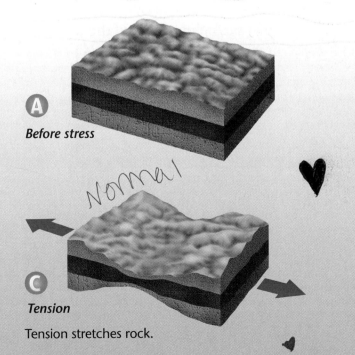

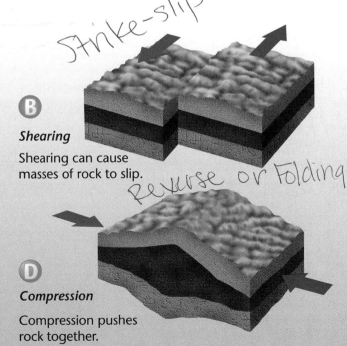

A
Before stress

B
Shearing
Shearing can cause masses of rock to slip.

C
Tension
Tension stretches rock.

D
Compression
Compression pushes rock together.

Chapter 2 **F ◆ 55**

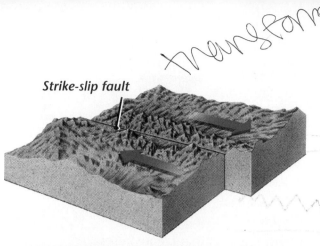

Strike-slip fault

transform (handwritten)

Figure 3 A strike-slip fault that is clearly visible at the surface is the San Andreas Fault in California.

Kinds of Faults

If you try to break a caramel candy bar in two, it may only bend and stretch at first. Like a candy bar, many types of rock can bend or fold. But beyond a certain limit, even these rocks will break. And it takes less stress to snap a brittle rock than it does to snap one that can bend.

When enough stress builds up in rock, the rock breaks, creating a fault. A **fault** is a break in Earth's crust where slabs of crust slip past each other. The rocks on both sides of a fault can move up or down or sideways. **Faults usually occur along plate boundaries, where the forces of plate motion compress, pull, or shear the crust so much that the crust breaks.** There are three main types of faults: strike-slip faults, normal faults, and reverse faults.

Strike-Slip Faults Shearing creates strike-slip faults. In a **strike-slip fault,** the rocks on either side of the fault slip past each other sideways with little up-or-down motion. Figure 3 shows the type of movement that occurs along a strike-slip fault. A strike-slip fault that forms the boundary between two plates is called a transform boundary. The San Andreas fault in California is an example of a strike-slip fault that is a transform boundary.

Normal Faults Tension forces in Earth's crust cause normal faults. In a **normal fault,** the fault is at an angle, so one block of rock lies above the fault while the other block lies below the fault. The half of the fault that lies above is called the **hanging wall.** The half of the fault that lies below is called the **footwall.** Look at Figure 4 to see how the hanging wall lies above the

Figure 4 A normal fault created the Sandia Mountains in New Mexico.

divergent (handwritten)

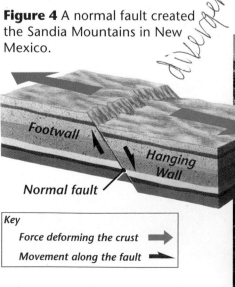

Footwall

Hanging Wall

Normal fault

Key

Force deforming the crust →

Movement along the fault →

footwall. When movement occurs along a normal fault, the hanging wall slips downward. Tension forces create normal faults where plates diverge, or pull apart. For example, normal faults occur along the Rio Grande rift valley in New Mexico, where two pieces of Earth's crust are diverging.

Reverse Faults Compression forces produce reverse faults. A **reverse fault** has the same structure as a normal fault, but the blocks move in the opposite direction. Look at Figure 5 to see how the rocks along a reverse fault move. As in a normal fault, one side of a reverse fault lies at an angle above the other side. The rock forming the hanging wall of a reverse fault slides up and over the footwall. Reverse faults produced part of the Appalachian Mountains in the eastern United States.

A type of reverse fault formed the majestic peaks in Glacier National Park in Montana shown in Figure 5. Over millions of years, a huge block of rock slid along the fault, moving up and over the surface rock. Parts of the overlying block then wore away, leaving the mountain peaks.

✓ *Checkpoint* *What are the three types of fault? What force of deformation produces each?*

Key
Force deforming the crust ➡
Movement along the fault ➤

Footwall   Hanging Wall

Reverse fault

Figure 5 A reverse fault formed Mt. Gould in Glacier National Park, beginning 60 million years ago.
Inferring *Which half of the reverse fault slid up and across to form this mountain, the hanging wall or the footwall? Explain.*

Figure 6 The San Andreas fault extends from the Salton Sea in southern California to the point in northern California where the plate boundary continues into the Pacific Ocean.

Friction Along Faults

INTEGRATING PHYSICS How rocks move along a fault depends on how much friction there is between the opposite sides of the fault. Friction is the force that opposes the motion of one surface as it moves across another surface. Friction exists because surfaces are not perfectly smooth.

Where friction along a fault is low, the rocks on both sides of the fault slide by each other without much sticking. Where friction is moderate, the sides of the fault jam together. Then from time to time they jerk free, producing small earthquakes. Where friction is high, the rocks lock together and do not move. In this case, stress increases until it is strong enough to overcome the friction force.

The San Andreas fault forms a transform boundary between the Pacific plate and the North American plate. In most places along the San Andreas fault, friction is high and the plates lock. Stress builds up until an earthquake releases the stress and the plates slide past each other.

Mountain Building

The forces of plate movement can build up Earth's surface. **Over millions of years, fault movement can change a flat plain into a towering mountain range.**

Mountains Formed by Faulting When normal faults uplift a block of rock, a **fault-block mountain** forms. You can see a diagram of this process in Figure 7. How does this process begin?

Figure 7 Two normal faults can form fault-block mountains, such as the Teton Range near the border of Wyoming and Idaho.

Normal faults

Key
Movement along normal faults ➡

Where two plates move away from each other, tension forces create many normal faults. When two of these normal faults form parallel to each other, a block of rock is left lying between them. As the hanging wall of each normal fault slips downward, the block in between moves upward. When a block of rock lying between two normal faults slides downward, a valley forms.

If you traveled by car from Salt Lake City to Los Angeles you would cross the Great Basin, a region with many ranges of fault-block mountains separated by broad valleys, or basins. This "basin and range" region covers much of Nevada and western Utah.

Mountains Formed by Folding Under certain conditions, plate movement causes the crust to fold. Have you ever skidded on a rug that wrinkled up as your feet pushed it across the floor? Much as the rug wrinkles, rock stressed by compression may bend slowly without breaking. **Folds** are bends in rock that form when compression shortens and thickens part of Earth's crust.

The collisions of two plates can cause compression and folding of the crust. Some of the world's largest mountain ranges, including the Himalayas in Asia and the Alps in Europe, formed when pieces of the crust folded during the collision of two plates. Such plate collisions also lead to earthquakes, because folding rock can fracture and produce faults.

Individual folds can be only a few centimeters across or hundreds of kilometers wide. You can often see small folds in the rock exposed where a highway has been cut through a hillside.

Sharpen your
Skills

Measuring
You can measure the force of friction.

ACTIVITY

1. Place a small weight on a smooth, flat tabletop. Use a spring scale to pull the weight across the surface. How much force is shown on the spring scale? (*Hint*: The unit of force is newtons.)

2. Tape a piece of sandpaper to the tabletop. Repeat Step 1, pulling the weight across the sandpaper.

Is the force of friction greater for a smooth surface or for a rough surface?

Figure 8 Compression forces cause folds in Earth's crust. **A.** Some mountains are made up of folded rock. **B.** The satellite image shows folded mountains west of Harrisburg, Pennsylvania.

Anticlines and Synclines Geologists use the terms anticline and syncline to describe upward and downward folds in rock. You can compare anticlines and synclines in the diagram in Figure 9. A fold in rock that bends upward into an arch is an **anticline**. A fold in rock that bends downward in the middle to form a bowl is a **syncline**. Anticlines and synclines are found on many parts of Earth's surface where compression forces have folded the crust.

One example of an anticline is the Black Hills of South Dakota. The Black Hills began to form about 65 million years ago. At that time, forces in Earth's crust produced a large dome-shaped anticline. Over millions of years, a variety of processes wore down and shaped the rock of this anticline into the Black Hills.

You may see a syncline where a valley dips between two parallel ranges of hills. But a syncline may also be a very large feature, as large as the state of Illinois. The Illinois Basin is a syncline that stretches from the western side of Indiana about 250 kilometers across the state of Illinois. The basin is filled with soil and rock that have accumulated over millions of years.

Figure 9 **A.** Over millions of years, compression and folding of the crust produce anticlines, which arch upward, and synclines, which dip downward. **B.** The folded rock layers of an anticline can be seen on this cliff on the coast of England.

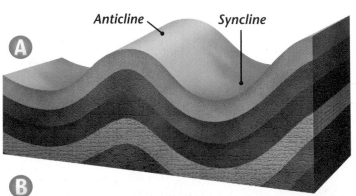

Anticline   Syncline

Figure 10 The flat land on the horizon is the Kaibab Plateau, which forms the North Rim of the Grand Canyon in Arizona. The Kaibab Plateau is part of the Colorado Plateau.

Plateaus The forces that raise mountains can also raise plateaus. A **plateau** is a large area of flat land elevated high above sea level. Some plateaus form when vertical faults push up a large, flat block of rock. Like a fancy sandwich, a plateau consists of many different flat layers, and is wider than it is tall.

Forces deforming the crust uplifted the Colorado Plateau in the "Four Corners" region of Arizona, Utah, Colorado, and New Mexico. The Colorado Plateau is a roughly circular area of uplifted rock more than 500 kilometers across. This vast slab of rock once formed part of a sea floor. Today, much of the plateau lies more than 1,500 meters above sea level.

Section 1 Review

1. What are the three main types of stress in rock?
2. Describe the movements that occur along each of the three types of faults.
3. How does Earth's surface change as a result of movement along faults?
4. **Thinking Critically Predicting** If plate motion compresses part of the crust, what landforms will form there in millions of years? Explain.

Check Your Progress

CHAPTER PROJECT 2

Discuss with your classmates the model you plan to build. What materials could you choose for your earthquake-resistant structure? Sketch your design. Does your design meet the guidelines provided by your teacher? How will you use your materials to build your model? (*Hint*: Draw the sketch of your model to scale).

MODELING MOVEMENT ALONG FAULTS

Faults are cracks in Earth's crust where masses of rock move over, under, or past each other. In this lab, you will make a model of the movements along faults.

Problem

How does the movement of rock along the sides of a fault compare for different types of faults?

Materials

Clay in two or more colors
Marking pen
Plastic butter knife

Procedure

1. Mold some clay into a sheet about 0.5 centimeter thick and about 6 centimeters square. Then make another sheet of the same size and thickness, using a different color.

2. Cut each square in half and stack the sheets on top of each other, alternating colors.
   CAUTION: *To avoid breaking the plastic knife, do not press too hard as you cut.* The sheets of clay stand for different layers of rock. The different colors will help you see where similar layers of rock end up after movement occurs along the model fault.

3. Press the layers of clay together to form a rectangular block that fits in the palm of your hand.

4. Use the butter knife to slice carefully through the block at an angle, as shown in the photograph.

5. Place the two blocks formed by the slice together, but don't let them stick together.

6. Review the descriptions and diagrams of faults in Section 1. Decide which piece of your block is the hanging wall and which is the footwall. Using the marking pen, label the side of each block. What part of your model stands for the fault itself?

7. What part of the model stands for the land surface? Along the top surface of the two blocks, draw a river flowing across the fault. Also draw an arrow on each block to show the direction of the river's flow. The arrow should point from the footwall toward the hanging wall.

8. Make a table that includes the headings Type of Fault, How the Sides of the Fault Move, and Changes in the Land Surface.

Type of Fault	How the Sides of the Fault Move	Changes in the Land Surface

9. Using your blocks, model the movement along a strike-slip fault. Record your motion and the results on the data table.
10. Repeat Step 9 for a normal fault.
11. Repeat Step 9 for a reverse fault.

Analyze and Conclude

Refer to your data table to draw a chart that will help you answer questions 1 through 4.

1. On your chart, show the direction in which the sides of the fault move for each type of fault.
2. On your chart, show how movement along a strike-slip fault is different from movement along the other two types of fault.
3. Add to your chart a column that shows how the river on the surface might change for each type of fault.
4. Assuming that the river is flowing from the footwall toward the hanging wall, which type of fault could produce small waterfalls in the surface river? (*Hint:* Recall how you tell which block is the hanging wall and which block is the footwall).
5. If you could observe only the land surface around a fault, how could you tell if the fault is a strike-slip fault? A normal fault?
6. If you slide the hanging wall of your fault model upward in relation to the footwall, what type of fault forms? If this movement continues, where will the slab of rock with the hanging wall end up?

7. From an airplane, you see a chain of several long, narrow lakes along a fault. What type of fault would cause these lakes to form?
8. **Think About It** In what ways does the model help you picture what is happening along a fault? In what ways does the model not accurately reflect what happens along a fault? How is the model still useful in spite of its inaccuracies?

More to Explore

On Earth's surface, individual faults do not exist all by themselves. With one or more of your classmates, combine your models to show how a fault-block mountain range or a rift valley could form. (*Hint:* Both involve normal faults.) How could you combine your models to show how reverse faults produce a mountain range?

2 Measuring Earthquakes

DISCOVER • ACTIVITY • • •

How Do Seismic Waves Travel Through Earth?

1. Stretch a spring toy across the floor while a classmate holds the other end. Do not overstretch the toy.

2. Gather together about 4 coils of the spring toy and release them. In what direction do the coils move?

3. Once the spring toy has stopped moving, jerk one end of the toy from side to side once. In what direction do the coils move? Be certain your classmate has a secure grip on the other end.

Think It Over

Observing Describe the two types of wave motion that you observed in the spring toy.

GUIDE FOR READING

◆ How does the energy of an earthquake travel through Earth?

◆ What are the different kinds of seismic waves?

◆ What are the scales used to measure the strength of an earthquake?

Reading Tip Before you read, rewrite the headings in the section as what, how, or why questions. As you read, look for answers to these questions.

Earth is never still. Every day, worldwide, there are about 8,000 earthquakes. Most of them are too small to notice. But when an earthquake is strong enough to rattle dishes in kitchen cabinets, people sit up and take notice. "How big was the quake?" and "Where was it centered?" are two questions just about everyone asks after an earthquake.

To know where an earthquake was centered, you need to know where it began. Earthquakes always begin in rock below the surface. Most earthquakes begin in the lithosphere within 100 kilometers of Earth's surface. An earthquake starts at one particular point. The **focus** (FOH kus) is the point beneath Earth's surface where rock that is under stress breaks, triggering an earthquake. The point on the surface directly above the focus is called the **epicenter** (EHP uh sen tur).

Seismic Waves

If you have ever played a drum, you know that the sound it makes depends on how hard you strike it. Like a drumbeat, an earthquake produces vibrations called waves. These waves carry energy as they travel outward through solid material. During an earthquake, seismic waves race out from the focus in all directions. **Seismic waves** are vibrations that travel through Earth carrying the energy released during an earthquake. The seismic waves move like ripples in a pond. Look at Figure 11 to see how seismic waves travel outward in all directions from the focus.

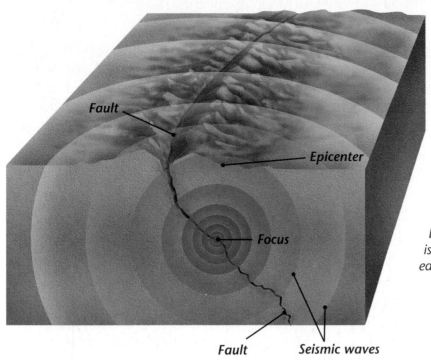

Fault

Epicenter

Focus

Fault   Seismic waves

Figure 11 An earthquake occurs when rocks fracture at the focus, deep in Earth's crust. *Interpreting Diagrams* What point is directly above the focus of the earthquake?

Seismic waves carry the energy of an earthquake away from the focus, through Earth's interior, and across the surface. The energy of the seismic waves that reach the surface is greatest at the epicenter. The most violent shaking during an earthquake, however, may occur kilometers away from the epicenter. The types of rock and soil around the epicenter determine where and how much the ground shakes. You will learn more about the effects of seismic waves in Section 3.

There are three categories of seismic waves: P waves, S waves, and surface waves. An earthquake sends out two types of waves from its focus: P waves and S waves. When these waves reach Earth's surface at the epicenter, surface waves develop.

Primary Waves The first waves to arrive are primary waves, or P waves. **P waves** are earthquake waves that compress and expand the ground like an accordion. P waves cause buildings to contract and expand. Look at Figure 12 to compare P waves and S waves.

Secondary Waves After P waves come secondary waves, or S waves. **S waves** are earthquake waves that vibrate from side to side as well as up and down. They shake the ground back and forth. When S waves reach the surface, they shake structures violently. Unlike P waves, which travel through both solids and liquids, S waves cannot move through liquids.

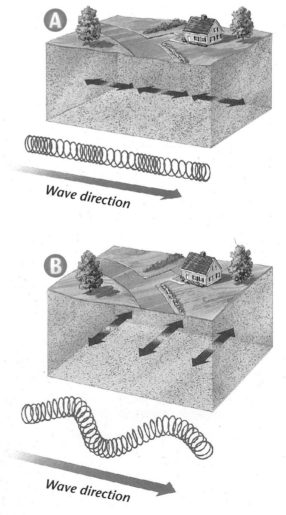

A

Wave direction

B

Wave direction

Figure 12 A. In P waves, the particles of the crust vibrate forward and back along the path of the wave. **B.** In S waves, the particles of the crust vibrate from side to side and up and down.

Surface Waves When P waves and S waves reach the surface, some of them are transformed into surface waves. **Surface waves** move more slowly than P waves and S waves, but they produce the most severe ground movements. Some surface waves make the ground roll like ocean waves. Other surface waves shake buildings from side to side.

☑ *Checkpoint* What are the three types of seismic waves?

Detecting Seismic Waves

To record and measure the vibrations of seismic waves, geologists use instruments called seismographs. A **seismograph** (SYZ muh graf) records the ground movements caused by seismic waves as they move through the Earth.

Until recently, scientists used mechanical seismographs. As shown in Figure 13, a mechanical seismograph consists of a heavy weight attached to a frame by a spring or wire. A pen connected to the weight rests its point on a rotating drum. When the drum is still, the pen draws a straight line on paper wrapped around the drum. During an earthquake, seismic waves cause the drum to vibrate. Meanwhile, the pen stays in place and records the drum's vibrations. The height of the jagged lines drawn on the seismograph's drum is greater for a more severe earthquake.

Today, scientists use electronic seismographs that work according to the same principle as the mechanical seismograph. The electronic seismograph converts ground movements into a signal that can be recorded and printed.

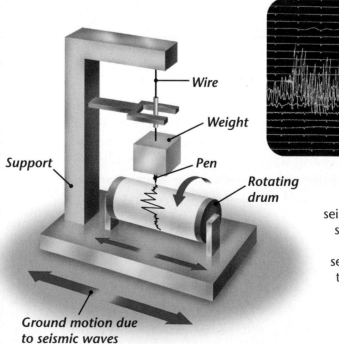

Figure 13 The mechanical seismograph records seismic waves. The record made by a seismograph shows the arrival times of different types of seismic waves.

The Mercalli Scale	
Earthquake Intensity	Earthquake Effects
I–II	Almost unnoticeable
III–IV	People notice vibrations like those from a passing truck. Unstable objects disturbed.
V–VI	Dishes and windows rattle. Books knocked off shelves. Slight damage.
VII–VIII	People run outdoors. Moderate to heavy damage.
IX–X	Buildings jolted off foundations or destroyed. Cracks appear in ground and landslides occur.
XI–XII	Severe damage. Wide cracks appear in ground. Waves seen on ground surface.

Figure 14 An earthquake in 1997 damaged the tower of this city hall in Foligno, Italy (left). The Mercalli scale (right) uses Roman numerals to rank earthquakes by how much damage they cause.
Applying Concepts How would you rate the damage to the Foligno city hall on the Mercalli scale?

Measuring Earthquakes

When geologists want to know the size of an earthquake, they must consider many factors. As a result, there are at least 20 different measures for rating earthquakes, each with its strengths and shortcomings. Three ways of measuring earthquakes, the Mercalli scale, the Richter scale, and the moment magnitude scale, are described here. **Magnitude** is a measurement of earthquake strength based on seismic waves and movement along faults.

The Mercalli Scale Early in the twentieth century, the **Mercalli scale** was developed to rate earthquakes according to their intensity. An earthquake's intensity is the strength of ground motion in a given place. The Mercalli scale is not a precise measurement. But the 12 steps of the Mercalli scale describe how earthquakes affect people, buildings, and the land surface. The same earthquake can have different Mercalli ratings because it causes different amounts of damage at different locations.

The Richter Scale The **Richter scale** is a rating of the size of seismic waves that was once measured by a type of mechanical seismograph. The Richter scale was developed in the 1930s. Geologists all over the world used this scale for about 50 years. Eventually, electronic seismographs replaced the mechanical seismographs used for the Richter scale. The Richter scale provides accurate measurements for small, nearby earthquakes. But the scale does not work well for large or distant earthquakes.

Earthquake Magnitudes	
Earthquake	**Moment Magnitude**
San Francisco, California, 1906	7.7
Southern Chile, 1960	9.5
Anchorage, Alaska, 1964	9.2
Loma Prieta, California, 1989	7.2
Northridge/ Los Angeles, California, 1994	6.7

Figure 15 The table lists the moment magnitudes for some of the twentieth century's biggest earthquakes.

The Moment Magnitude Scale Today, geologists use the **moment magnitude scale,** a rating system that estimates the total energy released by an earthquake. **The moment magnitude scale can be used to rate earthquakes of all sizes, near or far.** You may hear news reports that mention the Richter scale. But the magnitude number they quote is almost always the moment magnitude for that earthquake.

To rate an earthquake on the moment magnitude scale, geologists first study data from modern electronic seismographs. The data show what kinds of seismic waves the earthquake produced and how strong they were. The data also help geologists infer how much movement occurred along the fault and the strength of the rocks that broke when the fault slipped. Geologists combine all this information to rate the earthquake on the moment magnitude scale.

Earthquakes with a magnitude below 5.0 on the moment magnitude scale are small and cause little damage. Those with a magnitude above 5.0 can produce great destruction. A magnitude 6.0 quake releases 32 times as much energy as a magnitude 5.0 quake, and nearly 1,000 times as much as a magnitude 4.0 quake.

✓ *Checkpoint* What are three scales for measuring earthquakes?

Locating the Epicenter

Geologists use seismic waves to locate an earthquake's epicenter. Seismic waves travel at different speeds. P waves arrive first at a seismograph, with S waves following close behind. To tell how far the epicenter is from the seismograph, scientists measure the difference between the arrival times of the P waves and S waves.

Figure 16 In terms of magnitude, the 1906 San Francisco earthquake was not the strongest of the century. But it toppled buildings and caused fires that devastated the city.

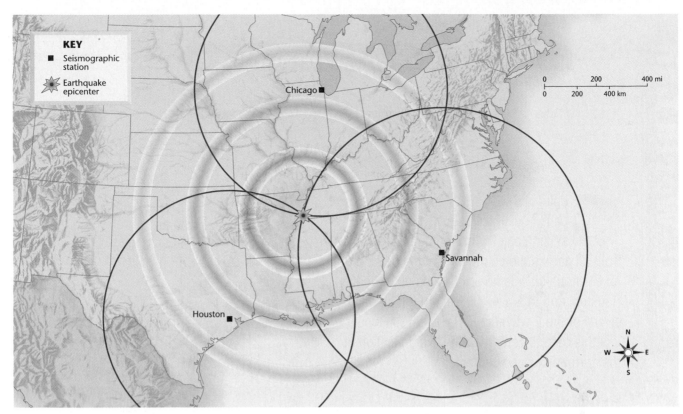

KEY
■ Seismographic station
✳ Earthquake epicenter

Chicago ■

Savannah ■

Houston ■

0   200   400 mi
0   200   400 km

The farther away an earthquake is, the greater the time between the arrival of the P waves and the S waves.

INTEGRATING MATHEMATICS Geologists then draw at least three circles using data from different seismographs set up at stations all over the world. The center of each circle is a particular seismograph's location. The radius of each circle is the distance from the seismograph to the epicenter. The point where the three circles intersect is the location of the epicenter. If you look at Figure 17, you can see why two circles would not give enough information to pinpoint the epicenter.

Figure 17 The map shows how to find the epicenter of an earthquake using data from three seismographic stations. *Measuring Use the map scale to determine the distances from Savannah and Houston to the epicenter. Which is closer?*

Section 2 Review

1. How does the energy from an earthquake reach Earth's surface?
2. Describe the three types of seismic waves.
3. What system do geologists use today for rating the magnitude of an earthquake?
4. **Thinking Critically Relating Cause and Effect** Describe how energy released at an earthquake's focus, deep inside Earth, can cause damage on the surface many kilometers from the epicenter.

Check Your Progress

CHAPTER PROJECT 2

Now it is time to complete your design and construct your model. From what you have learned about earthquakes, what changes will you make in your design? Have a classmate review your model and make suggestions for improvements. When you have made the changes, test your model's ability to withstand an earthquake. Take notes on how well it withstands the quake.

Locating an Epicenter

Geologists who study earthquakes are called seismologists. If you were a seismologist, you would receive data from all across the country. Within minutes after an earthquake, seismographs located in Denver, Houston, and Miami would record the times of arrival of the P waves and S waves. You would use this data to zero in on the exact location of the earthquake's epicenter.

Problem

How can you locate an earthquake's epicenter?

Skills Focus

interpreting data, drawing conclusions

Materials

drawing compass with pencil
outline map of the United States

Procedure ✂

1. Make a copy of the data table showing differences in earthquake arrival times.
2. The graph shows how the difference in arrival time between P waves and S waves depends on the distance from the epicenter of the earthquake. Find the difference in arrival time for Denver on the *y*-axis of the graph. Follow this line across to the point at which it crosses the curve. To find the distance to the epicenter, read down from this point to the *x*-axis of the graph. Enter this distance in the data table.

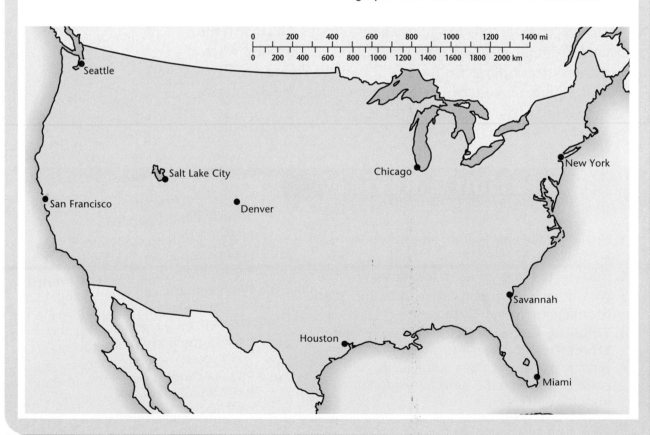

Data Table		
City	Difference in P and S Wave Arrival Times	Distance to Epicenter
Denver, Colorado	2 min 10 s	
Houston, Texas	3 min 55 s	
Miami, Florida	5 min 40 s	

3. Repeat Step 2 for Houston and Miami.
4. Set your compass at a radius equal to the distance from Denver to the earthquake epicenter that you recorded in your data table.
5. Draw a circle with the radius determined in Step 4, using Denver as the center. Draw the circle on your copy of the map. (*Hint:* Draw your circles carefully. You may need to draw some parts of the circles off the map.)
6. Repeat Steps 4 and 5 for Houston and Miami.

Analyze and Conclude

1. Observe the three circles you have drawn to locate the earthquake's epicenter.
2. Which city on the map is closest to the earthquake epicenter? How far, in kilometers, is this city from the epicenter?
3. In which of the three cities listed in the data table would seismographs detect the earthquake first? Last?
4. When you are trying to locate an epicenter, why is it necessary to know the distance from the epicenter for at least three recording stations?
5. About how far is the epicenter that you found from San Francisco? What would the difference in arrival times of the P waves and S waves be for a recording station in San Francisco?
6. What happens to the difference in arrival times between P waves and S waves as the distance from the earthquake increases?
7. **Apply** Working as a seismologist, you find the epicenters of many earthquakes in a region. What features of Earth's crust would you expect to find in this region?

More to Explore

You have just located an earthquake's epicenter. Find this earthquake's location on the earthquake risk map on page 81. Judging from the map, was this earthquake a freak event? What is the risk of earthquakes in the area of this quake? Now look at the map of Earth's plates on page 43. What conclusions can you draw from this map about the cause of earthquakes in this area?

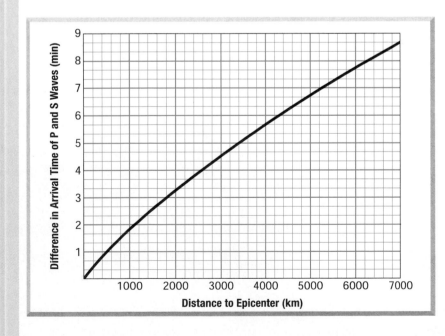

DISCOVER ·······················ACTIVITY····

Can Bracing Prevent Building Collapse?

1. Tape four straws together to make a square frame. Hold the frame upright on a flat surface in front of you.

2. Hold the bottom straw down with one hand while you push the top straw to the left with the other. Push it as far as it will go without breaking the frame.

3. Tape a fifth straw horizontally across the middle of the frame. Repeat Step 2.

Think It Over

Predicting What effect did the fifth straw have? What effect would a piece of cardboard taped to the frame have? Based on your observations, how would an earthquake affect the frame of a house?

GUIDE FOR READING

◆ What kinds of damage does an earthquake cause?

◆ What can be done to reduce earthquake hazards?

Reading Tip Before you read preview the headings of the section. Then predict some of the ways that people can reduce earthquake hazards.

On a cold, bleak morning in January 1995, a powerful earthquake awoke the 1.5 million residents of Kobe, Japan. In 20 terrifying seconds, the earthquake collapsed thousands of buildings, crumpled freeways, and sparked about 130 fires. More than 5,000 people perished.

Most of the buildings that toppled were more than 20 years old. Many were two-story, wood-frame houses with heavy tile roofs. These top-heavy houses were about as stable in an earthquake as a heavy book supported by a framework of pencils. In contrast, many of the more modern buildings remained standing. The newer buildings had been designed to withstand intense shaking.

Figure 18 Many buildings in Kobe, Japan, could not withstand the magnitude 6.9 earthquake that struck in 1995.

How Earthquakes Cause Damage

When a major earthquake strikes, it can cause great damage. **The severe shaking produced by seismic waves can damage or destroy buildings and bridges, topple utility poles, and fracture gas and water mains.** S waves, with their side-to-side and up-and-down movement, can cause severe damage near the epicenter. As the twisting forces of S waves sweep through the ground, the S waves put enough stress on buildings to tear them apart. Earthquakes can also trigger landslides or avalanches. In coastal regions, giant waves pushed up by earthquakes can cause more damage.

Local Soil Conditions When seismic waves move from hard, dense rock to loosely packed soil, they transmit their energy to the soil. The loose soil shakes more violently than the surrounding rock. The thicker the layer of soil, the more violent the shaking will be. This means a house built on solid rock will shake less than a house built on sandy soil.

Liquefaction In 1964, when a powerful earthquake roared through Anchorage, Alaska, cracks opened in the ground. Some of the cracks were 9 meters wide. The cracks were created by liquefaction. **Liquefaction** (lik wih FAK shun) occurs when an earthquake's violent shaking suddenly turns loose, soft soil into liquid mud. Liquefaction is likely where the soil is full of moisture. As the ground gives way, buildings sink and pull apart.

Liquefaction can also trigger landslides. During the 1964 Anchorage earthquake, liquefaction caused a landslide that swept an entire housing development down a cliff and into the sea. Figure 19 shows the damage liquefaction can cause.

Aftershocks Sometimes, buildings weakened by an earthquake collapse during an aftershock. An **aftershock** is an earthquake that occurs after a larger earthquake in the same area. Aftershocks may strike hours, days, or even months later.

Figure 19 An earthquake caused the soil beneath this house to liquefy. Liquefaction caused by seismic waves can change solid soil to liquid mud within seconds. *Posing Questions What are some questions people might ask before building a house in an area that is at risk for earthquakes?*

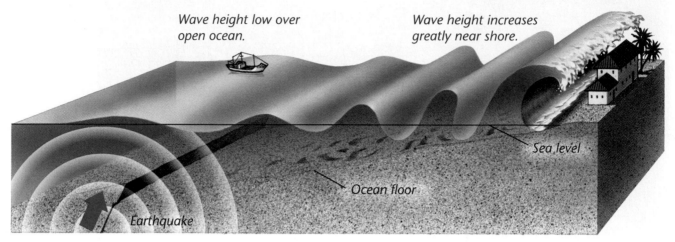

Wave height low over open ocean.

Wave height increases greatly near shore.

Sea level

Ocean floor

Earthquake

Figure 20 A tsunami begins as a low wave, but turns into a huge wave as it nears the shore.

Sharpen your Skills

Calculating ACTIVITY

The Tsunami Warning System alerts people who live near the Pacific Ocean. When geologists detect an earthquake on the ocean floor, they notify coastal areas.

An earthquake in the Gulf of Alaska occurs 3,600 kilometers from Hawaii. The quake's seismic waves travel about 560 kilometers per *minute*. The quake triggers a tsunami that travels at 640 kilometers per *hour*. The seismic waves arrive in Hawaii within minutes and are recorded on seismographs. The seismic waves' arrival warns of the dangerous tsunami that may follow. About how much advance warning will Hawaii have that a tsunami is on the way?

Tsunamis When an earthquake jolts the ocean floor, plate movement causes the ocean floor to rise slightly and push water out of its way. If the earthquake is strong enough, the water displaced by the quake forms large waves, called **tsunamis** (tsoo NAH meez). Figure 20 follows a tsunami from where it begins on the ocean floor.

A tsunami spreads out from an earthquake's epicenter and speeds across the ocean. In the open ocean, the distance between the waves of a tsunami is a very long—between 100 and 200 kilometers. But the height of the wave is low. Tsunamis rise only half a meter or so above the other waves. However, as they approach shallow water near a coastline, the waves become closer together. The tsunami grows into a mountain of water. Some are the height of a six-story building.

✓ *Checkpoint* What are the major causes of earthquake damage?

Making Buildings Safer

Most earthquake-related deaths and injuries result from damage to buildings or other structures. **To reduce earthquake damage, new buildings must be made stronger and more flexible. Older buildings must be modified to withstand stronger quakes.** A structure must be strong in order to resist violent shaking in a quake. It must also be flexible so it can twist and bend without breaking. *Exploring an Earthquake-Safe House* shows how a house can be made safer in an earthquake.

Choice of Location The location of a building affects the type of damage it may suffer during an earthquake. Steep slopes pose the danger of landslides. Filled land can shake violently. Therefore, people should avoid building on such sites. People should also avoid building structures near earthquake faults. As seismic waves pass through the earth, their strength decreases. So the farther a structure is from a fault, the less strong the shaking will be.

EXPLORING *an Earthquake-Safe House*

People can take a variety of steps to make their homes safer in an earthquake. Some steps strengthen the house itself. Others may help to keep objects from tipping or falling.

B. Secure brick chimneys with light, metal brackets.

C. In the attic, nail plywood to the ceiling joists around the chimney for protection against falling bricks.

D. Remove heavy items from the walls above beds. Locate beds away from plate-glass windows.

A. To prevent bookshelves, cabinets, and tall dressers from toppling, fasten them to wall studs with L-shaped brackets.

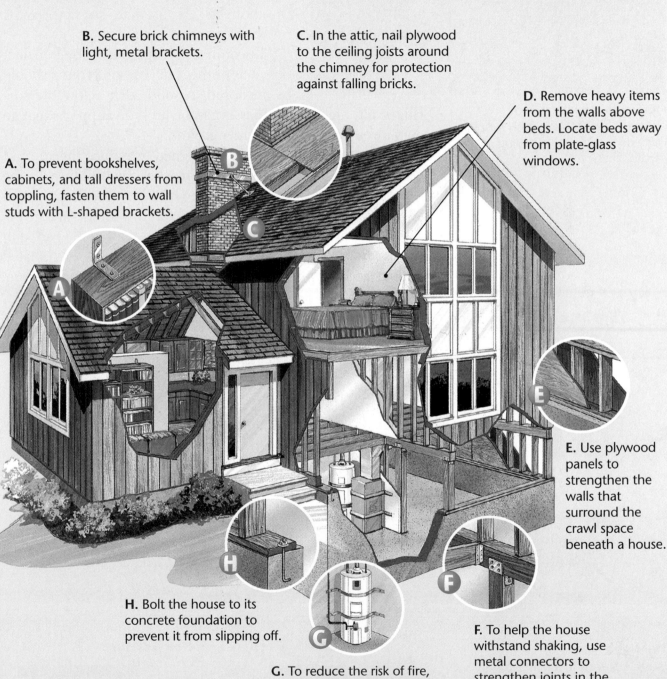

E. Use plywood panels to strengthen the walls that surround the crawl space beneath a house.

H. Bolt the house to its concrete foundation to prevent it from slipping off.

G. To reduce the risk of fire, strap the water heater to the wall to prevent it from toppling over and breaking a gas line. Learn how to shut off the gas, water, and electricity.

F. To help the house withstand shaking, use metal connectors to strengthen joints in the house's frame.

Figure 21 Architects and engineers work to design buildings that will be able to withstand earthquakes.

Construction Methods The way in which a building is constructed determines whether it can withstand an earthquake. During an earthquake, brick buildings as well as some wood-frame buildings may collapse if their walls have not been reinforced, or strengthened. Sometimes plywood sheets are used to strengthen the frames of wooden buildings.

To combat damage caused by liquefaction, new homes built on soft ground should be anchored to solid rock below the soil. Bridges and highway overpasses can be built on supports that go down through soft soil to firmer ground.

INTEGRATING TECHNOLOGY A building designed to reduce the amount of energy that reaches the building during an earthquake is called a **base-isolated building.** As you can see in Figure 22, a base-isolated building rests on shock-absorbing rubber pads or springs. Like the suspension of a car, the pads and springs smooth out a bumpy ride. During a quake, a base-isolated building moves gently back and forth without any violent shaking.

A Fixed-base building

Foundation

Ground movement

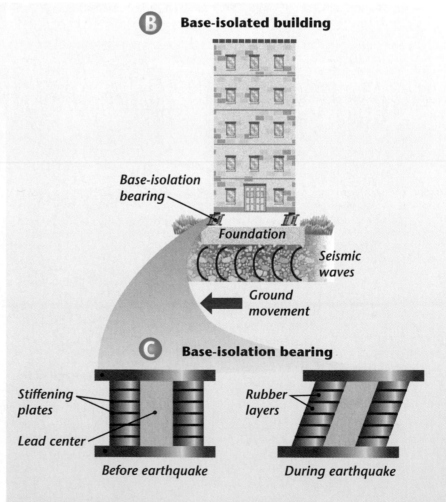

B Base-isolated building

Base-isolation bearing

Foundation

Seismic waves

Ground movement

C Base-isolation bearing

Stiffening plates

Lead center

Rubber layers

Before earthquake

During earthquake

Figure 22 A. The fixed-base building tilts and cracks during an earthquake. B. The base-isolated building remains upright during an earthquake. C. Base-isolation bearings bend and absorb the energy of seismic waves. *Inferring* How does a base-isolation bearing absorb an earthquake's energy?

Much earthquake damage is not the direct result of shaking. Earthquakes indirectly cause fire and flooding when gas pipes and water mains break. Flexible joints can be installed in gas and water lines to keep them from breaking. Automatic shut-off valves also can be installed on these lines to cut off gas and water flow.

Protecting Yourself During an Earthquake

What should you do if an earthquake strikes? The main danger is from falling objects and flying glass. **The best way to protect yourself is to drop, cover, and hold.** This means you should crouch beneath a sturdy table or desk and hold on to it so it doesn't jiggle away during the shaking. The desk or table will provide a barrier against falling objects. If no desk or table is available, crouch against an inner wall, away from the outside of a building, and cover your head and neck with your arms. Avoid windows, mirrors, wall hangings, and furniture that might topple.

If you are outdoors, move to an open area such as a playground. Avoid vehicles, power lines, trees, and buildings, especially ones with brick walls or chimneys. Sit down to avoid being thrown down.

INTEGRATING HEALTH After a major earthquake, water and power supplies may fail, food stores may be closed, and travel may be difficult. People may have to wait several days for these services to be restored. To prepare for such an emergency, families living in a region at high risk for damaging quakes may want to put together an earthquake kit. The kit should contain canned food, water, and first aid supplies and should be stored where it is easy to reach.

Figure 23 Drop, cover, and hold to protect yourself indoors during an earthquake. **A.** If possible, crouch under a desk or table. **B.** Or, crouch against an interior wall and cover your head and neck with your hands.

Section 3 Review

1. Explain how liquefaction occurs and how it causes damage during an earthquake.
2. What can residents do to reduce the risk of earthquake damage to their homes?
3. Describe safety measures you can take to protect yourself during an earthquake.
4. **Thinking Critically Problem Solving** You are a builder planning a housing development where earthquakes are likely. What types of land would you avoid for your development? Where would it be safe to build?

Science at Home

Show your family how an earthquake can affect two different structures—one with more weight on top, the other with more weight on the bottom. Make a model of a fault by placing two small, folded towels side by side on a flat surface. Pile a stack of books on the fault by placing the light books on the bottom and the heaviest ones on top. Then, gently pull the towels in opposite directions until the pile topples. Repeat the process, but this time with the heavier books on the bottom. Discuss with your family which makes a more stable structure.

SECTION
4 Monitoring Faults

DISCOVER ···ACTIVITY····

Can Stress Be Measured?

1. Unfold a facial tissue and lay it flat on your desk.

2. Measure the length of the tissue with a ruler.

3. Grasping the ends of the tissue with both hands, gently pull it. As you are stretching it, hold the tissue against the ruler and measure its length again.

4. Stretch the tissue once more, but this time give it a hard tug.

Think It Over

Drawing Conclusions How is the tissue like the ground along a fault? How might measuring stress in the ground help in predicting an earthquake?

GUIDE FOR READING

◆ How do geologists monitor faults?

◆ How do geologists determine earthquake risk?

Reading Tip As you read, make a list of devices for monitoring earthquakes. Write a sentence about each.

The small town of Parkfield, California, lies on the San Andreas fault about halfway between Los Angeles and San Francisco. Geologists are fascinated by Parkfield because the town had a strong earthquake about every 22 years between 1857 and 1966. Scientists have not found any other place on Earth where the time from one earthquake to the next has been so regular.

In the early 1980s, geologists predicted that a strong earthquake was going to occur in Parkfield between 1985 and 1993. The geologists eagerly set up their instruments—and waited. They waited year after year for the predicted earthquake. But it didn't happen. Finally, several medium-sized earthquakes rumbled along the San Andreas fault near Parkfield in 1993–1994.

Did these quakes take the place of the larger earthquake that geologists had expected? Or had the San Andreas fault itself changed, breaking the pattern of 22 years between quakes? Geologists still don't know the answers to these questions. Nonetheless, geologists continue to monitor the San Andreas fault. Someday, they may find a way to predict when and where an earthquake will occur.

Figure 24 This laser beam detects movement along the San Andreas Fault in Parkfield, California.

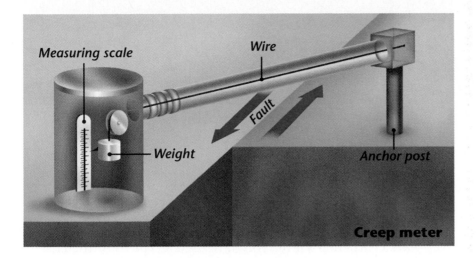

Figure 25 A creep meter can be used to measure movement along a strike-slip fault.

Devices that Monitor Faults

In trying to predict earthquakes, geologists have invented instruments to record the ground movements that occur along faults. **To observe these changes, geologists put in place instruments that measure stress and deformation in the crust.** Geologists hypothesize that such changes signal an approaching earthquake.

Unfortunately, earthquakes almost always strike without warning. The only clue may be a slight rise or fall in the elevation and tilt of the land. Instruments that geologists use to monitor these movements include creep meters, laser-ranging devices, tiltmeters, and satellites.

Creep Meters A creep meter uses a wire stretched across a fault to measure horizontal movement of the ground. On one side of the fault, the wire is anchored to a post. On the other side, the wire is attached to a weight that can slide if the fault moves. Geologists can measure the amount that the fault has moved by measuring how much the weight has moved against a measuring scale.

Laser-Ranging Devices A laser-ranging device uses a laser beam to detect even tiny fault movements. The device calculates any change in the time needed for the laser beam to travel to a reflector and bounce back. Thus, the device can detect any change in distance to the reflector.

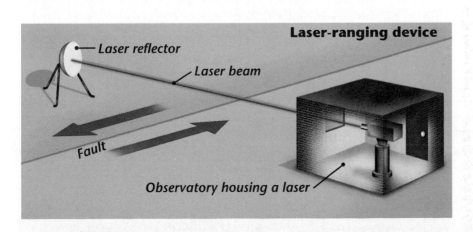

Figure 26 A laser-ranging device monitors fault movement by bouncing a laser beam off a reflector on the other side of the fault. *Comparing and Contrasting How are a laser-ranging device and a creep meter (shown above) similar? How are they different?*

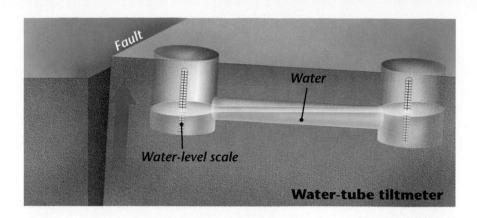

Figure 27 A tiltmeter monitors vertical movement along a fault.

Tiltmeters A tiltmeter measures tilting of the ground. If you have ever used a carpenter's level, you have used a type of tiltmeter. The tiltmeters used by seismologists consist of two bulbs that are filled with a liquid and connected by a hollow stem. Look at the drawing of a tiltmeter in Figure 27. Notice that if the land rises or falls even slightly, the liquid will flow from one bulb to the other. Each bulb contains a measuring scale to measure the depth of the liquid in that bulb. Geologists read the scales to measure the amount of tilt occurring along the fault.

INTEGRATING SPACE SCIENCE **Satellite Monitors** Besides ground-based instruments, geologists use satellites equipped with radar to make images of faults. The satellite bounces radio waves off the ground. As the waves echo back into space, the satellite records them. The time it takes for the radio waves to make their round trip provides precise measurements of the distance to the ground. The distance from the ground to the satellite changes with every change in the ground surface. By comparing different images of the same area taken at different times, geologists detect small changes in elevation. These changes in elevation result when stress deforms the ground along a fault.

 *Checkpoint* *What do fault-monitoring instruments measure?*

Monitoring Risk in the United States

Even with data from many sources, geologists can't predict when and where a quake will strike. Usually, stress along a fault increases until an earthquake occurs. Yet sometimes stress builds up along a fault, but an earthquake fails to occur. Or, one or more earthquakes may relieve stress along another part of the fault. Exactly what will happen remains uncertain—that's why geologists cannot predict earthquakes.

Geologists do know that earthquakes are likely wherever plate movement stores energy in the rock along faults. **Geologists can determine earthquake risk by locating where faults are active and where past earthquakes have occurred.** In the United States, the risk is highest along the Pacific coast in the states of California,

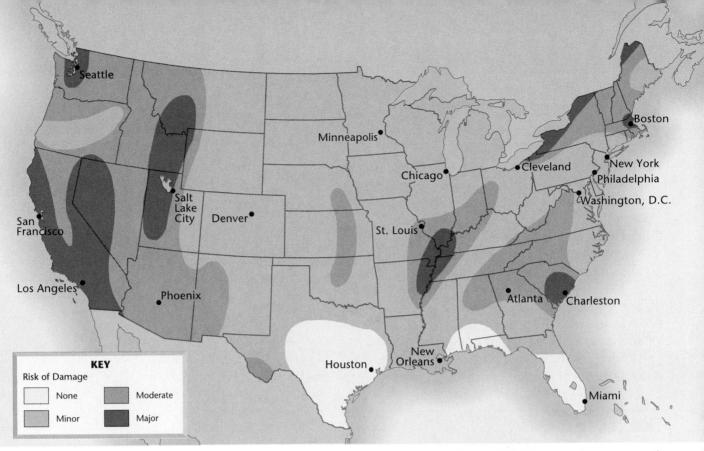

KEY

Risk of Damage

| | None | | Moderate |
| | Minor | | Major |

Figure 28 The map shows areas of the United States, excluding Alaska and Hawaii, where earthquakes are likely to occur and the relative damage they are likely to cause. *Interpreting Maps Where are damaging earthquakes least likely to occur? Most likely to occur?*

Washington, and Alaska. The risk of quakes is high because that's where the Pacific and North American plates meet.

Other regions of the United States also have some risk of earthquakes. Serious earthquakes are rare east of the Rockies. Nonetheless, the region has experienced some of the most powerful quakes in the nation's history. Scientists hypothesize that the continental plate forming most of North America is under stress. This stress could disturb faults that formed millions of years ago. Today, these faults lie hidden beneath thick layers of soil and rock. Find your state in Figure 28 to determine your area's risk of a damaging quake.

Section 4 Review

1. What equipment do geologists use to monitor the movement of faults?
2. What two factors do geologists consider when determining earthquake risk for a region?
3. Explain how satellites can be used to collect data on earthquake faults.
4. **Thinking Critically Making Generalizations** Why can't scientists predict the exact time and place an earthquake is going to occur?

Check Your Progress
Use what you have learned about making buildings earthquake resistant to repair and improve your structure. Test your model again. Are your changes successful in preventing damage? Make additional repairs and improvements to your structure.

CHAPTER PROJECT 2

What's the Risk of an Earthquake?

The New Madrid fault system stretches beneath the central Mississippi River Valley. East of the Rocky Mountains, this is the region of the United States most likely to experience an earthquake. But because the faults are hidden under soil and sediment, the hazards are not obvious.

This region has not had a serious earthquake since 1812. Yet scientists estimate that there is a 90 percent chance that a moderate earthquake will occur in this area in the next 50 years. Which locations might be at risk for heavy damage? No one knows for sure. What preparations, if any, should people of this region make?

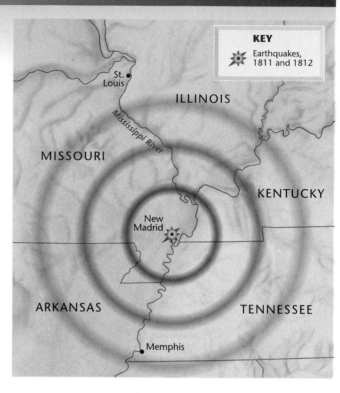

KEY
Earthquakes, 1811 and 1812

The Issues

How Much Money Should People Spend? In areas where earthquakes are rare, such as the New Madrid fault region, communities face hard choices. Should they spend money for earthquake preparation now in order to cut costs later? Or should they save the money and risk the consequences?

Which Buildings Should Be Modified? It's clear that the best way to save lives is to make buildings that can withstand severe shaking. Since damaged or collapsing buildings cause most injuries and deaths during earthquakes, modifying existing buildings could save lives. Unfortunately building renovations are costly.

Most new houses can withstand moderate earthquakes. But many older houses—especially brick or masonry houses—are not safe.

Unfortunately, few homeowners can afford the cost of making their houses safer. They might need financial aid or a tax break to help them make these changes.

What Other Structures Need Improvement? Imagine what would happen if your community were without utility stations and lines for electricity, gas, and water, or without bridges, schools, and hospitals. Engineers who understand earthquake hazards have worked out design standards to reduce damage to these structures. Today, many cities follow these standards in their building codes. But not all structures can be made earthquake-safe. Furthermore, some structures are more crucial for public health and safety than others.

You Decide

1. Identify the Problem
Summarize the dilemma that communities face in regard to earthquake preparations. Which structures in a community are most important to make earthquake-resistant?

2. Analyze the Options
Consider what would happen if communities spent more money, less money, or nothing on earthquake preparations. In each case, who would benefit? Who might be harmed?

3. Find a Solution
Your community near the New Madrid fault system has received a large sum of money to spend on earthquake preparedness. Develop a plan for building and modifying structures. Explain and defend your use of funds.

SECTION 1 Earth's Crust in Motion

Key Ideas

◆ Stresses on Earth's crust produce compression, tension, and shearing in rock.
◆ Faults are cracks in Earth's crust that result from stress.
◆ Faulting and folding of the crust cause mountains and other features to form on the surface.

Key Terms

earthquake	hanging wall
stress	footwall
shearing	reverse fault
tension	fault-block mountain
compression	folds
deformation	anticline
fault	syncline
strike-slip fault	plateau
normal fault	

SECTION 2 Measuring Earthquakes

Key Ideas

◆ As seismic waves travel through Earth, they carry the energy of an earthquake from the focus to the surface.
◆ Earthquakes produce two types of seismic waves, P waves and S waves, that travel out in all directions from the focus of an earthquake.
◆ Today, the moment magnitude scale is used to determine the magnitude of an earthquake. Other scales that geologists have used to rate earthquakes include the Mercalli scale and the Richter scale.

Key Terms

focus	seismograph
epicenter	magnitude
seismic waves	Mercalli scale
P waves	Richter scale
S waves	moment magnitude scale
surface waves	

SECTION 3 Earthquake Hazards and Safety

Key Ideas

◆ Earthquakes can damage structures through tsunamis, landslides or avalanches, and shaking or liquefaction of the ground.
◆ New buildings can be designed to withstand earthquakes; old buildings can be modified to make them more earthquake-resistant.
◆ For personal safety indoors during an earthquake, drop, cover, and hold under a desk or table, or against an interior wall.

Key Terms

liquefaction	tsunamis
aftershock	base-isolated building

SECTION 4 Monitoring Faults

INTEGRATING TECHNOLOGY

Key Ideas

◆ Geologists use instruments to measure deformation and stress along faults.
◆ Scientists determine earthquake risk by monitoring active faults and by studying faults where past earthquakes have occurred.

Organizing Information

Concept Map Copy the concept map about stress on a separate piece of paper. Then complete it and add a title. (For more on concept maps, see the Skills Handbook.)

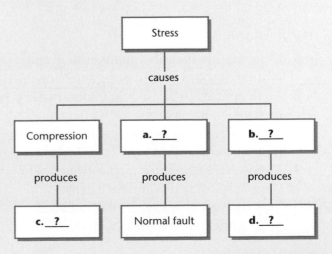

Reviewing Content

For more review of key concepts, see the Interactive Student Tutorial CD-ROM.

Multiple Choice

Chose the letter of the answer that best completes each statement.

1. Shearing is the force in Earth's crust that
   a. squeezes the crust together.
   b. pushes the crust in opposite directions.
   c. forces the crust to bend and fold.
   d. stretches the crust apart.
2. When the hanging wall of a fault slips down with respect to the footwall, the result is a
   a. reverse fault.　　b. syncline.
   c. normal fault.　　d. strike-slip fault.
3. A seismograph measures
   a. the depth of an earthquake.
   b. friction forces along a fault.
   c. ground motion during an earthquake.
   d. movement along a fault.
4. Geologists use the difference in the arrival times of P waves and S waves at a seismograph to determine
   a. the magnitude of the earthquake.
   b. the depth of the earthquake's focus.
   c. the strength of the surface waves.
   d. the distance to the epicenter.
5. To monitor the upward movement along a fault, geologists would probably use a
   a. laser-ranging device.　　b. tiltmeter.
   c. seismograph.　　d. creep meter.

True or False

If the statement is true, write true. If it is false, change the underlined word or words to make the statement true.

6. Deformation is the breaking, tilting, and folding of rocks caused by <u>liquefaction</u>.
7. Rock uplifted by <u>strike-slip faults</u> creates fault-block mountains.
8. An earthquake's <u>epicenter</u> is located deep underground.
9. As <u>S waves</u> move through the ground, they cause it to compress and then expand.
10. <u>Tsunamis</u> are triggered by earthquakes originating beneath the ocean floor.

Checking Concepts

11. How does stress affect Earth's crust?
12. Explain the process that forms a fault-block mountain.
13. What type of stress in the crust results in the formation of folded mountains? Explain your answer.
14. What are plateaus and how do they form?
15. Describe what happens along a fault beneath Earth's surface when an earthquake occurs.
16. Explain how the moment magnitude and Richter scales of earthquake measurement are similar and how they are different.
17. When geologists monitor a fault, what kinds of data do they collect? Explain.
18. **Writing to Learn** You are a geologist studying earthquake risk in an eastern state. Your data show that a major earthquake might happen there within 10 years. Write a letter to the governor of your state explaining why there is an earthquake hazard there and recommending how your state should prepare for the earthquake.

Thinking Critically

19. **Classifying** How would you classify a fault in which the hanging wall has slid up and over the footwall?
20. **Comparing and Contrasting** Compare and contrast P waves and S waves.
21. **Predicting** A community has just built a street across a strike-slip fault that has frequent earthquakes. How will movement along the fault affect the street?
22. **Applying Concepts** If you were building a house in an earthquake-prone area, what steps would you take to limit potential damage in an earthquake?
23. **Making Generalizations** How can filled land and loose, soft soil affect the amount of damage caused by an earthquake? Explain.
24. **Relating Cause and Effect** A geologist is monitoring a fault using radar waves bounced off Earth's surface by a satellite. If the satellite detects a change in elevation near the fault, what does this indicate? Explain.

Applying Skills

The graph shows the seismograph record for an earthquake. The y-axis of the graph shows the up-and-down shaking in millimeters at the seismograph station. The x-axis shows time in minutes.

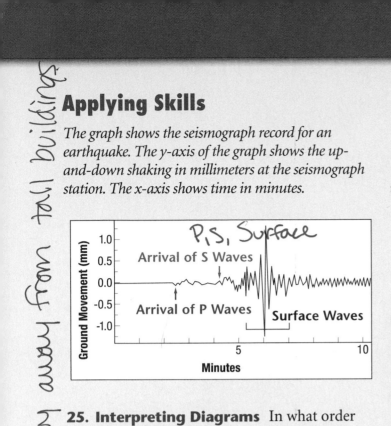

25. Interpreting Diagrams In what order do the seismic waves arrive at the seismograph station? Which type of seismic wave produces the largest ground movement?

26. Interpreting Diagrams What is the difference in arrival times for the P waves and S waves?

27. Predicting What would the seismograph record look like several hours after this earthquake? How would it change if an aftershock occurred?

28. Drawing Conclusions If the difference in arrival times for P waves and S waves is 5 minutes longer at a second seismograph station than at the first station, what can you conclude about the location of the second station?

Performance Assessment

CHAPTER PROJECT 2

Project Wrap Up Before testing how your model withstands an earthquake, explain to your classmates how and why you changed your model. When your model is tested, make notes of how it withstands the earthquake.

Reflect and Record How would a real earthquake compare with the method used to test your model? If it were a real building, could your structure withstand an earthquake? How could you improve your model?

Test Preparation

Use these questions to prepare for standardized tests.

Use the diagram of a fault to answer Questions 29–33.

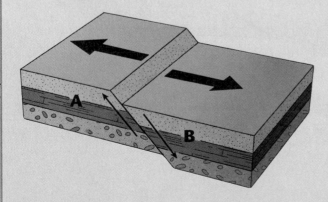

29. The rock on the side of the fault labeled B is the
a. footwall.
b. shearing wall.
c. hanging wall.
d. seismic wall.

30. The rock on the side of the fault labeled A is the
a. hanging wall.
b. strike-slip wall.
c. reverse wall.
d. footwall.

31. The thick arrows in the diagram stand for forces in Earth's crust pulling apart the two slabs of rock. This force is called
a. shearing.
b. compression.
c. elevation.
d. tension.

32. In the fault shown, the footwall
a. does not move.
b. moves down relative to the hanging wall.
c. moves up relative to the hanging wall.
d. slides sideways along the hanging wall.

33. The fault in the diagram is a(n)
a. normal fault.
b. strike-slip fault.
c. reverse fault.
d. inactive fault.

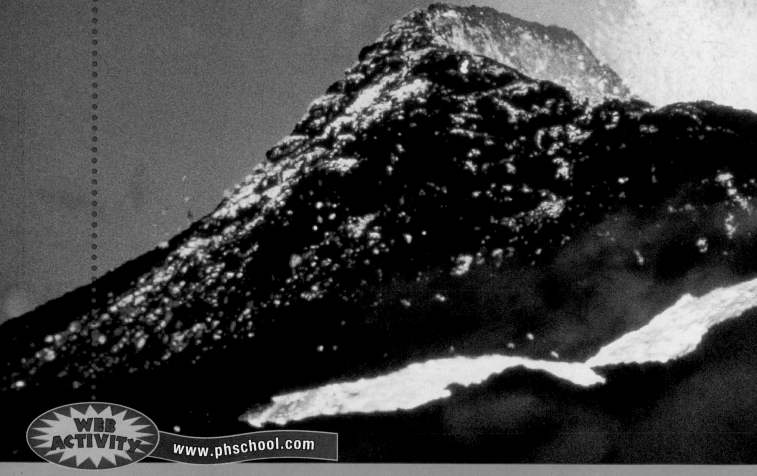

CHAPTER 3 Volcanoes

www.phschool.com

WEB ACTIVITY

Volcanoes and People

The frequent eruptions of Mount Kilauea can be spectacular. And they can be dangerous. Yet volcanoes and people have been closely connected throughout history, not only in Hawaii, but around the world. People often live near volcanoes because of the benefits they offer, from rich soil to minerals to hot springs. In your chapter project, you will research how volcanoes have affected the people living in a volcanic region.

Your Goal To make a documentary about life in a volcanic region.

Your project must
◆ describe the type of volcano you chose and give its history
◆ focus on one topic, such as how people have benefited from living near the volcano or how people show the volcano in their art and stories
◆ use a variety of media in your documentary presentation

Get Started Brainstorm with a group of other students which geographic area you would like to learn about. Your teacher may suggest some volcanic regions for you to check out. What research resources will your group need? Start planning what media you want to use to present your documentary. You might consider video, computer art, overhead transparencies, a rap song, a skit, or a mural. Be creative!

Check Your Progress You'll be working on this project as you study this chapter. To keep your project on track, look for Check Your Progress boxes at the following points.

Section 1 Review, page 91: Select the topic and region you will investigate and begin collecting information.
Section 3 Review, page 107: Use storyboards to organize your materials.
Section 4 Review, page 112: Prepare your visuals and narration.

Wrap Up At the end of the chapter (page 115), practice your presentation and then present your documentary to your class.

Kilauea volcano is on Hawaii, the largest of the Hawaiian Islands.

SECTION
4
Integrating Space Science
Volcanoes in the Solar System

Discover What Forces Shaped the Surface of Io?

Volcanoes and Plate Tectonics

Where Are Volcanoes Found on Earth's Surface?

1. Look at the map of Earth's volcanoes on page 89. What symbols are used to represent volcanoes? What other symbols are shown on the map?

2. Do the locations of the volcanoes form a pattern? Do the volcanoes seem related to any other features on Earth's surface?

Think About It

Developing Hypotheses Develop a hypothesis to explain where Earth's volcanoes are located. Are there any volcanoes on the map whose location cannot be explained by your hypothesis?

GUIDE FOR READING

◆ Where are Earth's volcanic regions found, and why are they found there?

Reading Tip Before you read, preview the headings in this section. Predict where volcanoes are likely to be located.

Before 1995, the island of Montserrat sat like a beautiful green gem in the Caribbean Sea. Some residents of the small island grew cotton, limes, and vegetables. Tourists flocked to the island to enjoy the scenery and tropical climate. What could possibly spoil this island paradise? A volcano named Soufrière (soo free EHR) Hills did. In 1995, Soufrière Hills began a series of eruptions that lasted more than two years. The volcano belched volcanic ash that fell like snow on roofs and gardens. Residents were evacuated as the volcano continued to erupt, and heavy falls of ash buried entire towns on the southern half of the island.

What Is a Volcano?

The eruption of a volcano is among the most dangerous and awe-inspiring events on Earth. A **volcano** is a weak spot in the crust where molten material, or magma, comes to the surface. **Magma** is a molten mixture of rock-forming substances, gases, and water from the mantle. When magma reaches the surface, it is called **lava**. After lava has cooled, it forms solid rock. The lava released during volcanic activity builds up Earth's surface. Volcanic activity is a constructive force that adds new rock to existing land and forms new islands.

◀ **Soufrière Hills volcano**

Location of Volcanoes

There are about 600 active volcanoes on land. Many more lie beneath the sea. Figure 1 is a map that shows the location of Earth's volcanoes. Notice how volcanoes occur in belts that extend across continents and oceans. One major volcanic belt is the **Ring of Fire,** formed by the many volcanoes that rim the Pacific Ocean. Can you find other volcanic belts on the map?

Volcanic belts form along the boundaries of Earth's plates. At plate boundaries, huge pieces of the crust diverge (pull apart) or converge (push together). Here, the crust is weak and fractured, allowing magma to reach the surface. **Most volcanoes occur along diverging plate boundaries, such as the mid-ocean ridge, or in subduction zones around the edges of oceans.** But there are exceptions to this pattern. Some volcanoes form at "hot spots" far from the boundaries of continental or oceanic plates.

Volcanoes at Diverging Plate Boundaries

Volcanoes form along the mid-ocean ridge, which marks a diverging plate boundary. Recall from Chapter 1 that the ridge is a long, underwater rift valley that winds through the oceans. Along the ridge, lava pours out of cracks in the ocean floor. Only in a few places, as in Iceland and the Azores Islands in the Atlantic Ocean, do the volcanoes of the mid-ocean ridge rise above the ocean's surface.

Language Arts
CONNECTION

The word *volcano* comes from the name of the Roman god of fire, Vulcan. According to Roman mythology, Vulcan lived beneath Mount Etna, a huge volcano on the island of Sicily in the Mediterranean Sea. Vulcan used the heat of Mount Etna to make metal armor and weapons for the ancient gods and heroes.

In Your Journal

Use the dictionary to find the definition of *plutonic* rock. Explain why the name of another Roman god was used for this term.

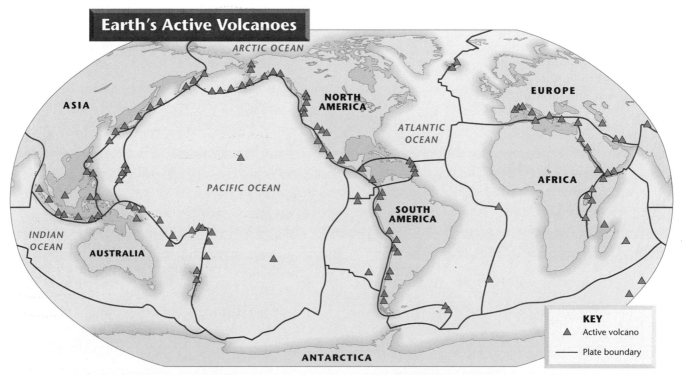

Earth's Active Volcanoes

KEY
▲ Active volcano
— Plate boundary

Figure 1 The Ring of Fire is a belt of volcanoes that circles the Pacific Ocean.
Observing What other patterns can you see in the locations of Earth's volcanoes?

Volcanoes at Converging Boundaries

Many volcanoes form near the plate boundaries where oceanic crust returns to the mantle. Subduction causes slabs of oceanic crust to sink through a deep-ocean trench into the mantle. The crust melts and forms magma, which then rises back toward the surface. When the magma from the melted crust erupts as lava, volcanoes are formed. Figure 2 shows how converging plates produce volcanoes.

Many volcanoes occur on islands, near boundaries where two oceanic plates collide. The older, denser plate dives under the other plate, creating a deep-ocean trench. The lower plate sinks beneath the deep-ocean trench into the asthenosphere. There it begins to melt, forming magma. Because it is less dense than the surrounding rock, the magma seeps upward through cracks in the crust. Eventually, the magma breaks through the ocean floor, creating volcanoes.

The resulting volcanoes create a string of islands called an **island arc**. The curve of an island arc echoes the curve of its deep-ocean trench. Major island arcs include Japan, New Zealand, Indonesia, the Caribbean islands, the Philippines, and the Aleutians.

Subduction also occurs where the edge of a continental plate collides with an oceanic plate. Collisions between oceanic and continental plates produced both the volcanoes of the Andes mountains on the west coast of South America and the volcanoes of the Pacific Northwest in the United States.

✓ *Checkpoint* How can oceanic crust eventually become magma?

Figure 2 Converging plates often form volcanoes when two oceanic plates collide or when an oceanic plate collides with a continental plate. In both situations, oceanic crust sinks through a deep-ocean trench, melts to form magma, and then erupts to the surface as lava.

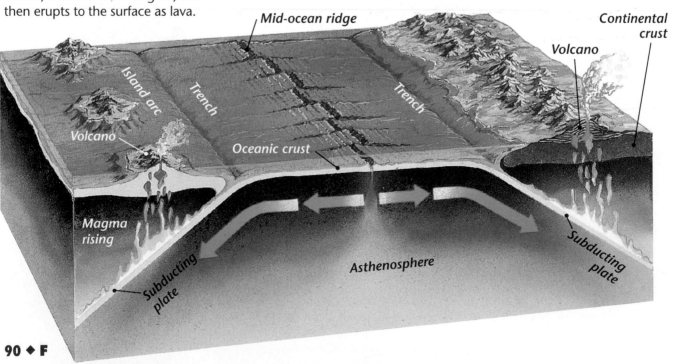

Mauna Kau

Pacific Ocean

Kauai   Oahu   Maui

Hawaii

Hawaiian Islands

Pacific plate

Hot spot

Figure 3 Hawaii sits on the moving Pacific plate. Beneath it is a powerful hot spot. Eventually, the plate's movement will carry the island of Hawaii away from the hot spot. *Inferring Which island on the map formed first?*

Hot Spot Volcanoes

Some volcanoes result from "hot spots" in Earth's mantle. A **hot spot** is an area where magma from deep within the mantle melts through the crust like a blow torch. Hot spots often lie in the middle of continental or oceanic plates far from any plate boundaries. Unlike the volcanoes in an island arc, the volcanoes at a hot spot do not result from subduction.

A hot spot volcano in the ocean floor can gradually form a series of volcanic mountains. For example, the Hawaiian Islands formed one by one over millions of years as the Pacific plate drifted over a hot spot.

Hot spots can also form under the continents. Yellowstone National Park in Wyoming marks a major hot spot under the North American plate. The last volcanic eruption in Yellowstone occurred about 75,000 years ago.

Hot Spot in a Box

ACTIVITY

1. Fill a plastic box half full of cold water. This represents the ocean.
2. Mix red food coloring with hot water in a small, narrow-necked bottle to represent magma.
3. Hold your finger over the mouth of the bottle as you place the bottle in the center of the box. The mouth of the bottle must be under water.
4. Float a flat piece of plastic foam on the water to model a tectonic plate. Make sure the "plate" is floating above the bottle.
5. Take your finger off the bottle and observe what happens to the "magma."

Making Models Move the plastic foam slowly along. Where does the magma touch the "plate"? How does this model a hot spot volcano?

 Section 1 Review

1. Where do most volcanoes occur on Earth's surface?
2. What process forms island arcs?
3. What causes hot spot volcanoes to form?
4. **Thinking Critically Predicting** What will eventually happen to the active volcano on the island of Hawaii, which is now over the hot spot?

Check Your Progress

CHAPTER PROJECT 3

Start by selecting the volcanic region you will study. Possible topics to investigate are myths and legends about volcanoes, the importance of volcanic soils, mineral resources from volcanoes, tourism, and geothermal power. Choose the topic that interests you the most. Begin your research and take notes on the information you collect.

Mapping Earthquakes and Volcanoes

In this lab, you will interpret data on the locations of earthquakes and volcanoes to find patterns.

Problem

Is there a pattern in the locations of earthquakes and volcanoes?

Materials

outline world map showing longitude and latitude
4 pencils of different colors

Procedure

1. Use the information in the table to mark the location of each earthquake on the world map. Use one of the colored pencils to draw a letter E inside a circle at each earthquake location.
2. Use a pencil of a second color to mark the locations of the volcanoes on the world map. Indicate each volcano with the letter V inside a circle.
3. Use a third pencil to lightly shade the areas in which earthquakes are found.
4. Use a fourth colored pencil to lightly shade the areas in which volcanoes are found.

Analyze and Conclude

1. How are earthquakes distributed on the map? Are they scattered evenly over Earth's surface? Are they concentrated in zones?
2. How are volcanoes distributed? Are they scattered evenly or concentrated in zones?
3. From your data, what can you infer about the relationship between earthquakes and volcanoes?

4. **Apply** Based on the data, which area of the North American continent would have the greatest risk of earthquake damage? Of volcano damage? Why would knowing this information be important to urban planners, engineers, and builders in this area?

More to Explore

On a map of the United States, locate active volcanoes and areas of earthquake activity. Determine the distance from your home to the nearest active volcano.

Earthquakes		Volcanoes	
Longitude	Latitude	Longitude	Latitude
120° W	40° N	150° W	60° N
110° E	5° S	70° W	35° S
77° W	4° S	120° W	45° N
88° E	23° N	61° W	15° N
121° E	14° S	105° W	20° N
34° E	7° N	75° W	0°
74° W	44° N	122° W	40° N
70° W	30° S	30° E	40° N
10° E	45° N	60° E	30° N
85° W	13° N	160° E	55° N
125° E	23° N	37° E	3° S
30° E	35° N	145° E	40° N
140° E	35° N	120° E	10° S
12° E	46° N	14° E	41° N
75° E	28° N	105° E	5° S
150° W	61° N	35° E	15° N
68° W	47° S	70° W	30° S
175° E	41° S	175° E	39° S
121° E	17° N	123° E	38° N

② Volcanic Activity

DISCOVER ·········· **ACTIVITY**

Pumice ▼

▲ Obsidian

What Are Volcanic Rocks Like?

Volcanoes produce lava, which hardens into rock. Two of these rocks are pumice and obsidian.

1. Observe samples of pumice and obsidian with a hand lens.

2. How would you describe the texture of the pumice? What could have caused this texture?

3. Observe the surface of the obsidian. How does the surface of the obsidian differ from pumice?

Think It Over

Developing Hypotheses What could have produced the difference in texture between the two rocks? Explain your answer.

VOCAB ▽ REVIEW SEC. 2 1/12/05

I n Hawaii, there are many myths about Pele (PAY lay), the fire goddess of volcanoes. In these myths, Pele is the creator and the destroyer of the Hawaiian islands. She lives in the fiery depths of erupting volcanoes. According to legend, when Pele is angry, she releases the fires of Earth through openings on the mountainside. Evidence of her presence is "Pele's hair," a fine, threadlike rock formed by lava. Pele's hair forms when lava sprays out of the ground like water from a fountain. As it cools, the lava stretches and hardens into thin strands.

How Magma Reaches Earth's Surface

Where does this fiery lava come from? Lava begins as magma in the mantle. There, magma forms in the asthenosphere, which lies beneath the lithosphere. The materials of the asthenosphere are under great pressure.

Magma Rises Because liquid magma is less dense than the surrounding solid material, magma flows upward into any cracks in the rock above. Magma rises until it reaches the surface, or until it becomes trapped beneath layers of rock.

GUIDE FOR READING

◆ **What happens when a volcano erupts?**

◆ **How do the two types of volcanic eruptions differ?**

◆ **What are some hazards of volcanoes?**

Reading Tip Before you read, preview *Exploring a Volcano* on page 95. Write a list of any questions you have about how a volcano erupts.

Figure 4 Pele's hair is a type of rock formed from lava. Each strand is as fine as spun glass.

Figure 5 Molten lava from Kilauea volcano in Hawaii.

A Volcano Erupts Just like the carbon dioxide trapped in a bottle of soda pop, the dissolved gases trapped in magma are under tremendous pressure. You cannot see the carbon dioxide gas in a bottle of soda pop because it is dissolved in the liquid. But when you open the bottle, the pressure is released. The carbon dioxide forms bubbles, which rush to the surface.

As magma rises toward the surface, the pressure decreases. The dissolved gases begin to separate out, forming bubbles. A volcano erupts when an opening develops in weak rock on the surface. **During a volcanic eruption, the gases dissolved in magma rush out, carrying the magma with them.** Once magma reaches the surface and becomes lava, the gases bubble out.

Inside a Volcano

All volcanoes have a pocket of magma beneath the surface and one or more cracks through which the magma forces its way. You can see these features in *Exploring a Volcano.* Beneath a volcano, magma collects in a pocket called a **magma chamber.** The magma moves through a **pipe,** a long tube in the ground that connects the magma chamber to Earth's surface. Molten rock and gas leave the volcano through an opening called a **vent.** Often, there is one central vent at the top of a volcano. However, many volcanoes also have other vents that open on the volcano's sides. A **lava flow** is the area covered by lava as it pours out of a vent. A **crater** is a bowl-shaped area that may form at the top of a volcano around the volcano's central vent.

✓ *Checkpoint* How does magma rise through the lithosphere?

EXPLORING *a Volcano*

A volcano forms where magma breaks through Earth's crust and lava flows over the surface.

Scientists prepare the robot Dante II for its descent into the crater of a volcano in Alaska.

Crater
Lava collects in the crater, the bowl-shaped area that forms around the volcano's vent.

Vent
The point on the surface where magma leaves the volcano's pipe is called the vent.

Side vent
Sometimes magma forces its way out of a volcano through a side vent.

Lava
Magma that reaches the surface is called lava.

Lava flow
The river of lava that pours down a volcano and over the land is called a lava flow.

Pipe
A pipe is a narrow, almost vertical crack in the crust through which magma rises to the surface.

Magma
Magma is extremely hot, molten material that also contains dissolved gases including water vapor.

Magma chamber
As magma rises toward the surface, it forms a large underground pocket called a magma chamber.

Figure 6 Rhyolite (top) forms from high-silica lava. Basalt (bottom) forms from low-silica lava. When this type of lava cools, it sometimes forms six-sided columns like the ones in the picture.

Characteristics of Magma

The force of a volcanic eruption depends partly on the amount of gas dissolved in the magma. But gas content is not the only thing that affects an eruption. How thick or thin the magma is, its temperature, and its silica content are also important factors.

Some types of magma are thick and flow very slowly. Other types of magma are fluid and flow almost as easily as water. Magma's temperature partly determines whether it is thick or fluid. The hotter the magma, the more fluid it is.

The amount of silica in magma also helps to determine how easily the magma flows. **Silica,** which is a material that is formed from the elements oxygen and silicon, is one of the most abundant materials in Earth's crust and mantle. The more silica magma contains, the thicker it is.

Magma that is high in silica produces light-colored lava that is too sticky to flow very far. When this type of lava cools, it forms the rock rhyolite, which has the same composition as granite. Pumice and obsidian, which you observed if you did the Discover activity, also form from high-silica lava. Obsidian forms when lava cools very quickly, giving it a smooth, glossy surface. Pumice forms when gas bubbles are trapped in cooling lava, leaving spaces in the rock.

Magma that is low in silica flows readily and produces dark-colored lava. When this kind of lava cools, rocks such as basalt are formed.

Types of Volcanic Eruptions

A volcano's magma influences how the volcano erupts. **The silica content of magma helps to determine whether the volcanic eruption is quiet or explosive.**

Quiet Eruptions A volcano erupts quietly if its magma flows easily. In this case, the gas dissolved in the magma bubbles out gently. Thin, runny lava oozes quietly from the vent. The islands of Hawaii and Iceland were formed from quiet eruptions. On the Big Island of Hawaii, lava pours out of the crater near the top of Mount Kilauea (kee loo AY uh), but also flows out of long cracks on the volcano's sides. Quiet eruptions like the ones that regularly take place on Mount Kilauea have built up the Big Island over hundreds of thousands of years. In Iceland, lava usually emerges from gigantic fissures many kilometers long. The fluid lava from a quiet eruption can flow many kilometers from the volcano's vent.

Quiet eruptions produce two different types of lava: pahoehoe and aa. **Pahoehoe** (pah HOH ee hoh ee) is fast-moving, hot lava. The surface of a lava flow formed from pahoehoe looks like a solid mass of wrinkles, billows, and ropelike coils. Lava that is cooler and slower-moving is called **aa** (AH ah). When aa hardens, it forms a rough surface consisting of jagged lava chunks. Figure 7 shows how different these types of lava can be.

✓ *Checkpoint* *What types of lava are produced by quiet eruptions?*

Figure 7 Both pahoehoe and aa can come from the same volcano.
A. Pahoehoe flows easily and hardens into a rippled surface.
B. Aa hardens into rough chunks.
Inferring *What accounts for the differences between these two types of lava?*

Figure 8 Mount St. Helens erupted at 8:30 A.M. on May 18, 1980. **A.** A large bulge that had formed on the north side of the mountain crashed downward.

B. As the mountainside collapsed, bottled up gas and magma inside began to escape.

Social Studies
CONNECTION

In A.D. 79, Mount Vesuvius in Italy erupted. A thick layer of ash from Vesuvius buried the Roman city of Pompeii, which lay between the volcano and the Mediterranean Sea. Beginning in the 1700s, about half of the buried city was dug out, and we now know the following: Pompeii was a walled city with shops, homes, paved streets, a forum (or public square), temples, and public baths. Perhaps 20,000 people lived there.

In Your Journal

Research Pompeii to find out what scientists have learned about daily life in the city. Write a paragraph summarizing your findings.

Explosive Eruptions If its magma is thick and sticky, a volcano erupts explosively. The thick magma does not flow out of the crater and down the mountain. Instead, it slowly builds up in the volcano's pipe, plugging it like a cork in a bottle. Dissolved gases cannot escape from the thick magma. The trapped gases build up pressure until they explode. The erupting gases push the magma out of the volcano with incredible force.

The explosion breaks the lava into fragments that quickly cool and harden into pieces of different sizes. The smallest pieces are volcanic ash—fine, rocky particles as small as a grain of sand. Cinders are pebble-sized particles. Larger pieces, called bombs, may range from the size of a baseball to the size of a car. A **pyroclastic flow** (py roh KLAS tik) occurs when an explosive eruption hurls out ash, cinders, and bombs as well as gases.

Look at Figure 8 to see the 1980 eruption of Mount St. Helens in the state of Washington. It was one of the most violent explosive eruptions that has ever occurred in the United States.

Checkpoint *What causes an explosive eruption?*

Stages of a Volcano

The activity of a volcano may last from less than a decade to more than 10 million years. Most long-lived volcanoes, however, do not erupt continuously. Geologists often describe volcanoes with terms usually reserved for living things, such as sleeping, awakening, alive, and dead. An **active,** or live, volcano is one that is erupting or has shown signs that it may erupt in the near future. A **dormant,** or sleeping, volcano is like a sleeping bear. Scientists expect a dormant volcano to awaken in the future and become active. However, there may be thousands of years between eruptions. An **extinct,** or dead, volcano is unlikely to erupt again.

C. Shattered rock and pyroclastic flows blasted out sideways from the volcano.

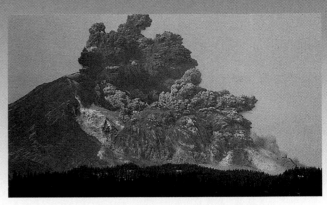

D. The blast traveled outward, leveling the surrounding forest and causing mudflows that affected a wide area around the volcano.

Other Types of Volcanic Activity

Hot springs and geysers are two examples of volcanic activity that do not involve the eruption of lava. These features may occur in any volcanic area—even around an extinct volcano.

A **hot spring** forms when groundwater heated by a nearby body of magma rises to the surface and collects in a natural pool. (Groundwater is water that has seeped into the spaces among rocks deep beneath Earth's surface.) Water from hot springs may contain dissolved gases and other substances from deep within Earth.

Sometimes, rising hot water and steam become trapped underground in a narrow crack. Pressure builds until the mixture suddenly sprays above the surface as a geyser. A **geyser** (GY zur) is a fountain of water and steam that erupts from the ground.

INTEGRATING TECHNOLOGY In volcanic areas, water heated by magma can provide a clean, reliable energy source called **geothermal energy.** The people of Reykjavik, Iceland, pipe this hot water directly into their homes for warmth. Geothermal energy is also a source of electricity in Iceland as well as northern California and New Zealand. Steam from deep underground is piped into turbines. Inside a turbine, the steam spins a wheel in the same way that blowing on a pinwheel makes the pinwheel turn. The moving wheel in the turbine turns a generator that changes the energy of motion into electrical energy.

Figure 9 Old Faithful, a geyser in Yellowstone National Park, erupts about every 33 to 93 minutes. That's how long it takes for the pressure to build up again after each eruption.

Monitoring Volcanoes

Geologists have been somewhat more successful in predicting volcanic eruptions than in predicting earthquakes. Changes in and around a volcano usually give warning a short time before the volcano erupts. Geologists use tiltmeters, laser-ranging devices, and other instruments to detect slight surface changes in elevation and tilt caused by magma moving underground. Geologists monitor the local magnetic field, water level in a volcano's crater lake, and any gases escaping from a volcano. They take the temperature of underground water to see if it is getting hotter—a sign that magma may be nearing the surface.

Geologists also monitor the many small earthquakes that occur in the area around a volcano before an eruption.

![SCIENCE & History]

The Power of Volcanoes

Within the last 150 years, major volcanic eruptions have greatly affected the land and people around them.

1883 Indonesia

The violent eruption of Krakatau volcano threw 18 cubic kilometers of ash skyward. The blast was heard 5,000 kilometers away.

1912 Alaska, U.S.A.

Today, a river in Alaska cuts through the thick layer of volcanic ash from the eruption of Mount Katmai. Mount Katmai blasted out almost as much ash as Krakatau.

1850   **1900**

1902 Martinique

Mount Pelée, a Caribbean volcano, spewed out a burning cloud of hot gas and pyroclastic flows. Within two minutes of the eruption, the cloud had killed the 29,000 residents of St. Pierre, a city on the volcano's flank. Only two people survived.

The movement of magma into the magma chamber and through the volcano's pipe triggers these quakes.

All these data help geologists predict that an eruption is about to occur. But geologists cannot be certain about the type of eruption or how powerful it will be.

Volcano Hazards

The time between volcanic eruptions may span hundreds of years. So people living near a dormant volcano may be unaware of the danger. Before 1980, the people who lived, worked, and vacationed in the region around Mount St. Helens viewed it as a peaceful mountain. Few imagined the destruction the volcano would bring when it awakened from its 123-year slumber.

In Your Journal

People have written eye-witness accounts of famous volcanic eruptions. Research one of the eruptions in the time line. Then write a letter describing what someone observing the eruption might have seen.

1991 Philippines

Mount Pinatubo was dormant for hundreds of years before erupting in June 1991. Pinatubo spewed out huge quantities of ash that rose high into the atmosphere and also buried the surrounding countryside.

1950   **2000**

1980 Washington, U.S.A.

When Mount St. Helens exploded, it blasted one cubic kilometer of rock fragments and volcanic material skyward. The eruption was not unexpected. For months, geologists had monitored releases of ash, small earthquakes, and a bulge on the mountain caused by the buildup of magma inside.

1995 Montserrat

For more than two years, eruptions of volcanic ash from the Soufrière Hills volcano poured down on this small Caribbean island. Geologists anxiously waited for the eruption to run its course, not knowing whether it would end in a huge explosion.

Figure 10 **A.** Mudflows were one of the hazards of Mt. Pinatubo's 1991 eruption. **B.** People around Mt. Pinatubo wore masks to protect themselves from breathing volcanic ash.

Although quiet eruptions and explosive eruptions involve different volcano hazards, both types of eruption can cause damage far from the crater's rim. During a quiet eruption, lava flows pour from vents, setting fire to and then burying everything in their path. During an explosive eruption, a volcano can belch out hot, burning clouds of volcanic gases as well as cinders and bombs.

Volcanic ash can bury entire towns, damage crops, and clog car engines. If it becomes wet, the heavy ash can cause roofs to collapse. If a jet plane sucks ash into its engine, the engine may stall. Eruptions can also cause landslides and avalanches of mud, melted snow, and rock. Figure 10 shows some effects of mud and ash from Mount Pinatubo's eruption. When Mount St. Helens erupted, gigantic mudflows carried ash, trees, and rock fragments 29 kilometers down the nearby Toutle River.

1/12/05

Section 2 Review

1. What are the stages that lead up to a volcanic eruption?
2. Compare and contrast quiet and explosive eruptions.
3. Describe some of the hazards posed by volcanoes.
4. **Thinking Critically Drawing Conclusions** A geologist times a passing lava flow at 15 kilometers per hour. The geologist also sees that lava near the edge of the flow is forming smooth-looking ripples as it hardens. What type of lava is this? What type of magma produced it? Explain your conclusions.

Science at Home

Place cold water in one cup and hot tap water in another. **CAUTION:** Handle the cup containing the hot water carefully to avoid spilling. Ask members of your family to predict what will happen when some melted candle wax drops into each cup of water. Have an adult family member drip melted wax from a candle into each cup. Explain how this models what happens when lava cools quickly or more slowly.

How Can Volcanic Activity Change Earth's Surface?

1. Use tape to secure the neck of a balloon over one end of a straw.
2. Place the balloon in the center of a box with the straw protruding.
3. Partially inflate the balloon.
4. Put damp sand on top of the balloon until it is covered.
5. Slowly inflate the balloon more. Observe what happens to the surface of the sand.

Think It Over
Making Models This activity models one of the ways in which volcanic activity can cause a mountain to form. What do you think the sand represents? What does the balloon represent?

Volcanoes have created some of Earth's most spectacular landforms. For example, the perfect volcanic cone of Mt. Fuji in Japan and the majestic profile of snow-capped Mt. Kilimanjaro rising above the grasslands of East Africa are famous around the world.

Some volcanic landforms arise when lava flows build up mountains and plateaus on Earth's surface. Other volcanic landforms are the result of the buildup of magma beneath the surface.

Landforms From Lava and Ash

Rock and other materials formed from lava create a variety of landforms including shield volcanoes, composite volcanoes, cinder cone volcanoes, and lava plateaus. Look at *Exploring Volcanic Mountains* on page 105 to see the similarities and differences among these features.

GUIDE FOR READING

◆ What landforms does lava create on Earth's surface?

◆ How does magma that hardens beneath the surface create landforms?

Reading Tip As you read, make a table comparing volcanic landforms. Include what formed each landform— lava, ash, or magma—as well as its characteristics.

◄ Mt. Fuji, Japan

Shield Volcanoes At some places on Earth's surface, thin layers of lava pour out of a vent and harden on top of previous layers. Such lava flows gradually build a wide, gently sloping mountain called a **shield volcano.** Shield volcanoes rising from a hot spot on the ocean floor created the Hawaiian Islands.

Cinder Cone Volcanoes A volcano can also be a **cinder cone,** a steep, cone-shaped hill or mountain. If a volcano's lava is thick and stiff, it may produce ash, cinders, and bombs. These materials pile up around the vent in a steep, cone-shaped pile. For example, Paricutín in Mexico erupted in 1943 in a farmer's cornfield. The volcano built up a cinder cone about 400 meters high.

Composite Volcanoes Sometimes, lava flows alternate with explosive eruptions of ash, cinder, and bombs. The result is a composite volcano. **Composite volcanoes** are tall, cone-shaped mountains in which layers of lava alternate with layers of ash. Examples of composite volcanoes include Mount Fuji in Japan and Mount St. Helens in Washington state.

Lava Plateaus Instead of forming mountains, some eruptions of lava form high, level areas called lava plateaus. First, lava flows out of several long cracks in an area. The thin, runny lava travels far before cooling and solidifying. Again and again, floods of lava flow on top of earlier floods. After millions of years, these layers of lava can form high plateaus. One example is the Columbia Plateau, which covers parts of Washington, Oregon, and Idaho.

Figure 11 Crater Lake in Oregon fills the caldera formed after an eruption that destroyed the top 2,000 meters of Mount Mazama nearly 7,000 years ago.
Developing Hypotheses *Develop a hypothesis to explain the formation of Wizard Island, the small island in Crater Lake.*

Calderas Enormous eruptions may empty the main vent and the magma chamber beneath a volcano. The mountain becomes a hollow shell. With nothing to support it, the top of the mountain collapses inward. The huge hole left by the collapse of a volcanic mountain is called a **caldera** (kal DAIR uh). The hole is filled with the pieces of the volcano that have fallen inward, as well as some lava and ash. In Figure 11 you can see one of the world's largest calderas.

✓ *Checkpoint* *What are the three types of volcanic mountains?*

EXPLORING *Volcanic Mountains*

Volcanic activity is responsible for building up much of Earth's surface. Lava from volcanoes cools and hardens into three types of mountains.

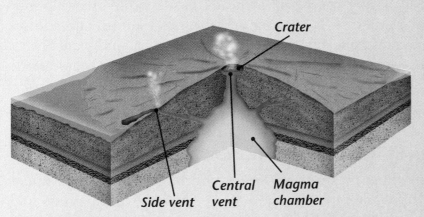

Crater

Side vent

Central vent

Magma chamber

▲ *Mauna Loa is one of the shield volcanoes that built the island Hawaii.*

Shield Volcano
Repeated lava flows during quiet eruptions gradually build up a broad, gently sloping volcanic mountain known as a shield volcano.

Cinder Cone Volcano
When cinders erupt explosively from a volcanic vent, they pile up around the vent, forming a cone-shaped hill called a cinder cone.

▲ *Sunset Crater is an extinct cinder cone in Arizona.*

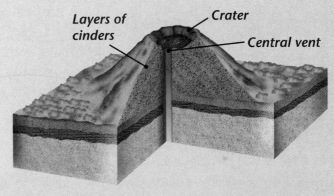

Layers of cinders

Crater

Central vent

Composite Volcano
Layers of lava alternate with layers of ash, cinders, and bombs in a composite volcano, which has both quiet and explosive eruptions.

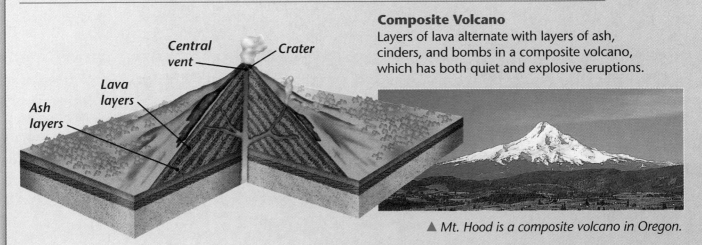

Central vent

Crater

Lava layers

Ash layers

▲ *Mt. Hood is a composite volcano in Oregon.*

Soils from Lava and Ash

 INTEGRATING ENVIRONMENTAL SCIENCE The lava, ash, and cinders that erupt from a volcano are initially barren. Over time, however, the hard surface of the lava flow breaks down to form soil. As soil develops, plants are able to grow. Some volcanic soils are among the richest soils in the world. Saying that soil is rich means that it's fertile, or able to support plant growth. Volcanic ash also breaks down and releases potassium, phosphorus, and other materials that plants need. Why would anyone live near an active volcano? People settle close to volcanoes to take advantage of the fertile volcanic soil.

✓ *Checkpoint* How does volcanic soil form?

Landforms from Magma

Sometimes magma forces its way through cracks in the upper crust, but fails to reach the surface. There the magma cools and hardens into rock. Or the forces that wear away Earth's surface—such as flowing water, ice, or wind—may strip away the layers of rock above the magma and finally expose it. **Features formed by magma include volcanic necks, dikes, and sills, as well as batholiths and dome mountains.**

Volcanic Necks, Dikes, and Sills A volcanic neck looks like a giant tooth stuck in the ground. A **volcanic neck** forms when magma hardens in a volcano's pipe. The softer rock around the pipe wears away, exposing the hard rock of the volcanic neck. Magma that forces itself across rock layers hardens into a **dike.** On the other hand, when magma squeezes between layers of rock, it forms a **sill.**

Figure 12 Magma that hardens beneath the surface may form volcanic necks, dikes, and sills. *Compare and Contrast What is the difference between a dike and a sill?*

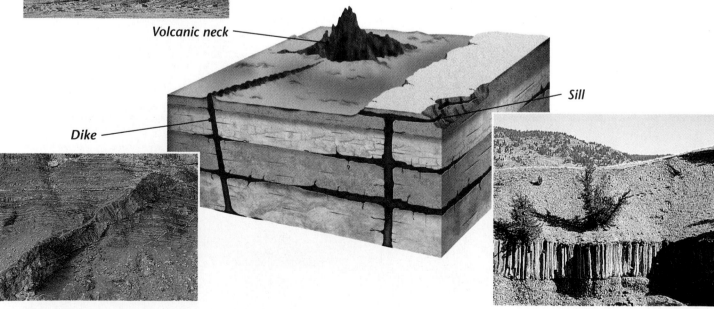

Volcanic neck

Sill

Dike

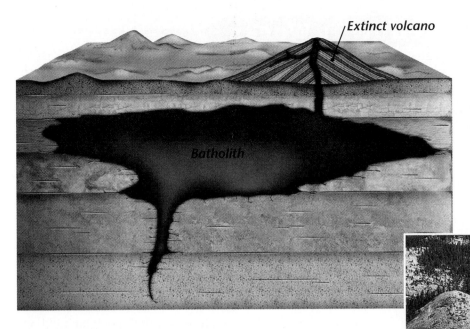

Extinct volcano

Batholith

Figure 13 A batholith forms when magma cools inside the crust. One of the largest batholiths in North America forms the core of the Sierra Nevada mountains in California. These mountains in Yosemite National Park are part of that granite batholith.

Batholiths Large rock masses called batholiths form the core of many mountain ranges. A **batholith** (BATH uh lith) is a mass of rock formed when a large body of magma cools inside the crust. The diagram in Figure 13 shows how a batholith looks when it forms. The photograph shows how it looks when the layers of rock above it have worn away.

Dome Mountains Other, smaller bodies of magma can create dome mountains. A dome mountain forms when rising magma is blocked by horizontal layers of rock. The magma forces the layers of rock to bend upward into a dome shape. Eventually, the rock above the dome mountain wears away, leaving it exposed. This process formed the Black Hills in South Dakota.

 Section 3 Review

1. Describe five landforms formed from lava and ash.
2. Describe the process that creates a lava plateau.
3. What features form as a result of magma hardening beneath Earth's surface?
4. Describe how a dome mountain can eventually form out of magma that hardened beneath Earth's surface.
5. **Thinking Critically Relating Cause and Effect** Explain the formation of a volcanic landform that can result when a volcano uses up the magma in its magma chamber.

Check Your Progress

CHAPTER PROJECT 3

By now you should have collected information about what it's like to live in a volcanic region. Do you need to do more research? Now begin to plan your presentation. One way to plan a presentation is to prepare storyboards. In a storyboard, you sketch each major step in the presentation on a separate sheet of paper. Decide who in your group is presenting each portion.

Gelatin Volcanoes

Does the magma inside a volcano move along fractures, or through tubes or pipes? How does the eruption of magma create features such as dikes and sills? You can use a gelatin volcano model and red-colored liquid "magma" to find answers to these questions.

Problem

How does magma move inside a volcano?

Skills Focus

developing hypotheses, making models, observing

Materials

plastic cup   tray or shallow pan
plastic knife
aluminum pizza pan with holes punched
   at 2.5-cm intervals
unflavored gelatin mold in bowl
red food coloring and water
plastic syringe, 10 cc
3 small cardboard oatmeal boxes
rubber gloves
unlined paper

Procedure

1. Before magma erupts as lava, how does it travel up from underground magma chambers? Record your hypothesis.
2. Remove the gelatin from the refrigerator. Loosen the gelatin from its container by briefly placing the container of gelatin in a larger bowl of hot water.
3. Place the pizza pan over the gelatin so the mold is near the center of the pizza pan. While holding the pizza pan against the top of the mold, carefully turn the mold and the pizza pan upside down.
4. Carefully lift the bowl off the gelatin mold to create a gelatin volcano.
5. Place the pizza pan with the gelatin mold on top of the oatmeal boxes as shown in the photograph.
6. Fill the syringe with the red water ("magma"). Remove air bubbles from the syringe by holding it upright and squirting out a small amount of water.
7. Insert the tip of the syringe through a hole in the pizza pan near the center of the gelatin volcano. Inject the magma into the gelatin very slowly. Observe what happens to the magma.
8. Repeat steps 6 and 7 as many times as possible. Observe the movement of the magma each time. Note any differences in the direction the magma takes when the syringe is inserted into different parts of the gelatin volcano. Record your observations.
9. Look down on your gelatin volcano from above. Make a sketch of the positions and shapes of the magma bodies. Label your drawing "Top View."
10. Carefully use a knife to cut your volcano in half. Separate the pieces and examine the cut surfaces for traces of the magma bodies.
11. Sketch the positions and shapes of the magma bodies on one of the cut faces. Label your drawing "Cross Section."

Analyze and Conclude

1. Describe how the magma moved through your model. Did the magma move straight up through the center of your model volcano or did it branch off in places? Explain why you think the magma moved in this way.
2. What knowledge or experience did you use to develop your hypothesis? How did the actual movement compare with your hypothesis?
3. Were there differences in the direction the magma flowed when the syringe was inserted in different parts of the gelatin volcano?
4. **Apply** How does what you observed in your model compare to the way magma moves through real volcanoes?

Plan to repeat the experiment using a mold made of two layers of gelatin. Before injecting the magma, predict what effect the layering will have on magma movement. Record your observations to determine if your hypothesis was correct. What volcanic feature is produced by this version of the model? Can you think of other volcanic features that you could model using gelatin layers?

SECTION 4 Volcanoes in the Solar System

What Forces Shaped the Surface of Io?

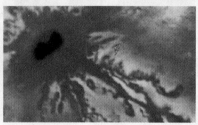

Io is a moon of Jupiter. Pictures taken by the *Voyager* space probe as it passed by Io in 1979 show signs of unusual features and activity on Io.

1. Observe the blue cloud rising above the rim of Io in the top photo. What do you think it could be?

2. Look at the feature on Io's surface shown in the bottom photo. What do you think it looks like?

Think It Over

Posing Questions Is the volcanic activity on Io similar to that on Earth? State several questions that you would like to answer in order to find out.

GUIDE FOR READING

◆ How do volcanoes on Mars and Venus compare with volcanoes on Earth?

◆ What volcanic activity is found on the moons of Jupiter and Neptune?

Reading Tip Before you read, preview the headings in the section. Then predict where, besides Earth, volcanoes are found in the solar system.

E arth is not the only body in the solar system to show signs of volcanic activity. Pictures taken by space probes show evidence of past volcanic activity on Mercury, Venus, and Mars. These planets—like Earth and its moon—have rocky crusts. Scientists think these planets once had hot, molten cores. The heat caused volcanic activity. But because these planets are smaller than Earth, their cores have cooled, bringing volcanic activity to an end.

Geologists are eager for information about other planets and moons. By comparing other bodies in the solar system with Earth, geologists can learn more about the processes that have shaped Earth over billions of years.

Earth's Moon

If you looked at the full moon through a telescope you would notice that much of the moon's surface is pockmarked with light-colored craters. Other, darker areas on the moon's surface look unusually smooth. The craters mark where meteorites have smashed into the moon over billions of years. The smooth areas are where lava flowed onto the moon's surface more than three billion years ago.

Figure 14 The dark areas on the moon's surface are flat plains made of basalt, a type of rock formed from lava.

Figure 15 The space probe *Magellan* observed volcanoes on Venus, but no recent or ongoing eruptions.

Volcanoes on Venus

Geologists were excited about the results of the space probe *Magellan's* mission to Venus in 1990. Venus shows signs of widespread volcanic activity that lasted for billions of years. Venus has thousands of volcanoes. There are about 150 large volcanoes measuring between 100 and 600 kilometers across and about half a kilometer high. The largest volcano on Venus, Theia Mons, is 800 kilometers across and 4 kilometers high. Scientists are trying to find evidence that volcanoes on Venus are still active.

Like Earth, Venus has volcanic mountains and other features that are probably made of thin, runny lava. Such lava produces gently sloping shield volcanoes with broad bases, as well as long, riverlike lava flows. One of the lava flows on Venus is more than 6,800 kilometers long!

☑ *Checkpoint* *What type of volcano is most common on Venus?*

Volcanoes on Mars

Mars is a planet with a long history of volcanic activity. However, there are far fewer volcanoes on Mars than on Venus. Volcanoes are found in only a few regions of Mars' surface.

Mars has a variety of volcanic features. **On Mars there are large shield volcanoes similar to those on Venus and Earth, as well as cone-shaped volcanoes and lava flows.** Mars also has lava plains that resemble the lava flows on the moon.

The biggest volcano on Mars is the largest mountain in the solar system. This volcano, Olympus Mons, is a shield volcano similar to Mauna Loa on the island of Hawaii, but much, much bigger! Olympus Mons covers an area as large as Ohio. This huge volcano, shown in Figure 16, is over eight times taller than Theia Mons on Venus.

Figure 16 Scientists estimate that Olympus Mons on Mars is about one billion years old. Around most of the base of Olympus Mons is a huge cliff that in places is 10 kilometers high—more than 5 times the height of the Grand Canyon.

Figure 17 The surface of Neptune's moon Triton has areas covered by frozen "lava lakes" that show where liquid material erupted from inside Triton. *Posing Questions Imagine that you are observing Triton from a spacecraft. What questions would you want to answer about volcanic activity there?*

Scientists estimate that volcanic activity on Mars probably goes back about 3.5 billion years, to about the same time as the volcanic activity on the moon. Martian volcanoes don't seem to be active. Lava flows on Olympus Mons may be more than 100 million years old.

Volcanoes on Distant Moons

Besides Earth, there are only two other bodies in the solar system where volcanic eruptions have been observed: Io, a moon of the planet Jupiter, and Triton, a moon of the planet Neptune. *Voyager 1* photographed eruptions on these moons as it sped past them in 1979. Geologists on Earth were amazed when they saw these pictures. **Io and Triton have volcanic features very different from those on Earth, Mars, and Venus.** On Io, sulfur volcanoes erupt like fountains or spread out like umbrellas above the colorful surface.

The eruptions on Triton involve nitrogen. On Earth, nitrogen is a gas. Triton is so cold, however, that most of the nitrogen there is frozen solid. Scientists hypothesize that Triton's surface, which is made up of frozen water and other materials, absorbs heat from the sun. This heat melts some of the frozen nitrogen underneath Triton's surface. The liquid nitrogen then expands and erupts through the planet's icy crust.

Other moons of Jupiter, Saturn, and Neptune show signs of volcanic activity, but space probes have not observed any eruptions in progress on these moons.

Section 4 Review

1. Describe volcanic features found on Venus and Mars. Do volcanic features on these planets resemble volcanic features on Earth? Explain.

2. How is volcanic activity on the moons of Jupiter and Neptune different from volcanic activity on Earth?

3. What is the largest volcano in the solar system? What type of volcano is it?

4. **Thinking Critically Comparing and Contrasting** How do the volcanoes on Venus compare with the volcanoes on Mars?

Check Your Progress CHAPTER PROJECT 3
By this time, your group should have planned your documentary and know what materials you will need. Put the finishing touches on your presentation. Make sure any posters, overhead transparencies, or computer art will be easy for your audience to read. If you are using video or audio, make your recordings now. Revise and polish any narrative, rap, or skit. (*Hint:* Check the length of your presentation.)

CHAPTER 3 STUDY GUIDE

SECTION 1 Volcanoes and Plate Tectonics

Key Ideas

◆ A volcano is an opening on Earth's surface where magma escapes from the interior. Magma that reaches Earth's surface is called lava.

◆ The constructive force of volcanoes adds new rock to existing land and forms new islands.

◆ Most volcanoes occur near the boundaries of Earth's plates and along the edges of continents, in island arcs, or along mid-ocean ridges.

Key Terms

volcano　　　lava　　　island arc
magma　　　Ring of Fire　　　hot spot

SECTION 2 Volcanic Activity

Key Ideas

◆ An eruption occurs when gases trapped in magma rush through an opening at the Earth's surface, carrying magma with them.

◆ Volcanoes can erupt quietly or explosively, depending on the amount of dissolved gases in the magma and on how thick or runny the magma is.

◆ When magma heats water underground, hot springs and geysers form.

◆ Volcano hazards include pyroclastic flows, avalanches of mud, damage from ash, lava flows, flooding, and deadly gases.

Key Terms

magma chamber　　　pyroclastic flow
pipe　　　active
vent　　　dormant
lava flow　　　extinct
crater　　　hot spring
silica　　　geyser
pahoehoe　　　geothermal energy
aa

SECTION 3 Volcanic Landforms

Key Ideas

◆ Lava and other volcanic materials on the surface create shield volcanoes, cinder cones, composite volcanoes, and plateaus.

◆ Magma that hardens beneath the surface creates batholiths, dome mountains, dikes, and sills, which are eventually exposed when the covering rock wears away.

Key Terms

shield volcano　　　caldera　　　sill
cinder cone　　　volcanic neck　　　batholith
composite volcano　　　dike

SECTION 4 Volcanoes in the Solar System

INTEGRATING SPACE SCIENCE

Key Ideas

◆ Venus and Mars both have extinct volcanoes similar to volcanoes on Earth.

◆ Spacecraft have photographed volcanic activity on moons of Jupiter and Neptune.

Organizing Information

Concept Map Copy the concept map about types of volcanic mountains onto a separate sheet of paper. Then complete it and add a title. (For more on concept maps, see the Skills Handbook.)

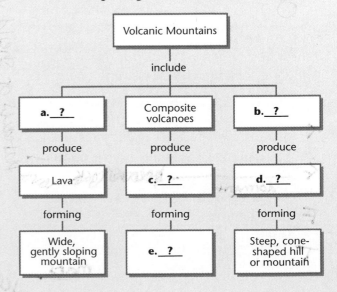

Chapter 3 **F ◆ 113**

CHAPTER 3 ASSESSMENT

Reviewing Content

For more review of key concepts, see the Interactive Student Tutorial CD-ROM.

Multiple Choice

Choose the letter of the best answer.

1. When two oceanic plates collide, the result may be
   a. volcanoes on the edge of a continent.
   b. a hot spot volcano.
   c. volcanoes in an island arc.
   d. a volcano along the mid-ocean ridge.
2. The force that causes magma to erupt at the surface is provided by
   a. heat.
   b. the shape of the pipe.
   c. geothermal energy.
   d. dissolved gases under pressure.
3. An eruption of thin, fluid lava would most likely be
   a. a cinder-cone eruption.
   b. an explosive eruption.
   c. a quiet eruption.
   d. a pyroclastic eruption.
4. Alternating layers of lava and volcanic ash are found in
   a. dome mountains.
   b. dikes and sills.
   c. shield volcanoes.
   d. composite volcanoes.
5. Which of the following has active volcanoes?
   a. Venus
   b. Mars
   c. Triton
   d. Earth's moon

True or False

If the statement is true, write true. If it is false, change the underlined word or words to make the statement true.

6. Many volcanoes are found in <u>island arcs</u> that form where two oceanic plates collide.
7. Thin, runny lava usually hardens into <u>ash, cinders, and bombs</u>. igneous rock
8. An <u>extinct</u> volcano is not likely to erupt in your lifetime. dormant
9. <u>Hot spots</u> form where a plume of magma rises through the crust from the mantle.
10. The volcano Olympus Mons is on <u>Venus</u>. Mars

Checking Concepts

11. What is the Ring of Fire?
12. How does plate tectonics explain the volcanoes that form along the mid-ocean ridge?
13. Where are hot spot volcanoes located in relation to Earth's plates? anywhere on the plate
14. What effect does silica content have on the characteristics of magma? Thick or thin explosive or quiet fast or slow
15. Describe the three stages in the "life-cycle" of a volcano.
16. How do hot springs and geysers form?
17. While observing a lava flow from a recently active volcano, you notice an area of lava with a rough, chunky surface. What type of lava is this and how does it form?
18. How does a shield volcano form?
19. Why can earthquakes be a warning sign that an eruption is about to happen?
20. **Writing to Learn** Pretend you are a newspaper reporter in 1980. You have been assigned to report on the eruption of Mount St. Helens. Write a news story describing your observations.

Thinking Critically

21. **Applying Concepts** Is a volcanic eruption likely to occur on the east coast of the United States? Explain your answer. No - no plate boundaries, no hot spots.
22. **Comparing and Contrasting** Compare the way in which an island arc forms with the way in which a hot spot volcano forms.
23. **Making Generalizations** How might a volcanic eruption affect the area around a volcano, including its plant and animal life?
24. **Relating Cause and Effect** Why doesn't the type of eruption that produces a lava plateau produce a volcanic mountain instead?
25. **Making Generalizations** What is one major difference between volcanic activity on Earth and volcanic activity on Mars, Venus, and the moon? Explain.

lava plateaus or shield volcanoes

I like these pens! Not! Yeah!

Applying Skills

Refer to the diagram to answer Questions 26–29.

26. Classifying What is this volcano made of? *Ash+hardened lava.* How do geologists classify a volcano made of these materials? *composite/strato*

27. Developing Hypotheses What is the feature labeled A in the diagram? What is the feature labeled B? How do these features form?

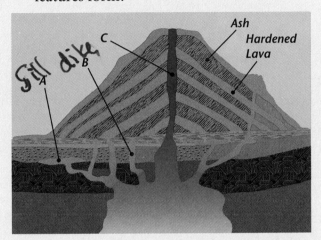

(handwritten labels: Sill dike, C, B, A; diagram labels: Ash, Hardened Lava)

28. Inferring This volcano is located where oceanic crust is subducted under continental crust. Would the volcano erupt quietly or explosively? Give reasons for your answer.

29. Predicting What is the feature labeled C in the diagram? If this feature becomes plugged with hardened magma, what could happen to the volcano? Explain.

CHAPTER PROJECT 3

Performance Assessment

Project Wrap Up Rehearse your documentary with your group before presenting it to the class. All group members should be able to answer questions about the visuals.

Reflect and Record In your journal, evaluate how well your documentary presented the information you collected. As you watched the other documentaries, did you see any similarities between how people in different regions live with volcanoes?

Test Preparation

Use these questions to prepare for standardized tests.

Read the passage. Then answer Questions 30–33.

Newsflash! At 8:30 A.M. today, May 8, 1980, Mount St. Helens in Washington State erupted. It blew away 400 meters of its top. A pyroclastic flow roared out of the volcano and burned leaves on trees 20 kilometers away. The volcano also blasted a cloud of ash 25 kilometers into the atmosphere. The cloud is drifting across several northwestern states, dumping a thick carpet of ash.

What led to this eruption? For 123 years, the snow-capped volcano had stood quietly. People thought it was dormant. But in March, the volcano began to rumble with small earthquakes. Scientists knew this meant magma was moving inside the volcano. In the weeks before the eruption, part of the mountain's northeastern slope also began to bulge. Then, in a moment, Mount St. Helens changed forever.

30. A good title for this passage is
a. "Volcanoes of Washington State."
b. "The Dramatic Eruption of Mount St. Helens."
c. "The Danger of Volcanic Ash."
d. "A Dormant Volcano."

31. The series of small earthquakes before the eruption of Mount St. Helens was the result of
a. movement along nearby faults.
b. water building up inside the volcano.
c. movement of magma inside the volcano.
d. the formation of a new caldera.

32. In the weeks before Mount St. Helens erupted, the volcano
a. let off some steam.   b. was very quiet.
c. glowed at night.   d. began to bulge.

33. Farm crops in nearby states would have been most affected by the volcano's
a. ash.   b. lava flows.
c. cinders and bombs.   d. pyroclastic flow.

Growing a Crystal Garden

Everyone has wondered at the beauty of minerals. Minerals occur in an amazing variety of colors and crystal shapes—from clear, tiny cubes of halite (table salt) to precious rubies and sapphires. Some crystals look like dandelion puffs. In this project, you will grow crystals to see how different types of chemicals form different crystal shapes.

Your Goal To design and grow a crystal garden.
To complete this project successfully, you must
◆ create a three-dimensional garden scene as a base on which to grow crystals
◆ prepare at least two different crystal-growth solutions
◆ observe and record the shapes and growth rates of your crystals
◆ follow the safety guidelines in Appendix A.

Get Started Begin by deciding what materials you will use to create your garden scene. Your teacher will suggest a variety of materials and also describe the types of crystal-growth solutions that you can use.

Check Your Progress You'll be working on this project as you study this chapter. To keep your project on track, look for Check Your Progress boxes at the following points.
Section 1 Review, page 126: Design and build a setting for your crystal garden and add the solutions.
Section 2 Review, page 132: Observe and record the growth of the crystals.

Wrap Up At the end of the chapter (page 143), display your finished crystal garden to your class. Be prepared to describe your procedure, observations, and conclusions.

These aurichalcite (oh rih KAL syt) crystals were found in a copper mine in Mexico. This mineral is formed from the metals zinc, copper, and other elements.

SECTION Properties of Minerals

SECTION 1 Properties of Minerals

DISCOVER • ACTIVITY

What Is the True Color of a Mineral?

1. Examine samples of magnetite and black hematite. Both minerals contain iron. Describe the color and appearance of the two minerals. Are they similar or different?

2. Rub the black hematite across the back of a porcelain or ceramic tile. Observe the color of the streak on the tile.

3. Wipe the tile clean before you test the next sample.

4. Rub the magnetite across the back of the tile. Observe the color of the streak on the tile.

Think It Over

Observing Does the color of each mineral's streak match its color? How could this streak test be helpful in identifying them as two different minerals?

GUIDE FOR READING

◆ What are the characteristics of a mineral?

◆ How are minerals identified?

Reading Tip As you read, use the headings to make an outline showing what minerals are and how they can be identified.

If you visit a science museum, you might wander into a room named the "hall of minerals." There you would see substances you have never heard of. For example, you might see deep-red crystals labeled "sphalerite" (SFAL uh ryt). You might be surprised to learn that sphalerite is a source of zinc and gallium. These metals are used in products from "tin" cans to computer chips! Although you may never have seen sphalerite, you are probably familiar with other common minerals. For example, you have probably seen turquoise, a blue-green mineral used in jewelry.

Figure 1 The Hall of Minerals at the American Museum of Natural History in New York City contains one of the world's largest collections of minerals.

Figure 2 **A.** Red crystals of the mineral sphalerite are called ruby zinc. **B.** Borax is a mineral that forms in dry lake beds. **C.** Coal is not a mineral because it is made of the remains of ancient plants. *Comparing and Contrasting How are sphalerite and borax similar? How are they different?*

What Is a Mineral?

Sphalerite and turquoise are just two of more than 3,000 minerals that geologists have identified. Of all these minerals, only about 100 are common. Most of the others are harder to find than gold. About 20 minerals make up most of the rocks of Earth's crust. These minerals are known as rock-forming minerals. Appendix B at the back of this book lists some of the most common rock-forming minerals.

A mineral is a naturally occurring, inorganic solid that has a crystal structure and a definite chemical composition. For a substance to be a mineral, it must have all five of these characteristics. In Figure 2, you can compare sphalerite with another mineral, borax, and with coal, which is not a mineral.

Naturally Occurring To be classified as a mineral, a substance must occur naturally. Cement, brick, steel, and glass all come from substances found in Earth's crust. However, these building materials are manufactured by people. Because they are not naturally occurring, such materials are not considered to be minerals.

Inorganic A mineral must also be **inorganic.** This means that the mineral cannot arise from materials that were once part of a living thing. For example, coal forms naturally in the crust. But geologists do not classify coal as a mineral because it comes from the remains of plants and animals that lived millions of years ago.

Solid A mineral is always a solid, with a definite volume and shape. The particles that make up a solid are packed together very tightly, so they cannot move like the particles that make up a liquid. A solid keeps its shape because its particles can't flow freely.

Crystal Structure The particles of a mineral line up in a pattern that repeats over and over again. The repeating pattern of a mineral's particles forms a solid called a **crystal.** A crystal has flat sides, called faces, that meet at sharp edges and corners.

Sometimes, the crystal structure is obvious from the mineral's appearance. In other minerals, however, the crystal structure is visible only under a microscope. A few minerals, such as opal, are considered minerals even though their particles are not arranged in a crystal structure.

Definite Chemical Composition A mineral has a definite

INTEGRATING CHEMISTRY

chemical composition. This means that a mineral always contains certain elements in definite proportions. An **element** is a substance composed of a single kind of atom. All the atoms of the same element have the same chemical and physical properties.

Almost all minerals are compounds. In a **compound,** two or more elements are combined so that the elements no longer have distinct properties. The elements that make up a compound are said to be chemically joined. For example, a crystal of the mineral quartz has one atom of silicon for every two atoms of oxygen. Each compound has its own properties, which usually differ greatly from the properties of the elements that form it. Figure 3 compares the mineral cinnabar to the elements that make it up.

Figure 3 Minerals are usually a compound of two or more elements. **A.** Mercury is a metal that is a silvery liquid at room temperature. **B.** The element sulfur is bright yellow. **C.** The mineral cinnabar is a compound of the elements mercury and sulfur. Cinnabar has red crystals.

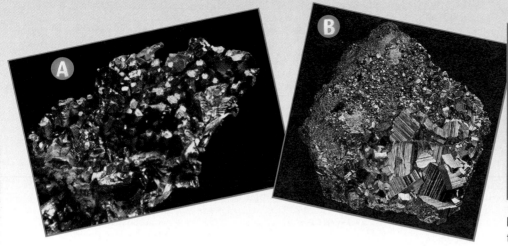

Figure 4 An old saying warns "All that glitters is not gold." **A.** Real gold can occur as a pure metal. **B.** Pyrite, or fool's gold, contains iron and sulfur. **C.** Chalcopyrite is a compound of copper, iron, and sulfur. *Observing These minerals are similar in color. But do you notice any differences in their appearance?*

Some elements occur in nature in a pure form, not as part of a compound with other elements. These elements, such as copper, silver, and gold, are considered to be minerals. Almost all pure elements are metals.

☑ *Checkpoint* *What does it mean to say that a mineral has a definite chemical composition?*

Identifying Minerals

During the California Gold Rush of 1849, thousands of people headed west to find gold in the California hills. Some found gold, but most found disappointment. Perhaps the most disappointed of all were the ones who found pyrite, or "fool's gold." All three minerals in Figure 4 look like gold, yet only one is the real thing.

Because there are so many different kinds of minerals, telling them apart can be a challenge. The color of a mineral alone often provides too little information to make an identification. **Each mineral has its own specific properties that can be used to identify it.** When you have learned to recognize the properties of minerals, you will be able to identify many common minerals around you.

You can see some of the properties of a mineral just by looking at a sample. To observe other properties, however, you need to conduct tests on that sample. As you read about the properties of minerals, think about how you could use them to identify a mineral.

Hardness When you identify a mineral, one of the best clues you can use is the mineral's hardness. In 1812, Friedrich Mohs, an Austrian mineral expert, invented a test to describe and compare the hardness of minerals. Called the **Mohs hardness scale,** this scale ranks ten minerals from softest to hardest. Look at the

Sharpen your Skills

Classifying

ACTIVITY

1. Use your fingernail to try to scratch talc, calcite, and quartz. Record which minerals you were able to scratch.

2. Now try to scratch the minerals with a penny. Were your results different? Explain.

3. Were there any minerals you were unable to scratch with either your fingernail or the penny?

4. How would you classify the three minerals in order of increasing hardness?

Figure 5 Mohs hardness scale rates the hardness of minerals on a scale of 1 to 10. *Drawing Conclusions You find a mineral that can be scratched by a steel knife, but not by a copper penny. What is this mineral's hardness on the Mohs scale?*

Mohs Hardness Scale		
Mineral	**Rating**	**Testing Method**
Talc	1	Softest known mineral. It flakes easily when scratched by a fingernail.
Gypsum	2	A fingernail can easily scratch it.
Calcite	3	A fingernail cannot scratch it, but a copper penny can.
Fluorite	4	A steel knife can easily scratch it.
Apatite	5	A steel knife can scratch it.
Feldspar	6	Cannot be scratched by a steel knife, but it can scratch window glass.
Quartz	7	Can scratch steel and hard glass easily.
Topaz	8	Can scratch quartz.
Corundum	9	Can scratch topaz.
Diamond	10	Hardest known mineral. Diamond can scratch all other substances.

table in Figure 5 to see which mineral is the softest and which is the hardest. A mineral can scratch any mineral softer than itself, but will be scratched by any mineral that is harder. How would you determine the hardness of a mineral not listed on the Mohs scale, such as sphalerite? You could try to scratch sphalerite with talc, gypsum, or calcite. But you would find that none of them scratch sphalerite. Apatite, the mineral rated 5 on the scale, does scratch sphalerite. Therefore, you would conclude that sphalerite's hardness is about 4 on Mohs hardness scale.

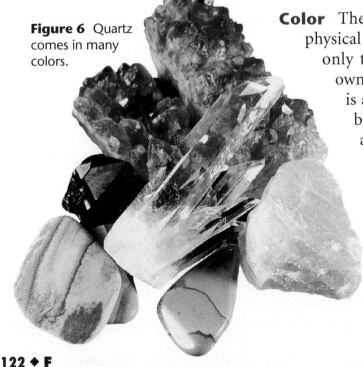

Figure 6 Quartz comes in many colors.

Color The color of a mineral is an easily observed physical property. But color can be used to identify only those few minerals that always have their own characteristic color. The mineral malachite is always green. The mineral azurite is always blue. No other minerals look quite the same as these. Many minerals, however, like the quartz in Figure 6, can occur in a variety of colors.

Streak A streak test can provide a clue to a mineral's identity. The **streak** of a mineral is the color of its powder. You can observe a streak by rubbing a mineral against a piece of unglazed tile called a streak plate. Even though the color of the mineral may vary, its streak does not. Surprisingly, the streak color

Figure 7 **A.** Galena, which contains lead, has a metallic luster. **B.** Malachite, which contains copper, has a silky luster.

and the mineral color are often different. For example, although pyrite has a gold color, it always produces a greenish black streak. Real gold, on the other hand, produces a golden yellow streak.

Luster Another simple test to identify a mineral is to check its luster. **Luster** is the term used to describe how a mineral reflects light from its surface. Minerals containing metals are often shiny. For example, galena is an ore of lead that has a bright, metallic luster. Look at Figure 7 to compare the luster of galena with the luster of malachite. Other minerals, such as quartz, have a glassy luster. Some of the other terms used to describe luster include earthy, waxy, and pearly.

Density Each mineral has a characteristic density. Recall from Chapter 1 that density is the mass in a given space, or mass per unit volume. No matter what the size of a mineral sample, the density of that mineral always remains the same.

You can compare the density of two mineral samples of about the same size. Just pick them up and heft them, or feel their weight, in your hands. You may be able to feel the difference between low-density quartz and high-density galena. If the two samples are the same size, the galena is almost three times as heavy as the quartz.

But heft provides only a rough measure of density. When geologists measure density, they use a balance to determine precisely the mass of a mineral sample. The mineral is also placed in water to determine how much water it displaces. The volume of the displaced water equals the volume of the sample. Dividing the sample's mass by its volume gives the density of the mineral.

☑ *Checkpoint* *How can you determine a mineral's density?*

Language **Arts**
CONNECTION

Geologists use adjectives such as glassy, dull, pearly, silky, greasy, and pitchlike to describe the luster of a mineral. When writers describe the surfaces of objects other than minerals, they also use words that describe luster. Luster can suggest how a surface looks. A new car, for example, might look glassy; an old car might look dull.

In Your Journal

Think of a familiar scene to describe—a room, building, tree, or street. Make a list of objects in your scene and a list of adjectives describing the surfaces of these objects. You might use some of the adjectives that geologists use to describe luster. Now write a paragraph using sensory words that make the scene seem real.

Crystal Systems The crystals of each mineral grow atom by atom to form that mineral's particular crystal structure. Geologists classify these structures into six groups based on the number and angle of the crystal faces. These groups are called crystal systems. For example, all halite crystals are cubic. Halite crystals have six sides that meet at right angles, forming a perfect cube. Sometimes you can see that a crystal has the particular crystal structure of its mineral. Crystals that grow in an open space can be almost perfectly formed. But crystals that grow in a tight space are often incompletely formed. Figure 8 shows minerals that belong to each of the six crystal systems.

Figure 8 This chart lists some common minerals and their properties. *Interpreting Data Which mineral is lowest in density and hardness? Which mineral could you identify by using a compass?*

Properties and Uses of Minerals

Name	 Magnetite	 Quartz	 Rutile	 Sulfur	 Azurite	 Microcline Feldspar
Hardness	6	7	$6 - 6\frac{1}{2}$	2	$3\frac{1}{2} - 4$	6
Color	Black	Transparent or in a range of colors	Black or reddish brown	Lemon yellow to yellowish brown	Blue	Green, red-brown, pink, or white
Streak	Black	Colorless	Light brown	White	Pale blue	Colorless
Crystal System	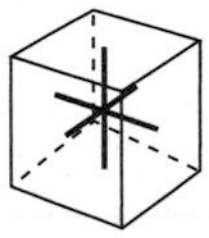 Cubic	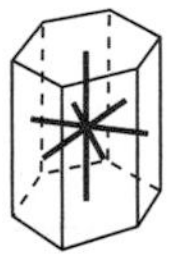 Hexagonal	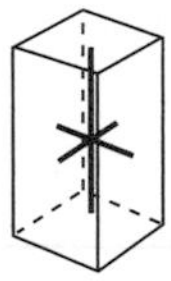 Tetragonal	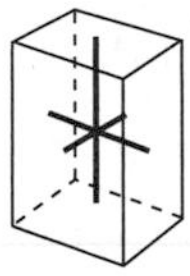 Orthorhombic	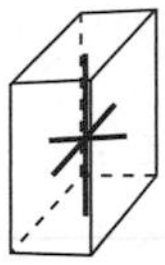 Monoclinic	 Triclinic
Luster	Metallic	Glassy	Metallic or gemlike	Greasy	Glassy to dull or earthy	Glassy
Special Properties	Magnetic	Fractures like broken glass	Not easily melted	Melts easily	Reacts to acid	Cleaves well in two directions
Density (g/cm³)	5.2	2.6	4.2–4.3	2.0–2.1	3.8	2.6
Uses	A source of iron used to make steel	Used in making glass and electronic equipment, or as a gem	Contains titanium, a hard, light-weight metal used in aircraft and cars	Used in fungicides, industrial chemicals, and rubber	A source of copper metal; also used as a gem	Used in pottery glaze, scouring powder, or as a gem

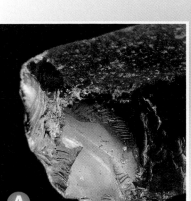

Figure 9 A. When quartz fractures, the break looks like the surface of a seashell. B. A piece of feldspar cleaves at right angles. C. Mica cleaves into thin, flat sheets that are almost transparent. *Applying Concepts How would you test a mineral to determine its cleavage and fracture?*

Cleavage and Fracture The way a mineral breaks apart can help to identify it. A mineral that splits easily along flat surfaces has the property called **cleavage.** Whether a mineral has cleavage depends on how the atoms in its crystals are arranged. Depending on the arrangement of atoms in the mineral, it will break apart more easily in one direction than another. Look at the minerals in Figure 9. Mica separates easily in only one direction, forming flat sheets. Feldspar splits at right angles, producing square corners. These minerals have cleavage.

Most minerals do not split apart evenly. Instead, they have a characteristic type of fracture. **Fracture** describes how a mineral looks when it breaks apart in an irregular way. Geologists use a variety of terms to describe fracture. For example, quartz has a shell-shaped fracture. When quartz breaks, it produces curved, shell-like surfaces that look like chipped glass. Pure metals, like copper and iron, have a hackly fracture—they form jagged points. Some soft minerals that crumble easily like clay have an earthy fracture. Minerals that form rough, irregular surfaces when broken have an uneven fracture.

✓ *Checkpoint How are cleavage and fracture similar? How are they different?*

Crystal Hands

You can grow ACTIVITY two different kinds of salt crystals.

1. Put on your goggles.

2. ☠ Pour a solution of halite (table salt) into one shallow pan and a solution of Epsom salts into another shallow pan.

3. Put a large piece of black construction paper on a flat surface.

4. Dip one hand in the halite solution. Shake off the excess liquid and make a palm print on the paper. Repeat with your other hand and the Epsom salt solution, placing your new print next to the first one. **CAUTION:** *Do not do this activity if you have a cut on your hand.* Wash your hands after making your hand prints.

5. Let the prints dry overnight.

Observing Use a hand lens to compare the shape of the crystals. Which hand prints have more crystals?

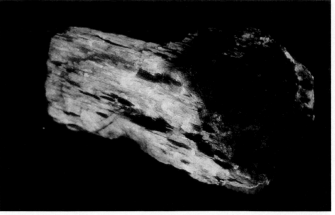

Figure 10 Scheelite looks quite ordinary in daylight, but glows with brilliant color under ultraviolet light.

Special Properties Some minerals can be identified by special physical properties. For example, minerals that glow under ultraviolet light have a property known as **fluorescence** (floo RES uns). The mineral scheelite is fluorescent. Magnetism occurs naturally in a few minerals. Lodestone, which is a form of magnetite, acts as a natural magnet. Early magnets—such as compass needles—were made by striking a piece of iron with lodestone. Uraninite and a few other minerals are radioactive. They set off a Geiger counter. Some minerals react chemically to acid. Calcite, a compound of calcium, carbon, and oxygen, fizzes and gives off carbon dioxide when a drop of vinegar is placed on it.

A few minerals, such as quartz, have electrical properties. Pressure applied to these crystals produces a small electric current. In addition, these crystals vibrate if they come in contact with an electric current. Because of these properties, quartz crystals are used in microphones, radio transmitters, and watches.

Section 1 Review

1. What characteristics must a substance have to be considered a mineral?
2. Describe how you can test a mineral to determine its hardness, density, and streak.
3. What is the major difference between an element and a compound?
4. **Thinking Critically Classifying** According to the definition of a mineral, can water be classified as a mineral? Explain your answer.
5. **Thinking Critically Making Generalizations** Explain why you can't rely on any single test or property when you are trying to identify a mineral.

Check Your Progress

CHAPTER PROJECT 4

Select a container for your crystal garden such as a plastic shoe box or a large-mouth jar. Make a sketch showing the shapes and locations of the "plants" you plan to grow. When you have designed your garden, decide what materials to put in the box for the crystals to grow on. Decide what crystal-growth solutions you will use. Halite, Epsom salts, and alum are possibilities. Check with your teacher to make sure the chemicals you plan to use are safe.

THE DENSITY OF MINERALS

In this lab, you will use water to help you measure the density of minerals.

Problem

How can you compare the density of different minerals?

Materials (per student)

graduated cylinder, 100 mL
3 mineral samples: pyrite, quartz, and galena
water
balance

Procedure

1. Check to make sure the mineral samples are small enough to fit in the graduated cylinder.
2. Copy the data table into your notebook. Place the pyrite on the balance and record its mass in the data table.
3. Fill the cylinder with water to the 50-mL mark.
4. Carefully place the pyrite into the cylinder of water. Try not to spill any of the water.
5. Read the level of the water on the scale of the graduated cylinder. Record the level of the water with the pyrite in it.
6. Calculate the volume of water displaced by the pyrite. To do this, subtract the volume of water without the pyrite from the volume of water with the pyrite. Record your answer.
7. Calculate the density of the pyrite by using this formula.

$$\text{Density} = \frac{\text{Mass of mineral}}{\text{Volume of water displaced by the mineral}}$$

(Note: Density is expressed as g/cm^3. One mL of water has a volume of 1 cm^3.)
8. Remove the water and mineral from the cylinder.
9. Repeat steps 2–8 for quartz and galena.

Analyze and Conclude

1. Which mineral had the highest density? The lowest density?
2. How does finding the volume of the water that was displaced help you find the volume of the mineral itself?
3. Why won't the procedure you used in this lab work for a substance that floats or one that dissolves in water?
4. **Apply** Pyrite is sometimes called "fool's gold" because its color and appearance are similar to real gold. How could a scientist determine if a sample was real gold?
5. **Think About It** Does the shape or size of a mineral sample affect its density? Explain.

More to Explore

Repeat the activity by finding the density of other minerals or materials. Then compare the densities of these materials with pyrite, quartz, and galena.

DATA TABLE			
	Pyrite	Quartz	Galena
Mass of Mineral (g)			
Volume of Water without Mineral (mL)	50	50	50
Volume of Water with Mineral (mL)			
Volume of Water Displaced (mL)			
Volume of Water Displaced (cm^3)			
Density (g/cm^3)			

2 How Minerals Form

How Does the Rate of Cooling Affect Crystals?

1. ☠ Put on your goggles. Use a plastic spoon to place a small amount of salol near one end of each of two microscope slides. You need just enough to form a spot 0.5 to 1.0 cm in diameter.

2. 🔥🧤 Carefully hold one slide with tongs. Warm it gently over a lit candle until the salol is almost completely melted. **CAUTION:** *Move the slide in and out of the flame to avoid cracking the glass.*

3. Set the slide aside to cool slowly.

4. While the first slide is cooling, hold the second slide with tongs and heat it as in Step 2. Cool the slide quickly by placing it on an ice cube. Carefully blow out the candle.

5. Observe the slides under a hand lens. Compare the appearance of the crystals that form on the two slides.

6. Wash your hands when you are finished.

Think It Over

Relating Cause and Effect
Which sample had larger crystals? If a mineral forms by rapid cooling, would you expect the crystals to be large or small?

◆ What are the processes by which minerals form?

Reading Tip Before you read, rewrite the headings of the section as how, why, or what questions. As you read, look for answers to these questions.

I magine digging for diamonds. At Crater of Diamonds State Park in Arkansas, that's exactly what people do. The park is one of the very few places in the United States where diamonds can be found. Visitors are permitted to prospect, or search, for diamonds. Since the area became a park in 1972, visitors have found more than 20,000 diamonds!

How did the diamonds get there? Millions of years ago, a volcanic pipe formed in the mantle at a depth of 120 kilometers or more. At that depth, great

Diamonds ▶

pressure and heat changed carbon atoms into the hardest known substance—diamond. Then the pipe erupted, carrying diamonds and other materials toward the surface. Today, geologists recognize this type of volcanic pipe as an area of unusual bluish-colored rock made up of a variety of minerals, including diamond. Volcanic pipes containing diamonds are found in only a few places on Earth. Most occur in South Africa and Australia, where many of the world's diamonds are mined today.

Processes That Form Minerals

You probably have handled products made from minerals. But you may not have thought about how the minerals formed. The minerals that people use today have been forming deep in Earth's crust or on the surface for several billion years. **In general, minerals can form in two ways: through crystallization of melted materials, and through crystallization of materials dissolved in water.** Crystallization is the process by which atoms are arranged to form a material with a crystal structure.

Minerals From Magma

Minerals form as hot magma cools inside the crust, or as lava hardens on the surface. When these liquids cool to the solid state, they form crystals. The size of the crystals depends on several factors. The rate at which the magma cools, the amount of gas the magma contains, and the chemical composition of the magma all affect crystal size.

When magma remains deep below the surface, it cools slowly over many thousands of years. Slow cooling leads to the formation of large crystals. If the crystals remain undisturbed while cooling, they grow by adding atoms according to a regular pattern.

Magma closer to the surface cools much faster than magma that hardens deep below ground. With more rapid cooling, there is no time for magma to form large crystals. Instead, small crystals form. If magma erupts to the surface and becomes lava, the lava will also cool quickly and form minerals with small crystals.

Figure 11 This crystal of the mineral spodumene is 24 cm long. But it's not the largest crystal. Spodumene crystals the size of telephone poles have been found in South Dakota.
Inferring Under what conditions did such large crystals probably form?

Figure 12 A. Silver sometimes occurs as a pure metal, forming delicate, treelike crystals. B. Solutions containing dissolved metals form veins like the ones in this silver mine in Idaho.

Minerals From Hot Water Solutions

Sometimes, the elements that form a mineral dissolve in hot water. Magma has heated the water to a high temperature beneath Earth's surface. These dissolved minerals form solutions. A **solution** is a mixture in which one substance dissolves in another. When a hot water solution begins to cool, the elements and compounds leave the solution and crystallize as minerals. The silver shown in Figure 12A formed by this process.

Pure metals that crystallize underground from hot water solutions often form veins. A **vein** is a narrow channel or slab of a mineral that is much different from the surrounding rock. Deep underground, solutions of hot water and metals often follow cracks within the rock. Then the metals crystallize into veins that resemble the streaks of fudge in vanilla fudge ice cream. Figure 12B shows a vein of silver in a mine.

Many minerals form from solutions at places where tectonic plates spread apart along the mid-ocean ridge. First, ocean water

Figure 13 Many minerals form at chimneys along the mid-ocean ridge. Chimneys occur in areas where sea-floor spreading causes cracks in the oceanic crust. *Interpreting Diagrams What is the energy source for this process?*

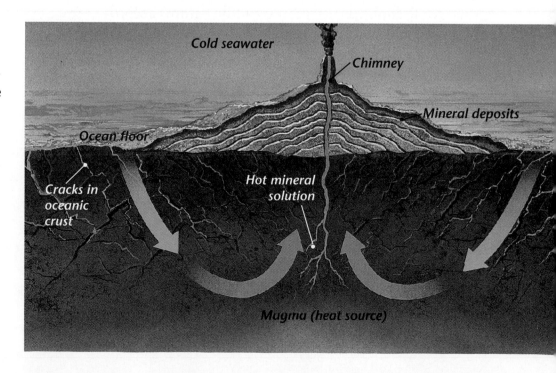

Figure 14 In Death Valley, California, water carries dissolved minerals from the surrounding mountains into the valley. When the water evaporates under the blazing desert sun, the minerals form a crust on the valley floor.

seeps down through cracks in the crust. There, the water comes in contact with magma that heats it to a very high temperature. The heated water dissolves minerals from the crust and rushes upward. This hot solution then billows out of vents, called "chimneys." When the hot solution hits the cold sea, minerals crystallize and settle to the ocean floor.

Minerals Formed by Evaporation

Minerals can also form when solutions evaporate. You know that if you stir salt crystals into a beaker of water, the salt dissolves, forming a solution. But if you allow the water in the solution to evaporate, it will leave salt crystals on the bottom of the beaker. In a similar way, thick deposits of the mineral halite formed over millions of years when ancient seas slowly evaporated. In the United States, such halite deposits occur in the Midwest, the Southwest, and along the Gulf Coast.

Several other useful minerals also form by the evaporation of seawater. These include gypsum, used in making building materials; calcite crystals, used in microscopes; and minerals containing potassium, used in making fertilizer.

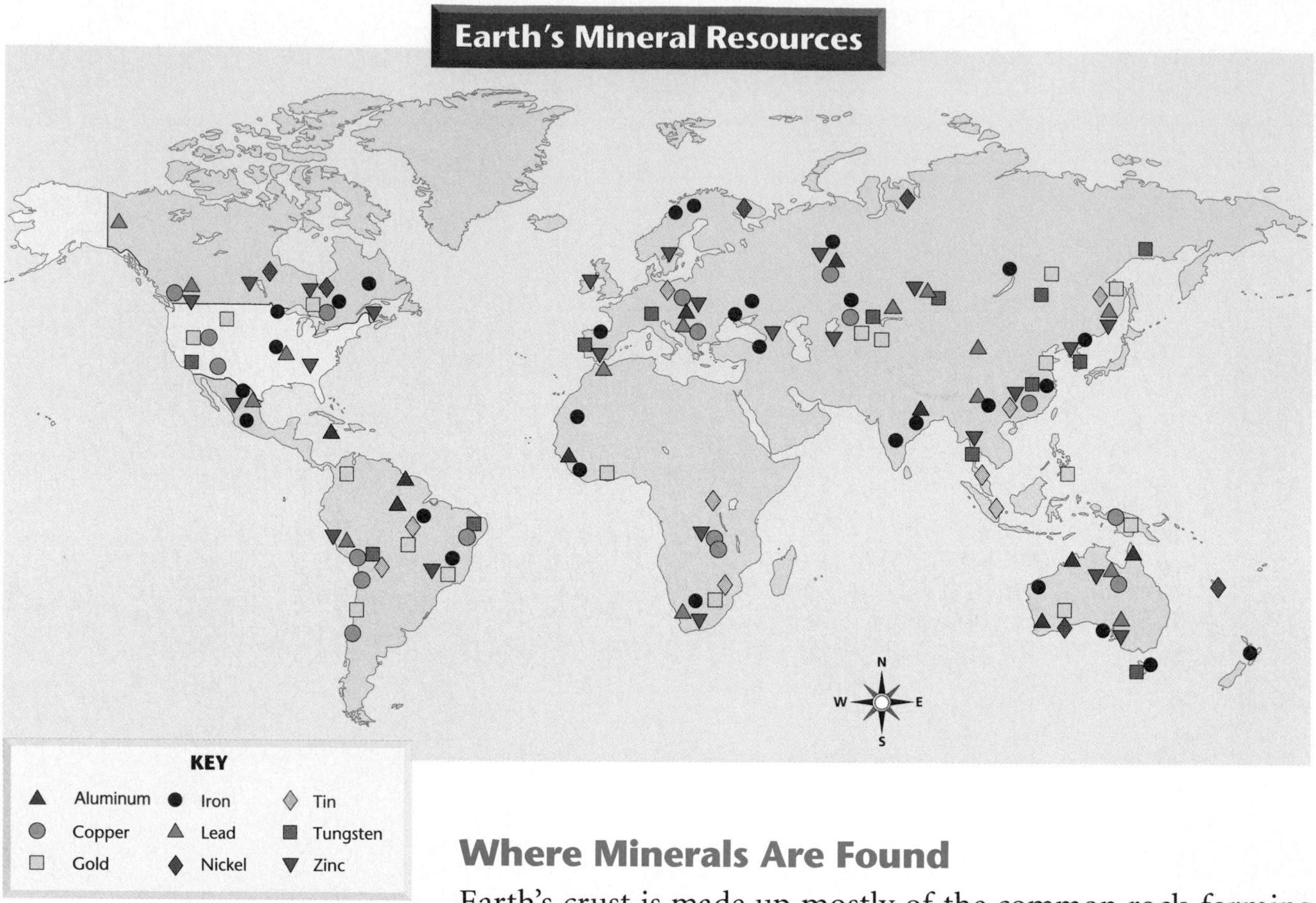

Earth's Mineral Resources

KEY

▲	Aluminum	●	Iron	◆	Tin
●	Copper	▲	Lead	■	Tungsten
□	Gold	◆	Nickel	▼	Zinc

Figure 15 The map shows where important mineral resources are found throughout the world. *Interpreting Maps Which metals are found in the United States? Which ones must be imported from other countries?*

Where Minerals Are Found

Earth's crust is made up mostly of the common rock-forming minerals combined in various types of rock. Less common and rare minerals, however, are not distributed evenly throughout the crust. Instead, there are several processes that concentrate minerals, or bring them together, in deposits. Look at the map of the world's mineral resources in Figure 15. Do you see any patterns in the distribution of minerals such as gold and copper? Many valuable minerals are found in or near areas of volcanic activity and mountain building. For example, rich copper deposits are found along the Andes mountains in Chile.

Section 2 Review

1. What are the two main ways in which minerals form?
2. Describe how the cooling rate of magma affects the size of the mineral crystals formed.
3. What are the steps by which mineral deposits form along mid-ocean ridges?
4. **Thinking Critically Relating Cause and Effect** A miner finds a vein of silver. Describe a process that could have formed the vein.

Check Your Progress

CHAPTER PROJECT **4**

Remember to record your daily observations of how your crystal garden grows. Sketch the shapes of the crystals and describe how the crystals grow. Compare the shapes and growth rates of the crystals grown from the various solutions. (*Hint:* If crystals do not begin growing, add more of the correct solution.)

Who Owns the Ocean's Minerals?

Rich mineral deposits lie on and just beneath the ocean floor. Many nations would like to mine these deposits. Coastal nations already have the right to mine deposits near their shores. Today, they are mining materials such as tin, titanium, diamonds, and sulfur from the continental shelf— the wide area of shallow water just off the shores of continents.

But the ocean floor beyond the continental shelves is open for all nations to explore. Mineral deposits in volcanic areas of the ocean floor include manganese, iron, cobalt, copper, nickel and platinum. Who owns these valuable underwater minerals?

▲ This sample from the floor of the Pacific Ocean near New Guinea may contain copper and gold.

The Issues

Who Can Afford to Mine? Although the ocean floor is open to all for exploration, mining the ocean floor will cost a huge amount of money. New technologies must be developed to obtain mineral deposits from the ocean floor.

Only wealthy industrial nations such as France, Germany, Japan, and the United States will be able to afford these costs. Industrial nations that have spent money and effort on mining think that they should be allowed to keep all the profits. However, developing nations that lack money and technology disagree. Landlocked nations that have no coastlines also object.

What Rights Do Other Nations Have?
As of 1996, 87 nations had signed the Law of the Sea treaty. Among other things, this treaty stated that ocean mineral deposits are the common property of all people. It also stated that mining profits must be shared among all nations.

Some people think that, because of the treaty, wealthy nations should share their technology and any profits they get from mining the ocean floor.

How Can the Wealth Be Shared?
What can nations do to prevent conflict over mining the ocean floor? They might arrange a compromise. Perhaps wealthy nations should contribute part of their profits to help developing or landlocked nations. Developing nations could pool their money for ocean-floor mining. Whatever nations decide, some regulations for ocean-floor mining are necessary. In the future, these resources will be important to everyone.

You Decide

1. **Identify the Problem**
   In your own words, state the controversy about ocean mineral rights.

2. **Analyze the Options**
   Compare the concerns of wealthy nations with those of developing nations. How could you reassure developing nations that they will not be left out?

3. **Find a Solution**
   Look at a map of the world. Who should share the mineral profits from the Pacific Ocean? From the Atlantic Ocean? Write one or two paragraphs stating your opinion. Support your ideas with facts.

SECTION 3 Mineral Resources

More than a thousand years ago, the Hopewell people lived in the Mississippi River valley. These ancient Native Americans are famous for the mysterious earthen mounds they built near the river. There these people left beautiful objects made from minerals: tools chipped from flint (a variety of quartz), the shape of a human hand cut out of a piece of translucent mica, or a flying bird made from a thin sheet of copper.

To obtain these minerals, the Hopewell people traded with peoples across North America. The copper, for example, came from near Lake Superior. There, copper could be found as a pure metal. Because copper is a soft metal, this copper was easy to shape into ornaments or weapons.

The Uses of Minerals

Like the Hopewell people, people today use minerals. You are surrounded by materials that come from minerals—for example, the metal body and window glass of a car. **Minerals are the source of metals, gemstones, and other materials used to make many products.** Are you familiar with any products that are made from minerals? You might be surprised at how important minerals are in everyday life.

Figure 16 The copper to make this Hopewell ornament may have come from an area in Michigan that is still a source of copper ore.

Gemstones Beautiful gemstones such as rubies and sapphires have captured the imagination of people throughout the ages. Usually, a **gemstone** is a hard, colorful mineral that has a brilliant or glassy luster. People value gemstones for their color, luster, and durability—and for the fact that they are rare. Once a gemstone is cut and polished, it is called a gem. Gems are used mainly for jewelry and decoration. They are also used for mechanical parts and for grinding and polishing.

Metals Some minerals are the sources of metals such as aluminum, iron, copper, or silver. Metals are useful because they can be stretched into wire, flattened into sheets, and hammered or molded without breaking. Metal tools and machinery, the metal filament in a light bulb, even the steel girders used to frame office buildings—all began as minerals inside Earth's crust.

Other Useful Minerals There are many other useful minerals besides metals and gems. People use materials from these minerals in foods, medicines, fertilizers, and building materials. The very soft mineral talc is ground up to make talcum powder. Fluorite is important in making aluminum and steel. Clear crystals of the mineral calcite are used in optical instruments such as microscopes. Quartz, a mineral found in sand, is used in making glass as well as in electronic equipment and watches. Kaolin occurs as white clay, which is used for making high-quality china and pottery. Gypsum, a soft, white mineral, is used to make wallboard, cement, and stucco. Corundum, the second hardest mineral after diamond, is often used in polishing and cleaning products.

✓ Checkpoint What is a gemstone? Why are gemstones valuable?

Figure 17 Gems like these red rubies and blue and yellow sapphires are among the most valuable minerals. These precious gems are varieties of the mineral corundum.

Ores

A rock that contains a metal or economically useful mineral is called an **ore**. Unlike the copper used by the Hopewell people, most metals do not occur in a pure form. A metal usually occurs as a mineral that is a combination of that metal and other elements. Much of the world's copper, for example, comes from ores containing the mineral chalcopyrite (kal kuh PY ryt). Before metals, gemstones, and other useful minerals can be separated from their ores, however, geologists must find them.

Prospecting

A prospector is anyone who searches, or prospects, for an ore deposit. Geologists prospect for ores by looking for certain features on Earth's surface. These geologists observe what kind of rocks are on the land surface. They examine plants growing in an area and test stream water for the presence of certain chemicals.

Geologists also employ some of the tools used to study Earth's interior. In one technique, they set off explosions below ground to create shock waves. The echoes of these shock waves are used to map the location, size, and shape of an ore deposit.

Mining

The geologist's map of an ore deposit helps miners decide how to mine the ore from the ground. **There are three types of mines: strip mines, open pit mines, and shaft mines.** In strip mining,

SCIENCE & History

Advances in Metal Technology

For thousands of years, people have been inventing and improving methods for smelting metals and making alloys.

4000 B.C. Cyprus

The island of Cyprus was one of the first places where copper was mined and smelted. In fact, the name of the island provided the name of the metal. In Latin, *aes cyprium* meant "metal of Cyprus." It was later shortened to *cuprum*, meaning "copper." The sculptured figure is carrying a large piece of smelted copper.

| 4000 B.C. | 2500 B.C. | 1000 B.C. |

3500 B.C.
Mesopotamia

Metalworkers in Sumer, a city between the Tigris and Euphrates rivers, made an alloy of tin and copper to produce a harder metal—bronze. Bronze was poured into molds to form statues, weapons, or vessels for food and drink.

1500 B.C.
Turkey

The Hittites learned to mine and smelt iron ore. Because iron is stronger than copper or bronze, its use spread rapidly. Tools and weapons could be made of iron. This iron dagger was made in Austria several hundred years after the Hittites' discovery.

earthmoving equipment scrapes away soil to expose ore. In open pit mining, miners use giant earthmoving equipment to dig a tremendous pit. Miners dig an open pit mine to remove ore deposits that may start near the surface, but extend down for hundreds of meters. Some open pit mines are more than a kilometer wide and nearly as deep. For ore deposits that occur in veins, miners dig shaft mines. Shaft mines often have a network of tunnels that extend deep into the ground, following the veins of ore.

 INTEGRATING ENVIRONMENTAL SCIENCE Mining for metals and other minerals can harm the environment. Strip mining and pit mining leave scars on the land. Waste materials from mining can pollute rivers and lakes. In the United States, laws now require that mine operators do as little damage to the environment as possible. To restore land damaged by strip mining, mine operators grade the surface and replace the soil.

In Your Journal

When people discover how to use metals in a new way, the discovery often produces big changes in the way those people live. Choose a development in the history of metals to research. Write a diary entry telling how the discovery happened and how it changed people's lives.

A.D. 1860s
England

Steel-making techniques invented by Henry Bessemer and William Siemens made it possible to produce steel cheaply on a large scale. Siemens' invention, the open-hearth furnace, is still widely used, although more modern methods account for most steel production today.

A.D. 500   **A.D. 2000**

A.D. 600s
Sri Lanka

Sri Lankans made steel in outdoor furnaces. Steady winds blowing over the top of the furnace's front wall created the high temperatures needed to make steel. Because their steel was so much harder than iron, the Sri Lankans were able to trade it throughout the Indian Ocean region.

A.D. 1960s TO THE PRESENT
United States

Scientists working on the space program have developed light and strong alloys for use in products ranging from bicycles to soda cans. For example, a new alloy of nickel and titanium can "remember" its shape. It is used for eyeglasses that return to their original shape after being bent.

Smelting

Ores must be processed before the metals they contain can be used. **After miners remove ore from a mine, smelting is necessary to remove the metal from the ore.** In the process of **smelting,** an ore is melted to separate the useful metal from other elements the ore contains. People around the world have used smelting to obtain metals from ores. Look at the time line in *Science and History* to see how this technology has developed from ancient times to the present.

How does smelting separate iron metal from hematite, a common form of iron ore? In general, smelting involves mixing an ore with other substances and then heating the mixture to a very high temperature. The heat melts the metal in the ore. The heat also causes the metal to separate from the oxygen with which it is combined. Metalworkers can then pour off the molten metal. Follow the steps in *Exploring Smelting Iron Ore.*

After smelting, additional processing is needed to remove impurities from the iron. The result is steel, which is harder and stronger than iron. Steel is an **alloy,** a solid mixture of two or more metals. Steelmakers mix iron with other elements to create alloys with special properties. For stronger steel, the metal manganese and a small amount of carbon are added. For rust-resistant steel, the metals chromium and nickel are added. You can compare plain steel with rust-resistant stainless steel in Figure 18.

Figure 18 Plain steel rusts easily. But stainless steel—an alloy of iron, chromium, and nickel—doesn't rust. The chromium and nickel slow down the process by which the oxygen in the air combines with iron in the steel to form iron oxide, or rust.

Section 3 Review

1. What are some of the ways that people use gems and metals?
2. Describe three different kinds of mines.
3. What process is used to separate useful metals from ores?
4. What are alloys, and why are they useful?
5. **Thinking Critically** In smelting, what causes a metal to separate from its ore?

Science at Home

You can demonstrate to your family how rust damages objects that contain iron. Obtain three iron nails. Coat one of the nails with petroleum jelly and coat the second nail with clear nail polish. Do not put anything on the third nail. Place all the nails in a glass of water with a little vinegar. (The vinegar speeds up the rusting process.) Allow the nails to stand in the glass overnight. Which nails show signs of rusting? Explain these results to your family.

EXPLORING Smelting Iron Ore

Iron usually occurs as the ores hematite or magnetite. Iron ores must be smelted to separate the iron from the oxygen and other substances in the ores. Then the iron is refined and processed into steel.

1. Iron ore is crushed and then mixed with crushed limestone and coke (baked coal), which is rich in carbon.

2. The coke and iron ore mixture is placed in a blast furnace, where extremely hot air is blown through, making the coke burn easily.

3. As the coke burns, chemical changes in the mixture produce carbon dioxide gas and molten iron.

4. The iron sinks to the bottom of the furnace. Impurities left in the ore combine with the limestone to create slag.

5. The slag and molten iron are poured off through taps in the blast furnace.

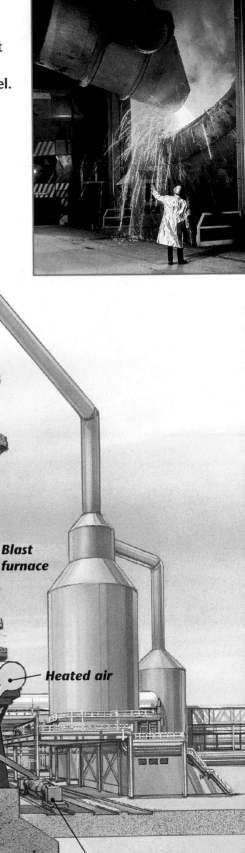

Skip hoist

Coke-limestone-iron ore mixture

Blast furnace

Heated air

Heated air

Slag

Molten iron

Coke

Iron ore and limestone

Slag ladle

Hot metal car

Careers in Science

COPPER RECOVERY

If you were a mining engineer, one of your tasks would be to make mining and processing ores more efficient. When copper ore is processed at copper mines, waste water containing copper sulfate is produced. Mining engineers have invented a way to recover copper metal from the waste water. They make the waste water flow over scrap iron.

Problem

How is copper recovered from a solution?

Skills Focus

observing, inferring, drawing conclusions

Materials

copper sulfate, 3 g	beaker, 400 mL
triple-beam balance	5 iron nails
graduated cylinder, 100 mL	water

Procedure

1. Place 3 g of copper sulfate in a beaker.
   CAUTION: *Copper sulfate is poisonous. Handle it with care.*
2. Add 50 mL of water to the beaker to dissolve the copper sulfate. Observe the color of the solution.
3. Add the iron nails to the beaker. The nails act as scrap iron. Describe the color of the solution after the nails have been added to the solution.
4. Follow your teacher's instructions for proper disposal. Wash your hands when you are finished.

Analyze and Conclude

1. What happened to the nails after you placed them in the solution? What is the material on the nails? Explain your answer.

2. How does the material on the nails compare with the copper sulfate?
3. Develop a plan that describes how a mine might recover copper from mine water using the method that you have just tried.
4. What additional step would you have to perform to obtain copper useful for making copper wire or pennies?
5. **Apply** Why do you think the operator of a copper mine would want to collect copper from the waste water?

Move to Explore

Repeat the experiment. This time test the solution with litmus paper both before and after you add the nails. Litmus paper indicates if a solution is acidic, basic, or neutral. Record your results. Why do you think a mining engineer would test the water from this process before releasing it into the environment?

SECTION 1 Properties of Minerals

Key Ideas

◆ A mineral is a naturally occurring inorganic solid that has a distinct chemical composition and crystal shape.

◆ Each mineral can be identified by its own physical and chemical properties.

◆ Some of the properties of minerals include hardness, color, streak, luster, density, cleavage and fracture, and crystal structure. Hardness is measured by the Mohs hardness scale.

◆ Minerals usually consist of two or more elements joined together in a compound.

Key Terms

mineral	Mohs hardness scale
inorganic	streak
crystal	luster
element	cleavage
compound	fracture
	fluorescence

SECTION 2 How Minerals Form

Key Ideas

◆ Minerals form inside Earth through crystallization as magma or lava cools.

◆ Minerals form on Earth's surface when materials dissolved in water crystallize through evaporation.

◆ Mineral deposits form on the ocean floor from solutions heated by magma. The hot-water solutions containing minerals erupt through chimneys on the ocean floor, then crystallize when they come in contact with cold sea water.

Key Terms
solution
vein

SECTION 3 Mineral Resources

INTEGRATING TECHNOLOGY

Key Ideas

◆ Minerals are useful as the source of all metals, gemstones, and of many other materials.

◆ Geologists locate ore deposits by prospecting—looking for certain features on and beneath Earth's surface.

◆ Ores can be removed from the ground through open pit mines, strip mines, or shaft mines.

◆ Smelting is the process of heating an ore to extract a metal.

Key Terms
gemstone
ore
smelting
alloy

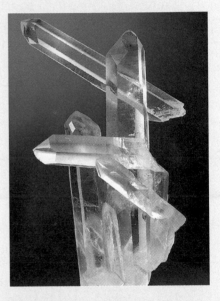

Organizing Information

Venn Diagram Copy the Venn diagram comparing the mineral hematite and the human-made material brick onto a separate piece of paper. Then complete it and add a title. (For more on Venn diagrams, see the Skills Handbook.)

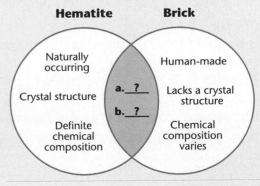

Hematite

Naturally occurring

Crystal structure

Definite chemical composition

a. ?

b. ?

Brick

Human-made

Lacks a crystal structure

Chemical composition varies

Reviewing Content

 For more review of key concepts, see the Interactive Student Tutorial CD-ROM.

Multiple Choice

Choose the letter of the answer that best completes each statement.

1. In a mineral, the particles line up in a repeating pattern to form
   a. an element.
   b. a crystal.
   c. a mixture.
   d. a compound.
2. The softest mineral in the Mohs hardness scale is
   a. quartz.
   b. talc.
   c. apatite.
   d. gypsum.
3. Halite is a mineral formed by
   a. chimneys on the ocean floor.
   b. cooling of magma.
   c. evaporation.
   d. cooling of lava.
4. Metals are useful for tools because they
   a. are compounds.
   b. have a metallic luster.
   c. are hard yet can be easily shaped.
   d. are elements.
5. Minerals from which metals can be removed in usable amounts are called
   a. gemstones.
   b. crystals.
   c. alloys.
   d. ores.

True or False

If the statement is true, write true. If it is false, change the underlined word or words to make the statement true.

6. <u>Luster</u> is the term that describes how a mineral reflects light from its surface.
7. A piece of unglazed tile is used to test a mineral's <u>hardness</u>.
8. If magma cools very slowly, minerals with <u>small</u> crystals will form.
9. Minerals form from <u>hot-water solutions</u> at chimneys on the ocean floor.
10. The process of removing an ore deposit from the ground is known as <u>prospecting</u>.

Checking Concepts

11. What is the difference in composition between most minerals and a pure element?
12. How can the streak test be helpful in identifying minerals?
13. Compare cleavage and fracture.
14. Describe two different ways that minerals can form.
15. Describe the process used to extract metal from hematite ore. What metal would be obtained?
16. **Writing to Learn** You are a prospector searching for gold. In a letter home, describe where you plan to look, how you will know if you have found gold, and how you will feel about your discovery.

Thinking Critically

17. **Comparing and Contrasting** Color and luster are both properties of minerals. How are these properties similar? How are they different? How can each be used to help identify a mineral?
18. **Classifying** Obsidian forms when magma cools very quickly, creating a type of glass. In glass, the particles are not arranged in an orderly pattern as in a crystal. Obsidian is a solid, inorganic substance that occurs naturally in volcanic areas. Should it be classified as a mineral? Explain why or why not.
19. **Relating Cause and Effect** Describe how a vein of ore forms underground. What is the energy source for this process?
20. **Applying Concepts** Explain the roles of elements, solutions, and compounds in the process that forms minerals around chimneys on the ocean floor.
21. **Predicting** What would happen if steel-makers forgot to add enough chromium and nickel to a batch of stainless steel?

Applying Skills

Working as a geologist, you have found a sample of the mineral wulfenite. Testing the wulfenite reveals that it has a hardness of about 3 on the Mohs hardness scale and a density of 6.8 grams per cubic centimeter. You also determine that the mineral contains oxygen as well as the metals lead and molybdenum.

Wulfenite

22. Observing Describe wulfenite's color, luster, and crystal structure.

23. Inferring Did the wulfenite form slowly or quickly? Explain your answer.

24. Drawing Conclusions Is wulfenite hard enough for use as a gem? What would you use these crystals for? Explain.

Performance ▾ CHAPTER PROJECT 4 Assessment

Project Wrap Up Before you present your crystal garden to the class, share it with a classmate. Can your classmate identify which solution created which crystals? Do your data show differences in crystal growth rates? What conclusions can you draw from your data? Now you are ready to present your project to your class.

Reflect and Record In your journal, identify any changes that would improve your crystal garden. Which materials worked best for crystals to grow on? Which ones did not work well?

Test Preparation
Use these questions to prepare for standardized tests.

Study the table. Then answer Questions 25–29.

Properties of Six Minerals				
Mineral	Hardness	Density (g/cm³)	Luster	Streak
Corundum	9.0	4.0	glassy	white
Quartz	7.0	2.6	glassy	white
Magnetite	6.0	5.2	metallic	black
Copper	2.8	8.9	metallic	red
Galena	2.5	7.5	metallic	lead gray
Talc	1.0	2.8	pearly	white

25. Which mineral in the table could be scratched by all the others?
  a. quartz **b.** galena
  c. copper **d.** talc

26. The mineral in the table with the greatest density is
  a. copper. **b.** galena.
  c. magnetite. **d.** talc.

27. To be suitable as a gemstone, a mineral usually must be very hard and have a glassy luster. Which mineral on the list would probably make the best gemstone?
  a. copper **b.** corundum
  c. magnetite **d.** galena

28. Quartz and talc have a similar density. What property or properties could you easily test to tell them apart?
  a. hardness and luster
  b. streak only
  c. density only
  d. none of the above

29. Suppose that you have found a dense, dark-colored mineral with a metallic luster. What property would you test quickly and easily to determine if the mineral were copper rather than galena?
  a. hardness **b.** luster
  c. streak **d.** density

CHAPTER 5 Rocks

WEB ACTIVITY
www.phschool.com

 SECTION 1 **Classifying Rocks**

Discover How Are Rocks Alike and Different?

 SECTION 2 **Igneous Rocks**

Discover How Do Igneous Rocks Form?
Sharpen Your Skills Observing

SECTION 3 **Sedimentary Rocks**

Discover How Does Pressure Affect Particles of Rock?
Try This Rock Absorber

144 ◆ F

Collecting Rocks

Each rock, whether a small pebble or a giant boulder, tells a story. By observing a rock's characteristics, geologists learn about the forces that shaped the portion of Earth's crust where the rock formed. The rocks in your own community tell the story of Earth's crust in your area.

In this chapter, you will learn how three different types of rocks form. You can apply what you learn about rocks to create your own rock collection and explore the properties of these rocks.

Your Goal To make a collection of the rocks in your area.

To complete this project, you must
- collect samples of rocks, keeping a record of where you found each sample
- describe the characteristics of your rocks, including their color, texture, and density
- classify each rock as igneous, sedimentary, or metamorphic
- create a display for your rock collection
- follow the safety guidelines in Appendix A

Get Started With your classmates and teacher, brainstorm locations in your community where rocks are likely to be found. Are there road cuts, outcroppings of bedrock, riverbanks, or beaches where you could safely and legally collect your rocks?

Check Your Progress You will be working on this project as you study the chapter. To keep your project on track, look for Check Your Progress boxes at the following points.

Section 1 Review, page 149: Plan your rock-hunting expeditions.
Section 3 Review, page 158: Collect your rocks.
Section 4 Review, page 161: Begin to describe, test, and catalog your rock collection.
Section 6 Review, page 169: Classify your rocks and plan your presentation.

Wrap Up At the end of the chapter (page 173), prepare a display of your rock collection. Be prepared to discuss the properties of the rocks you collected, how the rocks formed, and how people can use them.

Hikers cross a landscape of rock in the Cascade Range, a mountain range in Washington state.

Integrating Life Science

SECTION 4 Rocks From Reefs

Discover **What Can You Conclude From the Way a Rock Reacts to Acid?**

SECTION 5 Metamorphic Rocks

Discover **How Do the Grain Patterns of Gneiss and Granite Compare?**
Try This **A Sequined Rock**
Skills Lab **Mystery Rocks**

SECTION 6 The Rock Cycle

Discover **Which Rock Came First?**
Sharpen Your Skills **Classifying**
Real-World Lab **Testing Rock Flooring**

SECTION
1 Classifying Rocks

DISCOVER · ACTIVITY

How Are Rocks Alike and Different?

1. Look at samples of marble and conglomerate with a hand lens.

2. Describe the two rocks. What is the color and texture of each?

3. Try scratching the surface of each rock with the edge of a penny. Which rock seems harder?

4. Hold each rock in your hand. Allowing for the fact that the samples aren't exactly the same size, which rock seems denser?

Think It Over

Observing Based on your observations, how would you compare the physical properties of marble and conglomerate?

Figure 1 Geology students collect and study samples of rocks.

GUIDE FOR READING

◆ What characteristics are used to identify rocks?

◆ What are the three major groups of rocks?

Reading Tip Before you read, use the headings to make an outline about rocks. Then fill in details as you read.

Between 1969 and 1972, the Apollo missions to the moon returned to Earth with pieces of the moon's surface. Space scientists eagerly tested these samples. They wanted to learn what the moon is made of. They found that the moon's surface is made of material very similar to the material that makes up Earth's surface—rock. Some moon samples are dark rock called basalt. Other samples are light-colored rock made mostly of the mineral feldspar.

How Geologists Classify Rocks

For both Earth and its moon, rocks are important building blocks. On Earth, rock forms mountains, hills, valleys, beaches, even the ocean floor. Earth's crust is made of rock. Rocks are made of mixtures of minerals and other materials, although some rocks may contain only a single mineral. Granite, shown in Figure 2, is made up of the minerals quartz, feldspar, mica, and hornblende, and sometimes other minerals.

Geologists collect and study samples of rock in order to classify them. Imagine that you are a geologist exploring a mountain range for the first time. How would you study a particular type of rock found in these mountains? You might use a camera or notebook to record

Figure 2 Granite is made up of quartz, mica, feldspar, and hornblende. It may also contain other minerals. *Observing* Which mineral seems most abundant in the sample of granite shown?

information about the setting where the rock was found. (In classifying a rock, it's important for a geologist to know what other types of rock occur nearby). Then, you would use a chisel or the sharp end of a rock hammer to remove samples of the rock. Finally, you would break open the samples with a hammer to examine their inside surfaces. You must look at the inside of a rock because the effects of water and weather can change the outer surface of a rock.

When studying a rock sample, geologists observe the rock's color and texture and determine its mineral composition. Using these characteristics, geologists can classify a rock according to its origin, or where and how it formed.

Texture

As with minerals, color alone does not provide enough information to identify a rock. A rock's texture, however, is very useful in identifying the rock. To a geologist, a rock's **texture** is the look and feel of the rock's surface. Some rocks are smooth and glassy. Others are rough or chalky. Most rocks are made up of particles of minerals or other rocks, which geologists call **grains.** A rock's grains give the rock its texture. To describe a rock's texture, geologists use a number of terms based on the size, shape, and pattern of the rock's grains.

Figure 3 Texture helps geologists classify rocks. *Forming Operational Definitions* Looking at the rocks below, describe the characteristics of a rock that help you to define what a rock's "grain" is.

Fine-grained
Slate

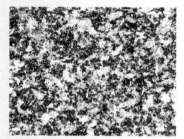

Coarse-grained
Diorite

No visible grain
Flint

Grain Size Often, the grains in a rock are large and easy to see. Such rocks are said to be coarse-grained. In other rocks, the grains are so small that they can only be seen with a microscope. These rocks are said to be fine-grained. Notice the difference in texture between the fine-grained slate and the coarse-grained diorite at left.

Grain Shape The grains in a rock vary widely in shape. Some grains look like tiny particles of fine sand. Others look like small seeds or exploding stars. In some rocks, such as granite, the grain results from the shapes of the crystals that form the rock. In other rocks, the grain shape results from fragments of other rock. These fragments can be smooth and rounded, like the fragments in conglomerate, or they can be jagged, like the fragments in breccia. You can compare conglomerate and breccia below.

Grain Pattern The grains in a rock often form patterns. Some grains lie in flat layers that look like a stack of pancakes. Other grains form wavy, swirling patterns. Some rocks have grains that look like rows of multicolored beads, as in the sample of gneiss shown below. Other rocks, in contrast, have grains that occur randomly throughout the rock.

No Visible Grain Some rocks have no grain, even when they are examined under a microscope. Some of these rocks have no crystal grains because when they form, they cool very quickly. This quick cooling gives these rocks the smooth, shiny texture of a thick piece of glass. Other rocks with no visible grain are made up of extremely small particles of silica that settle out of water. One familiar rock that forms in this manner is flint.

☑ *Checkpoint* *What terms describe a rock's texture?*

Rounded grain
Conglomerate

Jagged grain
Breccia

Nonbanded
Quartzite

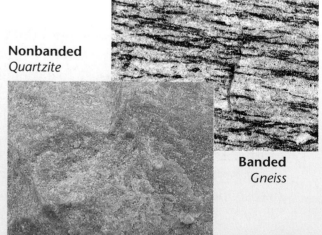

Banded
Gneiss

Mineral Composition

Often, geologists must look more closely at a rock to determine its mineral composition. By looking at a small sliver of a rock under a microscope, a geologist can observe the shape and size of crystals in the rock and identify the minerals it contains. To prepare a rock for viewing under the microscope, geologists cut the rock very thin, so that light can shine through its crystals.

In identifying rocks, geologists also use some of the tests that are used to identify minerals. For example, testing the rock's surface with acid determines whether the rock includes minerals made of compounds called carbonates. Testing with a magnet detects the elements iron or nickel.

Origin

There are three major groups of rocks: igneous rock, sedimentary rock, and metamorphic rock. These terms refer to how the rocks in each group formed.

Rock belonging to each of these groups forms in a different way. **Igneous rock** forms from the cooling of molten rock—either magma below the surface or lava at the surface. Most **sedimentary rock** forms when particles of other rocks or the remains of plants and animals are pressed and cemented together. Sedimentary rock forms in layers below the surface. **Metamorphic rock** is formed when an existing rock is changed by heat, pressure, or chemical reactions. Most metamorphic rock forms deep underground.

Figure 4 A scientist is preparing to cut a thin slice from a piece of moon rock. He will then examine it under a microscope to determine its composition.

 Section 1 Review

1. What three characteristics do geologists use to identify a rock sample?
2. What are the three groups into which geologists classify rocks?
3. What is a rock's texture?
4. What methods do geologists use to determine the mineral composition of a rock?
5. **Thinking Critically Comparing and Contrasting** What do the three major groups of rocks have in common? How are they different?

Check Your Progress CHAPTER PROJECT 5
Your neighborhood might be a good place to begin your rock collection. Look for gravel and crushed rock in flower beds, driveways or parking lots, and beneath downspouts. **CAUTION:** *If the area you choose is not a public place, make sure that you have permission to be there.* Begin to collect samples of rocks with different colors and textures. Plan with your teacher or an adult family member to visit other parts of your community where you could collect rocks.

SECTION
2 Igneous Rocks

DISCOVER •••ACTIVITY•••

How Do Igneous Rocks Form?

1. Use a hand lens to examine samples of granite and obsidian.

2. Describe the texture of both rocks using the terms coarse, fine, or glassy.

3. Which rock has coarse-grained crystals? Which rock has no crystals or grains?

Think It Over

Inferring Granite and obsidian are igneous rocks. Given the physical properties of these rocks, what can you infer about how each type of rock formed?

GUIDE FOR READING

◆ What characteristics are used to classify igneous rocks?

Reading Tip As you read, make a list of the characteristics of igneous rocks. Write one sentence describing each characteristic.

Figure 5 A lava flow soon cools and hardens to form igneous rock.

You are in a spacecraft orbiting Earth 4.6 billion years ago. Do you see the blue and green globe of Earth that astronauts today see from space? No—instead, Earth looks like a glowing piece of charcoal from a barbecue, or a charred and bubbling marshmallow heated over the coals.

Soon after Earth formed, the planet became so hot that its surface was a glowing mass of molten material. Hundreds of millions of years passed before Earth cooled enough for a crust to solidify. Then lava probably flowed from Earth's interior, spread over the surface, and hardened. The movement of magma and lava has continued ever since.

A   B

C

Characteristics of Igneous Rock

The first rocks to form on Earth probably looked much like the igneous rocks that harden from lava today. Igneous rock (IG nee us) is any rock that forms from magma or lava. The name "igneous" comes from the Latin word *ignis*, meaning "fire."

Most igneous rocks are made of mineral crystals. The only exceptions to this rule are the different types of volcanic glass—igneous rock that lacks minerals with a crystal structure. **Igneous rocks are classified according to their origin, texture, and mineral composition.**

Origin Geologists classify igneous rocks according to where they formed. **Extrusive rock** is igneous rock formed from lava that erupted onto Earth's surface. Basalt is the most common extrusive rock. Basalt forms much of the crust, including the oceanic crust, shield volcanoes, and lava plateaus.

Igneous rock that formed when magma hardened beneath Earth's surface is called **intrusive rock.** Granite is the most abundant intrusive rock in continental crust. Recall from Chapter 3 that granite batholiths form the core of many mountain ranges.

Texture The texture of an igneous rock depends on the size and shape of its mineral crystals. Igneous rocks may be similar in mineral composition and yet have very different textures. The texture of an igneous rock may be fine-grained, coarse-grained, glassy, or porphyritic. Rapid cooling lava forms fine-grained igneous rocks with small crystals. Slow cooling magma forms coarse-grained rock with large crystals.

Intrusive and extrusive rocks usually have different textures. Intrusive rocks have larger crystals than extrusive rocks. If you examine a coarse-grained rock such as granite, you can easily see that the crystals vary in size and color.

Some intrusive rocks have a texture that looks like a gelatin dessert with chopped-up fruit mixed in. A rock with large crystals scattered on a background of much smaller crystals has a **porphyritic texture** (pawr fuh RIT ik). How can a rock have two

Figure 6 Igneous rocks can vary greatly in texture.
A. Rhyolite is a fine-grained igneous rock with a mineral composition similar to granite.
B. Pegmatite is a very coarse-grained variety of granite.
C. Porphyry has large crystals surrounded by fine-grained crystals.
Relating Cause and Effect *What conditions caused rhyolite to have a fine-grained texture?*

ACTIVITY

You can learn about a rock's mineral composition by looking at a thin section.

1. The diagram shows a thin section of an igneous rock. The key identifies different minerals. Which mineral makes up most of this rock? How did you decide?

2. Which mineral is present in the smallest amount?

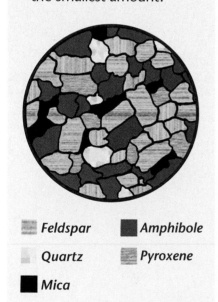

Feldspar	Amphibole
Quartz	Pyroxene
Mica	

Figure 7 This thin slice of granite, viewed under a microscope, contains quartz, feldspar, mica, and other minerals.

textures? Porphyritic rocks form when intrusive rocks cool in two stages. As the magma begins to cool, large crystals form slowly. The remaining magma, however, cools more quickly, forming small crystals. The change in the rate of cooling may occur as magma moves nearer to the surface.

Extrusive rocks have a fine-grained or glassy texture. Basalt is an extrusive rock. It consists of crystals too small to be seen without a microscope.

Mineral Composition Recall from Chapter 3 that the silica content of magma and lava affects how easily the magma or lava will flow. Lava that is low in silica usually forms dark-colored rocks such as basalt. Basalt contains feldspar as well as certain dark-colored minerals, but does not contain quartz.

INTEGRATING CHEMISTRY Magma that is high in silica usually forms light-colored rocks, such as granite. However, granite comes in many shades and colors. Granite can be dark to light gray, red, and pink. Granite's color changes along with its mineral composition. Granite that is rich in reddish feldspar is a speckled pink. But granite rich in hornblende and dark mica is light gray with dark specks. Quartz crystals in granite add light gray or smoky specks. Geologists can make thin slices of granite and study each type of crystal in the rock to determine its mineral composition more exactly.

✓ *Checkpoint* How do igneous rocks differ in origin, texture, and mineral composition?

Uses of Igneous Rocks

Many igneous rocks are hard, dense, and durable. For this reason, people throughout history have used igneous rock for tools and building materials. For example, ancient Native Americans used obsidian for making very sharp tools for cutting and scraping.

Granite, one of the most abundant igneous rocks, has a long history as a building material. More than 3,500 years ago, the ancient Egyptians used granite for statues like the one shown in Figure 8. About 600 years ago, the Incas of Peru carefully fitted together great blocks of granite and other igneous rocks to build a fortress near Cuzco, their capital city. In the United States during the 1800s and early 1900s, granite was widely used to build bridges and public buildings and for paving streets with cobblestones. Thin, polished sheets of granite are still used in decorative stonework, curbstones, and floors.

Igneous rocks such as basalt, pumice, and obsidian also have important uses. Basalt is crushed to make gravel that is used in construction. The rough surface of pumice makes it a good abrasive for cleaning and polishing. Perlite, formed from the heating of obsidian, is often mixed with soil for starting vegetable seeds.

Figure 8 The ancient Egyptians valued granite for its durability. These statues at a temple in Luxor, Egypt, were carved in granite.

Section 2 Review

1. What are the three major characteristics that geologists use to identify igneous rocks?
2. What is the difference between extrusive and intrusive rocks? Give an example of each.
3. Explain what causes an igneous rock to have a fine-grained or coarse-grained texture.
4. Why are some igneous rocks dark and others light?
5. **Thinking Critically Comparing and Contrasting** How are basalt and granite different in their origin, texture, and mineral composition? How are they similar?

Science at Home

When you and a family member visit a pharmacy or large food store, observe the various foot-care products. What kinds of foot products are available that are made from pumice? How do people use these products? Check other skin and body care products to see if they contain pumice or other igneous rocks. Explain to your family how pumice is formed.

SECTION
3 Sedimentary Rocks

DISCOVER ••**ACTIVITY**••••

How Does Pressure Affect Particles of Rock?

1. Place a sheet of paper over a slice of soft bread.

2. Put a stack of several heavy books on the top of the paper. After 10 minutes, remove the books. Observe what happened to the bread.

3. Slice the bread so you can observe its cross section.

4. Carefully slice a piece of fresh bread and compare its cross section to that of the pressed bread.

Think It Over

Observing How did the bread change after you removed the books? Describe the texture of the bread. How does the bread feel? What can you predict about how pressure affects the particles that make up sedimentary rocks?

GUIDE FOR READING

◆ How do sedimentary rocks form?

◆ What are the three major types of sedimentary rocks?

Reading Tip Before you read, preview the headings in the section and predict how you think sedimentary rocks form.

Visitors to Arches National Park in Utah see some of the strangest scenery on Earth. The park contains dozens of natural arches sculpted in colorful rock that is layered like a birthday cake. The layers of this cake are red, orange, pink, or tan. One arch, named Landscape Arch, is nearly 90 meters across and about 30 meters high. Delicate Arch looks like the legs of a striding giant. The forces that wear away rock on Earth's surface have been carving these arches out of solid rock for 100 million years. The arches are made of sandstone, one of the most common sedimentary rocks.

From Sediment to Rock

Sedimentary rocks form from particles deposited by water and wind. If you have ever walked along a stream or beach you may have noticed tiny sand grains, mud, and pebbles. These are some of the sediments that form sedimentary rock. **Sediment** is small, solid pieces of material that come from rocks or living things. Water, wind, and ice can carry sediment and deposit it in layers. But what turns these sediments into solid rock?

◀ Delicate Arch, Arches National Park, Utah

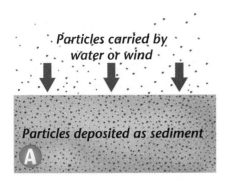

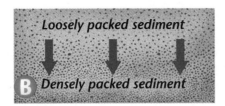

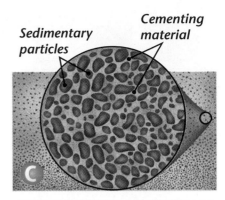

Figure 9 Sedimentary rocks form through the deposition, compaction, and cementation of sediments. **A.** Water or wind deposits sediment. **B.** The heavy sediments press down on the layers beneath. **C.** Dissolved minerals flow between the particles and cement them together.
Relating Cause and Effect What conditions are necessary for sedimentary rock to form?

Erosion Destructive forces are constantly breaking up and wearing away all the rocks on Earth's surface. These forces include heat and cold, rain, waves, and grinding ice. **Erosion** occurs when running water or wind loosen and carry away the fragments of rock.

Deposition Eventually, the moving water or wind slows and deposits the sediment. If water is carrying the sediment, rock fragments and other materials sink to the bottom of a lake or ocean. **Deposition** is the process by which sediment settles out of the water or wind carrying it. **After sediment has been deposited, the processes of compaction and cementation change the sediment into sedimentary rock.**

In addition to particles of rock, sediment may include shells, bones, leaves, stems, and other remains of living things. Over time, any remains of living things in the sediment may slowly harden and change into fossils trapped in the rock.

Compaction At first the sediments fit together loosely. But gradually, over millions of years, thick layers of sediment build up. These layers are heavy and press down on the layers beneath them. Then compaction occurs. **Compaction** is the process that presses sediments together. Year after year more sediment falls on top, creating new layers. The weight of the layers further compacts the sediments, squeezing them tightly together. The layers often remain visible in the sedimentary rock.

Cementation While compaction is taking place, the minerals in the rock slowly dissolve in the water. The dissolved minerals seep into the spaces between particles of sediment. **Cementation** is the process in which dissolved minerals crystallize and glue particles of sediment together. It often takes millions of years for compaction and cementation to transform loose sediments into solid sedimentary rock.

✔️ *Checkpoint* What are the processes that change sediment to sedimentary rock?

Types of Sedimentary Rock

Geologists classify sedimentary rocks according to the type of sediments that make up the rock. **There are three major groups of sedimentary rocks: clastic rocks, organic rocks, and chemical rocks.** Different processes form each of these types of sedimentary rocks.

Clastic Rocks

Most sedimentary rocks are made up of the broken pieces of other rocks. A **clastic rock** is a sedimentary rock that forms when rock fragments are squeezed together. These fragments can range in size from clay particles too small to be seen without a microscope to large boulders too heavy for you to lift. Clastic rocks are grouped by the size of the rock fragments, or particles, of which they are made.

Shale One common clastic rock is shale. Shale forms from tiny particles of clay. For shale to form, water must deposit clay particles in very thin, flat layers, one on top of another. No cementation is needed to hold clay particles together. Even so, the spaces between the particles in the resulting shale are so small that water cannot pass through them. Shale feels smooth, and splits easily into flat pieces.

Sandstone Sandstone forms from the sand on beaches, on the ocean floor, in riverbeds, and in sand dunes. Sandstone is a clastic rock formed from the compaction and cementation of small particles of sand. Most sand particles consist of quartz. Because the cementation process does not fill all the spaces between sand grains, sandstone contains many small holes. Sandstone can easily absorb water through these holes.

Conglomerate and Breccia Some sedimentary rocks contain a mixture of rock fragments of different sizes. The fragments can range in size from sand and pebbles to boulders. If the fragments have rounded edges, they form a clastic rock called conglomerate. A rock made up of large fragments with sharp edges is called breccia (BRECH ee uh).

Figure 10 Puddingstone is a form of the clastic rock conglomerate. *Observing What types of particles can you observe in this sample of puddingstone?*

Organic Rocks

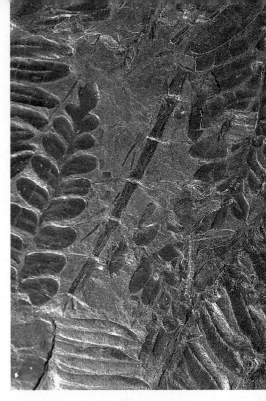

INTEGRATING LIFE SCIENCE Not all sedimentary rocks are made from particles of other rocks. **Organic rock** forms where the remains of plants and animals are deposited in thick layers. The term "organic" refers to substances that once were part of living things or were made by living things. Two important organic sedimentary rocks are coal and limestone.

Coal Coal forms from the remains of swamp plants buried in water. As layer upon layer of plant remains build up, the weight of the layers squeezes the decaying plants. Over millions of years, they slowly change into coal.

Limestone The hard shells of living things produce some kinds of limestone. How does limestone form? In the ocean, many living things, including coral, clams, oysters, and snails, have shells or skeletons made of calcite. When these animals die, their shells pile up as sediment on the ocean floor. Over millions of years, these layers of sediment can grow to a depth of hundreds of meters. Slowly, the pressure of overlying layers compacts the sediment. Some of the shells dissolve, forming a solution of calcite that seeps into the spaces between the shell fragments. Later, the dissolved material comes out of solution, forming calcite. The calcite cements the shell particles together, forming limestone.

Everyone knows one type of limestone: chalk. Chalk forms from sediments made of the skeletons of microscopic living things found in the oceans.

Figure 11 When broken apart, a piece of shale from a coal mine may reveal the impression of an ancient plant. Geologists estimate that it takes about 20 meters of decayed plants to form a layer of coal about one meter thick.

✔ Checkpoint What are two important organic sedimentary rocks?

Figure 12 These limestone cliffs are along the Eleven Point River in Missouri.

Figure 13 These rock "towers" in Mono Lake, California, are made of tufa, a type of limestone. Tufa forms from solutions containing dissolved minerals. *Classifying* *What type of sedimentary rock is tufa?*

Chemical Rocks

Chemical rock forms when minerals that are dissolved in a solution crystallize. For example, limestone can form when calcite that is dissolved in lakes, seas, or underground water comes out of solution and forms crystals. This kind of limestone is considered a chemical rock.

Chemical rocks can also form from mineral deposits left when seas or lakes evaporate. Rock salt is a chemical rock made of the mineral halite, which forms by evaporation. Gypsum is another chemical rock formed by evaporation. Large deposits of rocks formed by evaporation form only in dry climates.

Uses of Sedimentary Rocks

For thousands of years, people have used sandstone and limestone as building materials. Both types of stone are soft enough to be easily cut into blocks or slabs. You may be surprised to learn that the White House in Washington, D.C., is built of sandstone. Builders today use sandstone and limestone for decorating or for covering the outside walls of buildings.

Limestone also has many industrial uses. Recall from Chapter 4 that limestone is important in smelting iron ore. Limestone is also used in making cement.

Section 3 Review

1. Once sediment has been deposited, what processes change it into sedimentary rock?
2. What are the three major kinds of sedimentary rocks?
3. Describe two ways in which limestone can form.
4. **Thinking Critically Comparing and Contrasting** Compare and contrast shale and sandstone. Include what they are made of and how they form.

Check Your Progress

CHAPTER PROJECT 5

With an adult, visit an area where you can collect samples of rocks. As you collect your samples, observe whether the rock is loose on the ground, broken off a ledge, or in a stream. Begin to classify your rocks into groups. Do any of your rocks consist of a single mineral? Do you recognize any of the minerals in these rocks? Notice the texture of each rock. Did you find any rocks made of pieces of other rocks?

SECTION 4 Rocks From Reefs

DISCOVER •••••••••••••••••••••••••••••ACTIVITY•••

What Can You Conclude From the Way a Rock Reacts to Acid?

1. Using a hand lens, observe the color and texture of samples of limestone and coquina.

2. Put on your goggles and apron.

3. 🔖 Obtain a small amount of dilute hydrochloric acid from your teacher. Hydrochloric acid is used to test rocks for the presence of the mineral calcite.

4. Using a plastic dropper, place a few drops of dilute hydrochloric acid on the limestone. **CAUTION**: *Hydrochloric acid can cause burns.*

5. Record your observations.

6. Repeat Steps 2 through 4 with the sample of coquina and observe the results.

7. Rinse the samples of limestone and coquina with lots of water before returning them to your teacher. Wash your hands.

Think It Over
Drawing Conclusions
How did the color and texture of the two rocks compare? How did they react to the test? A piece of coral reacts to hydrochloric acid the same way as limestone and coquina. What could you conclude about the mineral composition of coral?

O ff the coast of Florida lies a "city" in the sea. It is a coral reef providing both food and shelter for many sea animals. The reef shimmers with life—clams, sponges, sea urchins, starfish, marine worms and, of course, fish. Schools of brilliantly colored fish dart in and out of forests of equally colorful corals. Octopuses lurk in underwater caves, scooping up crabs that pass too close. A reef forms a sturdy wall that protects the shoreline from battering waves. This city was built by billions of tiny, soft-bodied animals that have outer skeletons made of calcite.

GUIDE FOR READING

◆ How do coral reefs form?

◆ How do coral reefs become organic limestone deposits on land?

Reading Tip As you read, make a list of main ideas and supporting details about coral.

Figure 14 A coral reef in the Florida Keys provides food and shelter for many different kinds of living things.

Living Coral

Coral animals are tiny relatives of jellyfish that live together in vast numbers. Most coral animals are the size of your fingernail, or even smaller. Each one looks like a small sack with a mouth surrounded by tentacles. These animals use their tentacles to capture and eat microscopic creatures that float by. They produce skeletons that grow together to form a structure called a **coral reef.**

Coral reefs form only in the warm, shallow water of tropical oceans. Coral animals cannot grow in cold water or water low in salt. Reefs are most abundant around islands and along the eastern coasts of continents. In the United States, only the coasts of southern Florida and Hawaii have coral reefs.

Tiny algae grow within the body of each coral animal. The algae provide substances that the coral animals need to live. In turn, the coral animals provide a framework for the algae to grow on. Like plants, algae need sunlight. Below 40 meters, not enough light penetrates the water for the algae to grow. For this reason, almost all growth in a coral reef occurs within 40 meters of the water's surface.

How a Coral Reef Forms

Coral animals absorb the element calcium from the ocean water. The calcium is then changed into calcite and forms their skeletons. **When coral animals die, their skeletons remain, and more corals build on top of them.** Over thousands of years, reefs may grow to be hundreds of kilometers long and hundreds of meters thick. Reefs usually grow outward toward the open ocean. If the sea level rises or if the sea floor sinks, the reef will grow upward, too.

Figure 15 Coral animals feed on even smaller living things carried their way by the movement of ocean water. (This view has been magnified to show detail.)

Figure 16 The island of Bora Bora in the South Pacific Ocean is ringed by a fringing reef. Someday, erosion will wear away the island, leaving an atoll. *Inferring As the sea floor beneath an atoll sinks, what happens to the living part of the coral reef?*

There are three types of coral reefs: fringing reefs, barrier reefs and atolls. Fringing reefs lie close to shore, separated from land by shallow water. Barrier reefs lie farther out, at least 10 kilometers from the land. The Great Barrier Reef that stretches 2,000 kilometers along the coast of Australia is a barrier reef. An **atoll** is a ring-shaped coral island found far from land. An atoll develops when coral grows on top of a volcanic island that has sunk beneath the ocean's surface. How can a volcanic island sink? As the oceanic crust moves away from the mid-ocean ridge, it cools and becomes more dense. This causes the sea floor to sink.

☑ *Checkpoint* *What are the three types of coral reefs?*

Limestone Deposits From Coral Reefs

Over time, coral buried by sediments can turn into limestone. Like modern-day coral animals, ancient coral animals thrived in warm, tropical oceans. Their limestone fossils are among the most common fossils on Earth. **Limestone that began as coral can be found on continents in places where uplift has raised ancient sea floors above sea level.**

In parts of the United States, reefs that formed under water millions of years ago now make up part of the land. The movement of Earth's plates slowly uplifted the ocean floor where these reefs grew until the ocean floor became dry land. There are exposed reefs in Wisconsin, Illinois, and Indiana, as well as in Texas, New Mexico, and many other places.

Figure 17 A striking band of white rock tops El Capitan Peak in the Guadalupe Mountains of Texas. This massive layer of limestone formed from coral reefs that grew in a warm, shallow sea more than 250 million years ago.

Section 4 Review

1. Explain how coral reefs form.
2. How does coral become limestone?
3. Why are living coral animals only found in water that is less than 40 meters deep?
4. **Thinking Critically Predicting** The Amazon is a great river that flows through the tropical forests of Brazil. The river dumps huge amounts of fresh water, made cloudy by particles of sediment, into the South Atlantic Ocean. Would you expect to find coral reefs growing in the ocean near the mouth of the Amazon? Explain your answer.

Check Your Progress CHAPTER PROJECT 5

Begin to make an information card for each of your rocks, and decide how to store the rocks. Each rock's card should include the following information: where and when the rock was found; the type of geologic feature where you found the rock; a description of the rock's texture; a description of the minerals that make up the rock; and the results of any tests you performed on the rock. Are any of your rocks organic rocks? How could you tell?

DISCOVER ···················· ACTIVITY····

How Do the Grain Patterns of Gneiss and Granite Compare?

1. Using a hand lens, observe samples of gneiss and granite. Look carefully at the grains or crystals in both rocks.

2. Observe how the grains or crystals are arranged in both rocks. Draw a sketch of both rocks and describe their textures.

Think It Over

Inferring Within the crust, some granite becomes gneiss. What do you think must happen to cause this change?

GUIDE FOR READING

◆ Under what conditions do metamorphic rocks form?

◆ How do geologists classify metamorphic rocks?

Reading Tip Before you read, rewrite the headings in the section as questions. As you read, look for answers to those questions.

Every metamorphic rock is a rock that has changed its form. In fact, the word *metamorphic* comes from the Greek words *meta*, meaning "change," and *morphosis*, meaning "form." But what causes a rock to change into metamorphic rock? The answer lies inside Earth.

How Metamorphic Rocks Form

Heat and pressure deep beneath Earth's surface can change any rock into metamorphic rock. When rock changes into metamorphic rock, its appearance, texture, crystal structure, and mineral content change. Metamorphic rock can form out of igneous, sedimentary, or other metamorphic rock.

Collisions between Earth's plates can push the rock down toward the heat of the mantle. Pockets of magma rising through the crust also provide heat that can produce metamorphic rocks.

The deeper rock is buried in the crust, the greater the pressure on that rock. Under pressure hundreds or thousands of times greater than at Earth's surface, the minerals in a rock can change into other minerals. The rock has become a metamorphic rock.

Figure 18 Great heat and pressure can change one type lof rock into another. Granite becomes gneiss, shale becomes slate, and sandstone changes to quartzite. *Observing How does quartzite differ from sandstone?*

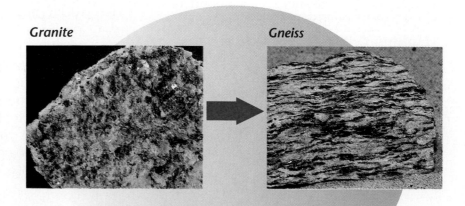

Granite   *Gneiss*

Classifying Metamorphic Rocks

While metamorphic rocks are forming, high temperatures change the size and shape of the grains, or mineral crystals, in the rock. In addition, tremendous pressure squeezes rock so tightly that the mineral grains may line up in flat, parallel layers. **Geologists classify metamorphic rocks by the arrangement of the grains that make up the rocks.**

Metamorphic rocks that have their grains arranged in parallel layers or bands are said to be **foliated.** The term *foliated* comes from the Latin word for "leaf." It describes the thin, flat layering found in most metamorphic rocks. Foliated rocks—including slate, schist, and gneiss—may split apart along these bands. In Figure 18, notice how the crystals in granite have been flattened to create the foliated texture of gneiss.

One common foliated rock is slate. Heat and pressure change the sedimentary rock shale into slate. Slate is basically a denser, more compact version of shale. During the change, new minerals such as mica and hornblende form in the slate.

Sometimes metamorphic rocks are nonfoliated. The mineral grains in these rocks are arranged randomly. Metamorphic rocks that are nonfoliated do not split into layers. Marble and quartzite both have a nonfoliated texture. Quartzite forms out of sandstone. The weakly cemented quartz particles in the sandstone recrystallize to form quartzite, which is extremely hard. Notice in Figure 18 how much smoother quartzite looks than sandstone.

☑ *Checkpoint* What is a foliated rock?

A Sequined Rock

1. Make three balls of clay about 3 cm in diameter. Gently mix about 25 sequins into one ball.
2. Use a 30-cm piece of string to cut the ball in half. How are the sequins arranged?
3. Roll the clay with the sequins back into a ball. Stack the three balls with the sequin ball in the middle. Set these on a block of wood. With another block of wood, press slowly down until the stack is about 3 cm high.
4. Use the string to cut the stack in half. Observe the arrangement of the sequins.

Making a Model What do the sequins in your model rock represent? Is this rock foliated or nonfoliated?

Shale

Slate

Sandstone

Quartzite

Figure 19 The pure white marble for the Taj Mahal came from a quarry 300 kilometers away. It took 20,000 workers more than 20 years to build the Taj Mahal.

Visual Arts
CONNECTION

The architect of the Taj Mahal used symmetry and repetition to design a beautiful building. Notice how the left side mirrors the right side, creating balance. Also notice how different parts of the building, such as domes, arches, and minarets (towers), are repeated. Repetition of these shapes creates rhythms as you look at the building.

In Your Journal

Write a letter to a friend describing what you feel walking toward the Taj Mahal. Explain how the building's symmetry and other features help to create this effect.

Uses of Metamorphic Rock

Marble and slate are two of the most useful metamorphic rocks. Marble usually forms when limestone is subjected to heat and pressure deep beneath the surface. Because marble has a fine, even grain, it is relatively easy to cut into thin slabs. And marble can be easily polished. These qualities have led architects and sculptors to use marble for many buildings and statues. For example, one of the most beautiful buildings in the world is the Taj Mahal in Agra, India. An emperor of India had the Taj Mahal built during the 1600s as a memorial to his wife, who had died in childbirth. The Taj Mahal, shown in Figure 19, is made of gleaming white marble.

Slate, because it is foliated, splits easily into flat pieces that can be used for flooring, roofing, outdoor walkways, or chalkboards. Like marble, slate comes in a variety of colors, including gray, black, red, and purple, so it has been used as trim for stone buildings.

Section 5 Review

1. Describe the process by which metamorphic rocks form.
2. What characteristics are used to classify metamorphic rocks? *Geologists classify*
3. Which properties of a rock may change as the rock becomes metamorphic?
4. How does pressure change rock?
5. **Thinking Critically Relating Cause and Effect** Why are you less likely to find fossils in metamorphic rocks than in sedimentary rocks?

Science at Home

How are rocks used in your neighborhood? Take a walk with your family to see how many uses you can observe. Identify statues, walls, and buildings made from rocks. Can you identify which type of rock is used? Look for limestone, sandstone, granite, and marble. Share a list of the rocks you found with your class. For each rock, include a description of its color and texture, where you observed the rock, and how it was used.

MYSTERY ROCKS

Problem

What properties can be used to classify rocks?

Materials

1 "mystery rock"   hand lens
2 unknown igneous rocks
2 unknown sedimentary rocks
2 unknown metamorphic rocks

Procedure

1. For this activity, you will be given six rocks and one sample that is not a rock. They are labeled A through G.
2. Copy the data table into your notebook.
3. Using the hand lens, examine each rock for clues that show the rock formed from molten material. Record the rock's color and texture. Observe if there are any crystals or grains in the rock.
4. Use the hand lens to look for clues that show the rock formed from particles of other rocks. Observe the texture of the rock to see if it has any tiny, well-rounded grains.
5. Use the hand lens to look for clues that show the rock formed under heat and pressure. Observe if the rock has a flat layer of crystals or shows colored bands.
6. Record your observations in the data table.

Analyze and Conclude

1. Infer from your observations which group each rock belongs in.
2. Decide which sample is not a rock. How did you determine that the sample you chose is not a rock? What do you think the "mystery rock" is? Explain.
3. Which of the samples could be classified as igneous rocks? What physical properties do these rock share with the other samples? How are they different?
4. Which of the samples could be classified as sedimentary rocks? How do you think these rocks formed? What are the physical properties of these rocks?
5. Which of the samples could be classified as metamorphic rocks? What are their physical properties?
6. **Think About It** What physical property was most useful in classifying rocks? Why?

More to Explore

Can you name each rock? Use a field guide to rocks and minerals to find the specific name of each rock sample.

Sample	Color (dark, medium, light, or mixed colors)	Texture (fine, medium, or coarse-grained)	Foliated or Banded	Rock Group (igneous, metamorphic, sedimentary)
A				
B				

SECTION 6 The Rock Cycle

DISCOVER •••••••••••••••••••••••••••••••••••••• ACTIVITY ••••

Which Rock Came First?

1. Referring to the photos below, make sketches of quartzite, granite, and sandstone on three index cards.

2. In your sketches, try to portray the color and texture of each rock. Look for similarities and differences.

3. To which major group does each rock belong?

Think It Over

Developing Hypotheses How are quartzite, granite, and sandstone related? Arrange your cards in the order in which these three rocks formed. Given enough time in Earth's crust, what might happen to the third rock in your series?

Quartzite

Granite

Sandstone

GUIDE FOR READING

◆ What is the rock cycle?

◆ What is the role of plate tectonics in the rock cycle?

Reading Tip Before you read, preview *Exploring the Rock Cycle* on page 168. Write a list of questions you have about the rock cycle. Then look for answers to the questions as you read.

The enormous granite dome that forms Stone Mountain in Georgia looks as if it will be there forever. The granite formed hundreds of millions of years ago as a batholith— a mass of igneous rock beneath Earth's surface. But this rock has stood exposed to the weather for millions of years. Bit by bit, the granite is flaking off. Washed away in streams, the bits of granite will eventually be ground down into sand. But that's not the end of the story. What will become of those sand particles from Stone Mountain? They are part of a series of changes that happen to all the rocks of Earth's crust.

A Cycle of Many Pathways

Earth's rocks are not as unchanging as they seem. **Forces inside Earth and at the surface produce a rock cycle that builds, destroys, and changes the rocks in the crust.** The **rock cycle** is a series of processes on Earth's surface and inside the planet that slowly change rocks from one kind to another. What drives the rock cycle? Earth's constructive and destructive forces—including plate tectonics—move rocks through the rock cycle.

The rock cycle can follow many different pathways. You can follow the rock of Stone Mountain along one of the pathways of the rock cycle.

Figure 20 Stone Mountain, near Atlanta, Georgia, rises 210 meters above the surrounding land.

One Pathway Through the Rock Cycle

In the case of Stone Mountain, the rock cycle began millions of years ago. First, a granite batholith formed beneath Earth's surface. Then the forces of mountain building slowly pushed the granite upward. Over millions of years, water and weather began to wear away the granite of Stone Mountain. Today, particles of granite still break off the mountain and become sand. Streams carry the sand to the ocean.

Over millions of years, layers of sediment will pile up on the ocean floor. Slowly, the sediments will be compacted by their own weight. Dissolved calcite in the ocean water will cement the particles together. Eventually, the quartz that once formed the granite of Stone Mountain will become sandstone, a sedimentary rock.

More and more sediment will pile up on the sandstone. As sandstone becomes deeply buried, pressure on the rocks will increase. The rock will become hot. Pressure will compact the particles in the sandstone until no spaces are left between them. Silica, the main ingredient in quartz, will replace the calcite as the cement holding the rock together. The rock's texture will change from gritty to smooth. After millions of years, the sandstone will have changed into the metamorphic rock quartzite.

What will happen next? You could wait tens of millions of years to find out how the quartzite completes the rock cycle. Or you can trace alternative pathways in *Exploring the Rock Cycle.*

Sharpen your Skills

Classifying

ACTIVITY

Some metamorphic rocks form out of igneous rocks, and other metamorphic rocks form out of sedimentary rocks.

1. If you find a fine-grained metamorphic rock with thin, flaky layers, from which group of rocks did it probably form? Explain.

2. If you find a metamorphic rock with distinct grains of different colors and sizes arranged in parallel bands, from which group of rocks did it probably form? Explain.

EXPLORING *the Rock Cycle*

Earth's constructive and destructive forces build up and wear down the crust. Igneous, sedimentary, and metamorphic rocks change continuously through the rock cycle. Rocks can follow many different pathways. The outer circle shows a complete cycle. The arrows within the circle show alternate pathways.

Igneous Rock

Sedimentary Rock

Erosion

Melting

Heat and pressure

Volcanic activity

Melting

Erosion

Heat and pressure

Magma

Metamorphic Rock

Melting

The Rock Cycle and Plate Tectonics

The changes of the rock cycle are closely related to plate tectonics. Recall that plate tectonics causes the movement of sections of Earth's lithosphere called plates. **Plate movements drive the rock cycle by pushing rocks back into the mantle, where they melt and become magma again. Plate movements also cause the folding, faulting, and uplift of the crust that move rocks through the rock cycle.** At least two types of plate movement advance the rock cycle. One type is a collision between subducting oceanic plates. The other type is a collision between continental plates.

Figure 21 This fossil trilobite lived on an ocean floor about 500 million years ago. As plate tectonics moved pieces of Earth's crust, the rock containing this fossil became part of a mountain.

Subducting Oceanic Plates Consider what could happen to the sand grains that once were part of Stone Mountain. The sand may become sandstone attached to oceanic crust. On this pathway through the rock cycle, the oceanic crust carrying the sandstone drifts toward a deep-ocean trench. At the trench, subduction returns some of the sandstone to the mantle. There, it melts and forms magma, which eventually becomes igneous rock.

Colliding Continental Plates Collisions between continental plates can also change a rock's path through the rock cycle. Such a collision can squeeze some sandstone from the ocean floor. As a result, the sandstone will change to quartzite. Eventually, the collision could form a mountain range or plateau. Then, as the mountains or plateaus containing quartzite are worn away, the rock cycle continues.

Section 6 Review

1. What process gradually changes rocks from one form to another?
2. How can plate movements move rocks through the rock cycle?
3. What rock comes before quartzite in the rock cycle? What rock or rocks could come just after quartzite in the rock cycle? Explain your answer.
4. **Thinking Critically Applying Concepts** Begin with a grain of sand on a beach. Describe what happens as you follow the grain through the rock cycle until it returns to a beach as a grain of sand again.
5. **Thinking Critically Making Judgments** In your opinion, at what point does the rock cycle really begin? Give reasons for your answer.

Check Your Progress

CHAPTER PROJECT 5

Now that you have collected, described, tested, and recorded your rocks, classify them as igneous, sedimentary, or metamorphic. Are any of your rocks foliated? Try to identify specific types of rock. Compare your rock samples with pictures of rocks in a field guide or other library reference sources.

TESTING ROCK FLOORING

You are building your own house. For the kitchen floor, you want to use some building stones such as granite, marble, or limestone. You need to know which material is easiest to maintain and keep clean.

Problem

What kind of building stone makes the best flooring?

Skills Focus

designing experiments, forming operational definitions drawing conclusions

Suggested Materials

steel nail   wire brush   water
plastic dropper   hand lens
samples of igneous, sedimentary, and metamorphic rocks with flat surfaces
materials that form stains, such as ink and paints
greasy materials such as butter and crayons

Procedure

1. Brainstorm with your partner the qualities of good flooring. For example, good flooring should resist stains, scratches, and grease marks, and be safe to walk on when wet.
2. Predict what you think is the best building stone for a kitchen floor. Why?
3. Write the steps you plan to follow to answer the problem question. As you design your plan, consider the following factors:
   - What igneous, sedimentary, and metamorphic rocks will you test? (Pick at least one rock from each group.)
   - What materials or equipment will you need to acquire, and in what amounts?
   - What tests will you perform on the samples?
   - How will you control the variables in each test?
   - How will you measure each sample's resistance to staining, grease, and scratches?
   - How will you measure slipperiness?
4. Review your plan. Will it lead to an answer to the problem question?
5. Check your procedure and safety plan with your teacher.
6. Create a data table that includes a column in which you predict how each material will perform in each test.

Analyze and Conclude

1. Which material performed the best on each test? Which performed the worst on each test?
2. Which material is best for the kitchen flooring? Which material would you least want to use?
3. Do your answers support your initial prediction? Why or why not?
4. The person installing the floor might want stone that is easy to cut to the correct size or shape. What other qualities would matter to the flooring installer?
5. **Apply** Based on your results for flooring, what materials would you use for kitchen counters? How might the qualities needed for countertops differ from those for flooring?

More to Explore

Find out the cost per square meter of some materials used to build kitchen floors in your community. How does cost influence your decision on which material to use? What other factors can influence the choice of materials?

Classifying Rocks

Key Ideas
- A rock is a hard piece of Earth's crust.
- Geologists classify rocks according to their color, texture, mineral composition, and origin.
- The three kinds of rocks are igneous, sedimentary, and metamorphic.

Key Terms
texture   igneous rock   metamorphic rock
grain   sedimentary rock

 ### Igneous Rocks

Key Ideas
- Igneous rocks form from magma or lava.
- Igneous rocks are classified according to their origin, texture, and composition.

Key Terms
extrusive rock   intrusive rock   porphyritic texture

 ### Sedimentary Rocks

Key Ideas
- Most sedimentary rocks form from sediments that are compacted and cemented together.
- The three types of sedimentary rocks are clastic rocks, organic rocks, and chemical rocks.

Key Terms
sediment   compaction   organic rock
erosion   cementation   chemical rock
deposition   clastic rock

 ### Rocks From Reefs

INTEGRATING *LIFE SCIENCE*

Key Ideas
- When corals die, their skeletons remain. More corals grow on top of them, slowly forming a reef.

Key Terms
coral reef   atoll

 ### Metamorphic Rocks

Key Ideas
- In a process that takes place deep beneath the surface, heat and pressure can change any type of rock into metamorphic rock.
- Geologists classify metamorphic rock according to whether the rock is foliated or nonfoliated.

Key Term
foliated

 ### The Rock Cycle

Key Ideas
- The series of processes on and beneath Earth's surface that change rocks from one type of rock to another is called the rock cycle.

Key Term
rock cycle

Organizing Information

Cycle Diagram Construct a cycle diagram that shows one pathway through the rock cycle. Include the following steps in your diagram in the correct order: sediments build up; igneous rock wears away; sedimentary rock forms; igneous rock forms from magma and lava; lava erupts. (For tips on making cycle diagrams, see the Skills Handbook.)

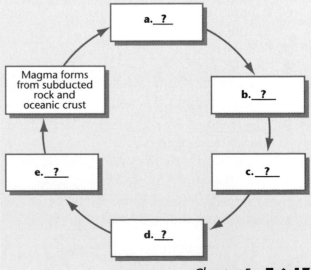

a. ?

b. ?

c. ?

d. ?

e. ?

Magma forms from subducted rock and oceanic crust

Reviewing Content

 For more review of key concepts, see the Interactive Student Tutorial CD-ROM.

Multiple Choice

Choose the letter of the best answer.

1. Which of the following sedimentary rocks is a chemical rock?
   a. shale
   b. sandstone
   c. rock salt
   d. breccia
2. Metamorphic rocks can be formed from
   a. igneous rocks.
   b. sedimentary rocks.
   c. metamorphic rocks.
   d. all rock groups.
3. The rock formed when granite changes to a metamorphic rock is
   a. marble.   b. basalt.
   c. gneiss.   d. pumice.
4. Which of the following helps create both metamorphic and sedimentary rocks?
   a. cementation   b. pressure
   c. evaporation   d. heat
5. Millions of years ago, a deposit of organic limestone was probably
   a. a swampy forest.   b. a lava flow.
   c. a coral reef.   d. an intrusive rock.

True or False

If the statement is true, write true. If it is false, change the underlined word or words to make the statement true.

6. Igneous rocks are classified by their origin, texture, and <u>shape</u>.
7. Granite is a <u>fine-grained</u> igneous rock.
8. Sedimentary rocks that form when minerals come out of solution are classified as <u>porphyritic</u>.
9. A <u>barrier reef</u> is a ring-shaped coral island found in the open ocean.
10. The series of processes that slowly change rocks from one kind to another is called the <u>rock cycle</u>.

Checking Concepts

11. What is the relationship between an igneous rock's texture and where it was formed?
12. Why can water pass easily through sandstone but not through shale?
13. Describe how a rock can form by evaporation. What type of rock is it?
14. How do the properties of a rock change when the rock changes to metamorphic?
15. What are the sources of the heat that helps metamorphic rocks to form?
16. **Writing to Learn** You are a camp counselor taking your campers on a mountain hike. One of your campers cracks open a rock and finds a fossil fish inside. The camper wants to know how a fish fossil from the sea floor ended up on the side of a mountain. What explanation would you give the camper?

Thinking Critically

17. **Applying Concepts** The sedimentary rocks limestone and sandstone are used as building materials. However, they wear away more rapidly than marble and quartzite, the metamorphic rocks that are formed from them. Why do you think this is so?
18. **Inferring** As a geologist exploring for rock and mineral deposits, you come across an area where the rocks are layers of coal and shale. What kind of environment probably existed in this area millions of years ago when these rocks formed?
19. **Comparing and Contrasting** How are clastic rocks and organic rocks similar? How are they different?
20. **Relating Cause and Effect** In the rock cycle, igneous, metamorphic, and sedimentary rocks can all become magma again. What step in the rock cycle causes this to happen? Explain your answer.

Applying Skills

Answer Questions 21–23 using the photos of three rocks.

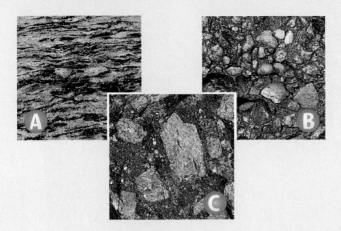

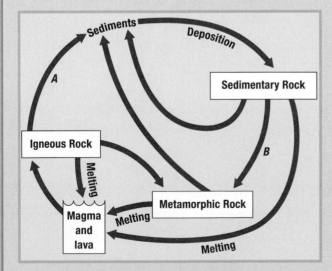

21. **Observing** How would you describe the texture of each rock?
22. **Classifying** Which of the three rocks would you classify as a metamorphic rock? Explain your answer.

23. **Inferring** A rock's texture gives clues about how the rock formed. What can you infer about the process by which rock B formed?

Performance CHAPTER PROJECT 5 Assessment

Project Wrap Up Construct a simple display for your rocks. Your display should clearly give your classification for each of your rock samples. In your presentation, describe where you went hunting for rocks and what kinds of rocks you found. Describe which of your discoveries surprised you the most.

Reflect and Record In your journal, write about how you developed your rock collection. Were there any rocks that were hard to classify? Did you find rocks from each of the three major groups? Can you think of any reason why certain types of rocks would not be found in your area?

Test Preparation
Use these questions to prepare for standardized tests.

Use the diagram to answer Questions 24–28.

Sediments
Deposition
A
Sedimentary Rock
Igneous Rock
B
Melting
Metamorphic Rock
Magma and lava
Melting
Melting

24. A good title for this diagram is
   a. Different Kinds of Rock
   b. Deposition of Sediment
   c. How Metamorphic Rock Forms
   d. Pathways of the Rock Cycle

25. The process shown by letter A is called
   a. extrusion.   b. crystallization.
   c. erosion.   d. intrusion.

26. The process shown by letter B involves
   a. cementation only.
   b. heat and pressure.
   c. erosion and deposition.
   d. compaction only.

27. According to the diagram, metamorphic rock forms from
   a. igneous rock and sedimentary rock.
   b. sedimentary rock only.
   c. magma and lava.
   d. melting rock.

28. According to the diagram, magma and lava may form through the melting of
   a. any type of rock.
   b. metamorphic rock only.
   c. sediments.
   d. igneous rock only.

The Noble Metal

You can find it . . .

- on people's wrists and on their ears
- in your computer ◆ around the edge of some dinner plates ◆ in outer space—on satellites and in spacesuits ◆

What is this mysterious substance? It's the rare, beautiful—and very useful— metal called Gold

Because it is both rare and beautiful, people have prized gold since ancient times. Gold was so valuable that it was used to make crowns for rulers and coins for trade. In some cultures, people wore gold bracelets and necklaces to show their wealth.

In spite of its many uses, gold is scarce. For every 23,000 metric tons of rock and minerals from the Earth's crust, you could produce only about 14 grams of gold, enough to make a small ring. Today, gold is found in many parts of the world. But even rich gold fields produce only small amounts of gold. In fact, if all the gold mined over the years were gathered and melted down, you would have a cube only about 15 meters on a side—about the size of a four-story square building.

This gold burial mask was crafted around 1550 B.C. by the Mycenaeans, people who lived in the eastern Mediterranean.

Properties of Gold

Why is gold used for everything from bracelets to space helmets to medicine? You'll find the answers in this precious metal's unusual chemical and physical properties. Gold is deep yellow in color and so shiny, or lustrous, that its Latin name, *aurum*, means "glowing dawn." Gold's chemical symbol—*Au*—comes from that Latin word.

Gold is very stable. Unlike iron, gold doesn't rust. It also doesn't tarnish in air as silver does, so its luster can last forever. Ancient chemists thought that gold was superior to other metals. They classified it as one of the "noble" metals.

Gold is very soft and malleable. That is, it's easy to bend or hammer into shapes without breaking. It can be pounded into very thin sheets called gold leaf. In fact, you can pound 30 grams of gold into a sheet that's large enough to cover the floor of a small room. Gold is also the most ductile metal. You can draw out 30 grams of gold into a fine thread as long as 8 kilometers without breaking it.

Ancient people of Egypt, Greece, and China found ways to dig gold from mines. But most of the gold that people have used in the last 6,000 years has come from Earth's surface, often from streams and riverbanks. Gold is very heavy—one of the densest metals. Over centuries, mountain streams have washed away dirt and pebbles from veins of gold-bearing rocks and minerals and left the heavy gold in the streambeds.

Gold reflects heat and, when combined with other materials, filters sunlight. For this reason, gold is used in spacesuits and face visors. This astronaut wears a face visor coated with gold. The window glass in some skyscrapers is tinted with gold to keep out heat and protect people's eyes.

Science Activity

Many of the gold hunters who flocked to California during the Gold Rush of 1849 were searching for gold in streams and rivers. Although they had very simple equipment, their technique worked because gold is so dense. Using pans, miners washed gold-bearing gravel in running water. Try your own gold panning.

Procedure:
Set up your own model of gold panning, using a large pan, a gravel mixture, and a very dense material as a substitute for gold. Use a sink trap. Under running water, shake and swirl the pan until the lighter materials wash away. What's left is your "gold."

◆ Why is "gold" left in the pan while other materials are washed away?

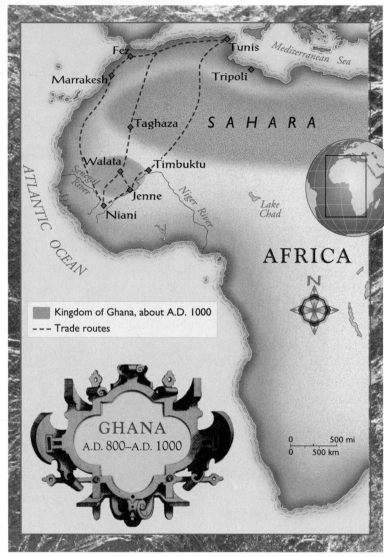

Kingdom of Ghana, about A.D. 1000
- - - Trade routes

GHANA
A.D. 800–A.D. 1000

0   500 mi
0   500 km

Social Studies Activity

How would you succeed as a gold or salt trader? Find out by carrying out your own silent trade. Work in teams of Salt Traders and Gold Miners. Before trading, each team should decide how much a bag of gold or a block of salt is worth. Then, for each silent trade, make up a situation that would change the value of gold or salt, such as, "Demand for gold in Europe increases."

◆ Suppose you are selling a product today. How would the supply of the product affect the value or sale price of the product?

Golden Trade Routes

In West Africa nearly 1,000 years ago, salt was said to be worth its weight in gold. If you get your salt from the supermarket shelf, it may be hard to imagine how valuable this mineral was to people. But if you lived in a very hot, dry climate, you would need salt. It would be as valuable to you as gold. In West Africa, salt and gold were the most important goods traded in a busy north-south trade.

Camel caravans crossed the desert going south, carrying slabs of salt from mines in the desert. Trade centers, such as Jenne and Timbuktu, flourished. In the area around Taghaza, people built houses with walls of salt slabs. But several hundred kilometers south in the Kingdom of Ghana, salt was scarce and gold was plentiful. Salt traders from the north traveled deep into the forests of Ghana to trade salt for gold.

African gold became the basis for several rich cultures and trading empires that grew up in West Africa between 800 and 1400. At that time, most of the gold that Europeans used for crowns, coins, and jewelry was carried north from Africa.

Around 1100, Arab travelers in Africa wrote about the fabulous wealth of the Kingdom of Ghana. The most popular tale was that the salt traders and gold miners never met, as a way of keeping secret the location of gold mines. Traders from the north left slabs of salt in an agreed-upon trading place, pounded their drums to indicate a trade, and then withdrew. Miners from the south arrived, left an amount of gold that seemed fair, and withdrew. The salt traders returned. If they thought the trade was fair, they took the gold and left. If they were not satisfied, the silent trade continued.

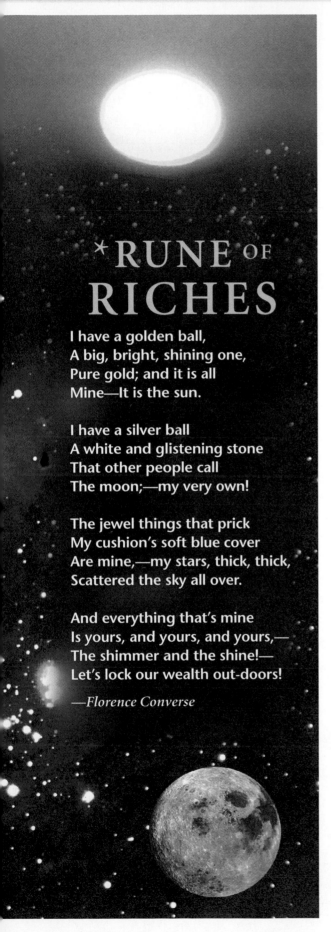

*RUNE OF RICHES

I have a golden ball,
A big, bright, shining one,
Pure gold; and it is all
Mine—It is the sun.

I have a silver ball
A white and glistening stone
That other people call
The moon;—my very own!

The jewel things that prick
My cushion's soft blue cover
Are mine,—my stars, thick, thick,
Scattered the sky all over.

And everything that's mine
Is yours, and yours, and yours,—
The shimmer and the shine!—
Let's lock our wealth out-doors!

—*Florence Converse*

Go for the gold

What do these sayings have in common?

◆ It's worth its weight in gold.

◆ Speech is silver, silence is golden.

◆ All that glitters is not gold.

◆ Go for the gold!

All of these sayings use gold as a symbol of perfection and value. Because gold has always been beautiful and scarce, it has for centuries been a symbol of excellence and richness—things that people want and search for. When writers use *gold* or *golden*, they are referring to something desirable, of value or worth. These words may also represent the beauty of gold.

In literature, writers and poets often use *gold* to make a comparison in a simile or metaphor. Similes and metaphors are figures of speech.

◆ A simile makes a comparison between two things, using *like* or *as* in the comparison. Here's an example: "An honest person's promise is as good as gold."

◆ A metaphor is a comparison without the use of like or as, such as, "When you're in trouble, true friends are golden."

Look for similes and metaphors in the poem by Florence Converse.

◆ What similes or metaphors has Converse made?

◆ What would this poem be like without the comparisons?

*A rune is a song or poem.

Language Arts Activity

What does gold symbolize for you? Think of some comparisons of your own in which you use gold in a simile or metaphor. After jotting down all of your ideas, choose one (or more) and decide what comparison you will make. Write a short saying, a proverb, or a short poem that includes your own simile or metaphor.

◆ How does your comparison make your saying or poem more interesting?

Mathematics

Measuring Gold

People often say that something is "worth its weight in gold." But how do you measure the weight of gold? Most gold that's mined today is used to make jewelry. But modern-day jewelry is seldom made of pure gold. Because gold is so soft, it is usually mixed with another metal to form an alloy—a mixture of two or more metals.

Most commonly the other metal in a gold alloy is copper, although alloys of gold can also contain silver, zinc, or other metals. A gold alloy keeps most of the properties of gold but is harder and resists denting and scratching. The other metals affect the color. More copper produces "red gold," while "white gold" may contain gold and copper along with nickel, palladium, or silver.

Suppose you are shopping for a gold ring. You see two rings that look the same and are exactly the same size. How do you decide which one to buy? If you look carefully at the gold jewelry, you'll probably see small letters that read "18 K," "20 K," "14 K," or "12 K." The "K" here stands for karat. That's the measure of how pure an alloy of gold is. Pure gold—used very rarely—is 24 karat. Gold that is 50 percent pure is $\frac{12}{24}$ gold, or 12 karat. The greater the amount of gold in a piece of jewelry, the higher the value.

Look at the display of rings above. The 18-karat ring has copper in it. What percent of the 18 K gold ring is gold? What percent is copper?

Analyze. You know that pure gold is $\frac{24}{24}$ gold. In order to find out what percent of an 18 K ring is gold, you need to write a proportion.

Write the proportion.

$$\frac{\text{number of gold parts}}{\text{number of parts in the whole}} \rightarrow \frac{18}{24}$$

Simplify and solve.

$$\frac{18}{24} = \frac{3}{4} = 75\%$$

Think about it. If 75% of the ring is gold, then 25% of the ring must be copper.

Math Activity

Look at the other gold rings to determine what percent of each is gold.

◆ What percent of the 14 K gold ring is gold? What percent is another metal? Round decimals to the nearest hundredth.

◆ What percent of the 12 K ring is gold? What percent of the 20 K ring is gold?

◆ Which ring would you like to own—the 12 K or the 20 K? Why?

◆ Which ring in the display would probably be the most expensive?

Gold Producers

1. South Africa
2. United States
3. Australia
4. Canada
5. Russia
6. China

A Treasure Hunt

Work in small groups to make a World Treasure Map of one of the countries where gold is mined today. Use the information above to get you started. Then use the library to learn about these gold-producing countries.

On a large map of the world, use push pins to mark the location of the gold sites. In the United States and Canada, mark the states and provinces that are the largest producers. Make up fact sheets with information that will answer questions such as the following:

◆ Where are gold sites located in each country?

◆ When was gold first discovered there?

◆ Did a gold rush influence the history of that area?

If possible, collect photographs to illustrate gold products in each country. Post your pictures and fact sheets at the side of the World Treasure Map.

Think Like a Scientist

*A*lthough you may not know it, you think like a scientist every day. Whenever you ask a question and explore possible answers, you use many of the same skills that scientists do. Some of these skills are described on this page.

Observing

When you use one or more of your five senses to gather information about the world, you are **observing.** Hearing a dog bark, counting twelve green seeds, and smelling smoke are all observations. To increase the power of their senses, scientists sometimes use microscopes, telescopes, or other instruments that help them make more detailed observations.

An observation must be an accurate report of what your senses detect. It is important to keep careful records of your observations in science class by writing or drawing in a notebook. The information collected through observations is called evidence, or data.

Inferring

When you interpret an observation, you are **inferring,** or making an inference. For example, if you hear your dog barking, you may infer that someone is at your front door. To make this inference, you combine the evidence—the barking dog—and your experience or knowledge—you know that your dog barks when strangers approach—to reach a logical conclusion.

Notice that an inference is not a fact; it is only one of many possible interpretations for an observation. For example, your dog may be barking because it wants to go for a walk. An inference may turn out to be incorrect even if it is based on accurate observations and logical reasoning. The only way to find out if an inference is correct is to investigate further.

Predicting

When you listen to the weather forecast, you hear many predictions about the next day's weather—what the temperature will be, whether it will rain, and how windy it will be. Weather forecasters use observations and knowledge of weather patterns to predict the weather. The skill of **predicting** involves making an inference about a future event based on current evidence or past experience.

Because a prediction is an inference, it may prove to be false. In science class, you can test some of your predictions by doing experiments. For example, suppose you predict that larger paper airplanes can fly farther than smaller airplanes. How could you test your prediction?

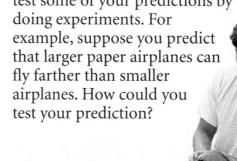

ACTIVITY Use the photograph to answer the questions below.

Observing Look closely at the photograph. List at least three observations.

Inferring Use your observations to make an inference about what has happened. What experience or knowledge did you use to make the inference?

Predicting Predict what will happen next. On what evidence or experience do you base your prediction?

Classifying

Could you imagine searching for a book in the library if the books were shelved in no particular order? Your trip to the library would be an all-day event! Luckily, librarians group together books on similar topics or by the same author. Grouping together items that are alike in some way is called **classifying.** You can classify items in many ways: by size, by shape, by use, and by other important characteristics.

Like librarians, scientists use the skill of classifying to organize information and objects. When things are sorted into groups, the relationships among them become easier to understand.

ACTIVITY

Classify the objects in the photograph into two groups based on any characteristic you choose. Then use another characteristic to classify the objects into three groups.

Making Models

Have you ever drawn a picture to help someone understand what you were saying? Such a drawing is one type of model. A model is a picture, diagram, computer image, or other representation of a complex object or process. **Making models** helps people understand things that they cannot observe directly.

Scientists often use models to represent things that are either very large or very small, such as the planets in the solar system, or the parts of a cell. Such models are physical models—drawings or three-dimensional structures that look like the real thing. Other models are mental models—mathematical equations or words that describe how something works.

ACTIVITY

This student is using a model to demonstrate what causes day and night on Earth. What do the flashlight and the tennis ball in the model represent?

Communicating

Whenever you talk on the phone, write a letter, or listen to your teacher at school, you are communicating. **Communicating** is the process of sharing ideas and information with other people. Communicating effectively requires many skills, including writing, reading, speaking, listening, and making models.

Scientists communicate to share results, information, and opinions. Scientists often communicate about their work in journals, over the telephone, in

letters, and on the Internet. They also attend scientific meetings where they share their ideas with one another in person.

ACTIVITY

On a sheet of paper, write out clear, detailed directions for tying your shoe. Then exchange directions with a partner. Follow your partner's directions exactly. How successful were you at tying your shoe? How could your partner have communicated more clearly?

Making Measurements

When scientists make observations, it is not sufficient to say that something is "big" or "heavy." Instead, scientists use instruments to measure just how big or heavy an object is. By measuring, scientists can express their observations more precisely and communicate more information about what they observe.

Measuring in SI

The standard system of measurement used by scientists around the world is known as the International System of Units, which is abbreviated as SI (in French, *Système International d'Unités*). SI units are easy to use because they are based on multiples of 10. Each unit is ten times larger than the next smallest unit and one tenth the size of the next largest unit. The table lists the prefixes used to name the most common SI units.

Common SI Prefixes		
Prefix	**Symbol**	**Meaning**
kilo-	k	1,000
hecto-	h	100
deka-	da	10
deci-	d	0.1 (one tenth)
centi-	c	0.01 (one hundredth)
milli-	m	0.001 (one thousandth)

Length To measure length, or the distance between two points, the unit of measure is the **meter (m).** The distance from the floor to a doorknob is approximately one meter. Long distances, such as the distance between two cities, are measured in kilometers (km). Small lengths are measured in centimeters (cm) or millimeters (mm). Scientists use metric rulers and meter sticks to measure length.

Common Conversions
1 km = 1,000 m
1 m = 100 cm
1 m = 1,000 mm
1 cm = 10 mm

Liquid Volume To measure the volume of a liquid, or the amount of space it takes up, you will use a unit of measure known as the **liter (L).** One liter is the approximate volume of a medium-size carton of milk. Smaller volumes are measured in milliliters (mL). Scientists use graduated cylinders to measure liquid volume.

Common Conversion
1 L = 1,000 mL

ACTIVITY

The larger lines on the metric ruler in the picture show centimeter divisions, while the smaller, unnumbered lines show millimeter divisions. How many centimeters long is the shell? How many millimeters long is it?

ACTIVITY

The graduated cylinder in the picture is marked in milliliter divisions. Notice that the water in the cylinder has a curved surface. This curved surface is called the *meniscus.* To measure the volume, you must read the level at the lowest point of the meniscus. What is the volume of water in this graduated cylinder?

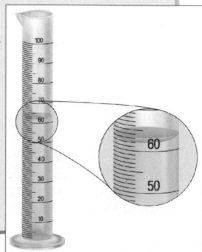

Mass To measure mass, or the amount of matter in an object, you will use a unit of measure known as the **gram (g)**. One gram is approximately the mass of a paper clip. Larger masses are measured in kilograms (kg). Scientists use a balance to find the mass of an object.

Common Conversion

1 kg = 1,000 g

The mass of the apple in the picture is measured in kilograms. What is the mass of the apple? Suppose a recipe for applesauce called for one kilogram of apples. About how many apples would you need?

Temperature
To measure the temperature of a substance, you will use the **Celsius scale**. Temperature is measured in degrees Celsius (°C) using a Celsius thermometer. Water freezes at 0°C and boils at 100°C.

ACTIVITY

What is the temperature of the liquid in degrees Celsius?

Converting SI Units

To use the SI system, you must know how to convert between units. Converting from one unit to another involves the skill of **calculating**, or using mathematical operations. Converting between SI units is similar to converting between dollars and dimes because both systems are based on multiples of ten.

Suppose you want to convert a length of 80 centimeters to meters. Follow these steps to convert between units.

1. Begin by writing down the measurement you want to convert—in this example, 80 centimeters.
2. Write a conversion factor that represents the relationship between the two units you are converting. In this example, the relationship is *1 meter = 100 centimeters*. Write this conversion factor as a fraction, making sure to place the units you are converting from (centimeters, in this example) in the denominator.

3. Multiply the measurement you want to convert by the fraction. When you do this, the units in the first measurement will cancel out with the units in the denominator. Your answer will be in the units you are converting to (meters, in this example).

Example

80 centimeters = ___?___ meters

$$80 \text{ centimeters} \times \frac{1 \text{ meter}}{100 \text{ centimeters}} = \frac{80 \text{ meters}}{100}$$

$$= 0.8 \text{ meters}$$

Convert between the following units.

ACTIVITY

1. 600 millimeters = _?_ meters
2. 0.35 liters = _?_ milliliters
3. 1,050 grams = _?_ kilograms

Conducting a Scientific Investigation

In some ways, scientists are like detectives, piecing together clues to learn about a process or event. One way that scientists gather clues is by carrying out experiments. An experiment tests an idea in a careful, orderly manner. Although experiments do not all follow the same steps in the same order, many follow a pattern similar to the one described here.

Posing Questions

Experiments begin by asking a scientific question. A scientific question is one that can be answered by gathering evidence. For example, the question "Which freezes faster—fresh water or salt water?" is a scientific question because you can carry out an investigation and gather information to answer the question.

Developing a Hypothesis

The next step is to form a hypothesis. A **hypothesis** is a possible explanation for a set of observations or answer to a scientific question. In science, a hypothesis must be something that can be tested. A hypothesis can be worded as an *If . . . then . . .* statement. For example, a hypothesis might be "*If I add salt to fresh water, then the water will take longer to freeze.*" A hypothesis worded this way serves as a rough outline of the experiment you should perform.

Designing an Experiment

Next you need to plan a way to test your hypothesis. Your plan should be written out as a step-by-step procedure and should describe the observations or measurements you will make.

Two important steps involved in designing an experiment are controlling variables and forming operational definitions.

Controlling Variables In a well-designed experiment, you need to keep all variables the same except for one. A **variable** is any factor that can change in an experiment. The factor that you change is called the **manipulated variable.** In this experiment, the manipulated variable is the amount of salt added to the water. Other factors, such as the amount of water or the starting temperature, are kept constant.

The factor that changes as a result of the manipulated variable is called the responding variable. The **responding variable** is what you measure or observe to obtain your results. In this experiment, the responding variable is how long the water takes to freeze.

An experiment in which all factors except one are kept constant is a **controlled experiment.** Most controlled experiments include a test called the control. In this experiment, Container 3 is the control. Because no salt is added to Container 3, you can compare the results from the other containers to it. Any difference in results must be due to the addition of salt alone.

Forming Operational Definitions

Another important aspect of a well-designed experiment is having clear operational definitions. An **operational definition** is a statement that describes how a particular variable is to be measured or how a term is to be defined. For example, in this experiment, how will you determine if the water has frozen? You might decide to insert a stick in each container at the start of the experiment. Your operational definition of "frozen" would be the time at which the stick can no longer move.

EXPERIMENTAL PROCEDURE

1. Fill 3 containers with 300 milliliters of cold tap water.

2. Add 10 grams of salt to Container 1; stir. Add 20 grams of salt to Container 2; stir. Add no salt to Container 3.

3. Place the 3 containers in a freezer.

4. Check the containers every 15 minutes. Record your observations.

Interpreting Data

The observations and measurements you make in an experiment are called data. At the end of an experiment, you need to analyze the data to look for any patterns or trends. Patterns often become clear if you organize your data in a data table or graph. Then think through what the data reveal. Do they support your hypothesis? Do they point out a flaw in your experiment? Do you need to collect more data?

Drawing Conclusions

A conclusion is a statement that sums up what you have learned from an experiment. When you draw a conclusion, you need to decide whether the data you collected support your hypothesis or not. You may need to repeat an experiment several times before you can draw any conclusions from it. Conclusions often lead you to pose new questions and plan new experiments to answer them.

ACTIVITY

Is a ball's bounce affected by the height from which it is dropped? Using the steps just described, plan a controlled experiment to investigate this problem.

Thinking Critically

Has a friend ever asked for your advice about a problem? If so, you may have helped your friend think through the problem in a logical way. Without knowing it, you used critical-thinking skills to help your friend. Critical thinking involves the use of reasoning and logic to solve problems or make decisions. Some critical-thinking skills are described below.

Comparing and Contrasting

When you examine two objects for similarities and differences, you are using the skill of **comparing and contrasting.** Comparing involves identifying similarities, or common characteristics. Contrasting involves identifying differences. Analyzing objects in this way can help you discover details that you might otherwise overlook.

ACTIVITY

Compare and contrast the two animals in the photo. First list all the similarities that you see. Then list all the differences.

Applying Concepts

When you use your knowledge about one situation to make sense of a similar situation, you are using the skill of **applying concepts.** Being able to transfer your knowledge from one situation to another shows that you truly understand a concept. You may use this skill in answering test questions that present different problems from the ones you've reviewed in class.

ACTIVITY

You have just learned that water takes longer to freeze when other substances are mixed into it. Use this knowledge to explain why people need a substance called antifreeze in their car's radiator in the winter.

Interpreting Illustrations

Diagrams, photographs, and maps are included in textbooks to help clarify what you read. These illustrations show processes, places, and ideas in a visual manner. The skill called **interpreting illustrations** can help you learn from these visual elements. To understand an illustration, take the time to study the illustration along with all the written information that accompanies it. Captions identify the key concepts shown in the illustration. Labels point out the important parts of a diagram or map, while keys identify the symbols used in a map.

Bristles

Upper blood vessel

Reproductive organs

Arches

Brain

Mouth

Waste-removal organs

Intestine

Nerve cord

Digestive tract

Lower blood vessel

▲ **Internal anatomy of an earthworm**

ACTIVITY

Study the diagram above. Then write a short paragraph explaining what you have learned.

Relating Cause and Effect

If one event causes another event to occur, the two events are said to have a cause-and-effect relationship. When you determine that such a relationship exists between two events, you use a skill called **relating cause and effect.** For example, if you notice an itchy, red bump on your skin, you might infer that a mosquito bit you. The mosquito bite is the cause, and the bump is the effect.

It is important to note that two events do not necessarily have a cause-and-effect relationship just because they occur together. Scientists carry out experiments or use past experience to determine whether a cause-and-effect relationship exists.

ACTIVITY

You are on a camping trip and your flashlight has stopped working. List some possible causes for the flashlight malfunction. How could you determine which cause-and-effect relationship has left you in the dark?

Making Generalizations

When you draw a conclusion about an entire group based on information about only some of the group's members, you are using a skill called **making generalizations.** For a generalization to be valid, the sample you choose must be large enough and representative of the entire group. You might, for example, put this skill to work at a farm stand if you see a sign that says, "Sample some grapes before you buy." If you sample a few sweet grapes, you may conclude that all the grapes are sweet—and purchase a large bunch.

ACTIVITY

A team of scientists needs to determine whether the water in a large reservoir is safe to drink. How could they use the skill of making generalizations to help them? What should they do?

Making Judgments

When you evaluate something to decide whether it is good or bad, or right or wrong, you are using a skill called **making judgments.** For example, you make judgments when you decide to eat healthful foods or to pick up litter in a park. Before you make a judgment, you need to think through the pros and cons of a situation, and identify the values or standards that you hold.

ACTIVITY

Should children and teens be required to wear helmets when bicycling? Explain why you feel the way you do.

Problem Solving

When you use critical-thinking skills to resolve an issue or decide on a course of action, you are using a skill called **problem solving.** Some problems, such as how to convert a fraction into a decimal, are straightforward. Other problems, such as figuring out why your computer has stopped working, are complex. Some complex problems can be solved using the trial and error method—try out one solution first, and if that doesn't work, try another. Other useful problem-solving strategies include making models and brainstorming possible solutions with a partner.

Organizing Information

As you read this textbook, how can you make sense of all the information it contains? Some useful tools to help you organize information are shown on this page. These tools are called *graphic organizers* because they give you a visual picture of a topic, showing at a glance how key concepts are related.

Concept Maps

Concept maps are useful tools for organizing information on broad topics. A concept map begins with a general concept and shows how it can be broken down into more specific concepts. In that way, relationships between concepts become easier to understand.

A concept map is constructed by placing concept words (usually nouns) in ovals and connecting them with linking words. Often, the most general concept word is placed at the top, and the words become more specific as you move downward. Often the linking words, which are written on a line extending between two ovals, describe the relationship between the two concepts they connect. If you follow any string of concepts and linking words down the map, it should read like a sentence.

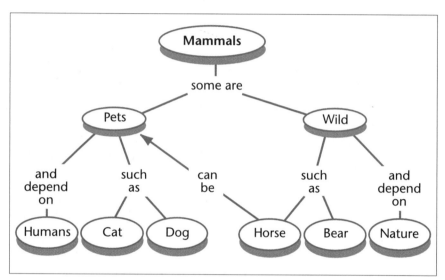

Some concept maps include linking words that connect a concept on one branch of the map to a concept on another branch. These linking words, called cross-linkages, show more complex interrelationships among concepts.

Compare/Contrast Tables

Compare/contrast tables are useful tools for sorting out the similarities and differences between two or more items. A table provides an organized framework in which to compare items based on specific characteristics that you identify.

To create a compare/contrast table, list the items to be compared across the top of a table. Then list the characteristics that will form the basis of your comparison in the left-hand

Characteristic	Baseball	Basketball
Number of Players	9	5
Playing Field	Baseball diamond	Basketball court
Equipment	Bat, baseball, mitts	Basket, basketball

column. Complete the table by filling in information about each characteristic, first for one item and then for the other.

Venn Diagrams

Another way to show similarities and differences between items is with a Venn diagram. A Venn diagram consists of two or more circles that partially overlap. Each circle represents a particular concept or idea. Common characteristics, or similarities, are written within the area of overlap between the two circles. Unique characteristics, or differences, are written in the parts of the circles outside the area of overlap.

To create a Venn diagram, draw two over-lapping circles. Label the circles with the names of the items being compared. Write the unique characteristics in each circle outside the area of overlap. Then write the shared characteristics within the area of overlap.

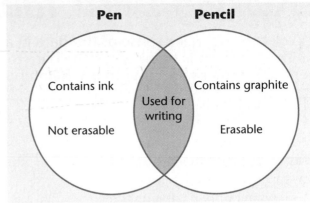

Flowcharts

A flowchart can help you understand the order in which certain events have occurred or should occur. Flowcharts are useful for outlining the stages in a process or the steps in a procedure.

To make a flowchart, write a brief description of each event in a box. Place the first event at the top of the page, followed by the second event, the third event, and so on. Then draw an arrow to connect each event to the one that occurs next.

Preparing Pasta

Boil water

↓

Cook pasta

↓

Drain water

↓

Add sauce

Cycle Diagrams

A cycle diagram can be used to show a sequence of events that is continuous, or cyclical. A continuous sequence does not have an end because, when the final event is over, the first event begins again. Like a flowchart, a cycle diagram can help you understand the order of events.

To create a cycle diagram, write a brief description of each event in a box. Place one event at the top of the page in the center. Then, moving in a clockwise direction around an imaginary circle, write each event in its proper sequence. Draw arrows that connect each event to the one that occurs next, forming a continuous circle.

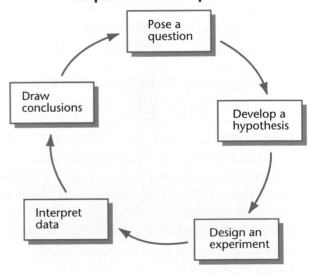

Steps in a Science Experiment

Creating Data Tables and Graphs

How can you make sense of the data in a science experiment? The first step is to organize the data to help you understand them. Data tables and graphs are helpful tools for organizing data.

Data Tables

You have gathered your materials and set up your experiment. But before you start, you need to plan a way to record what happens during the experiment. By creating a data table, you can record your observations and measurements in an orderly way.

Suppose, for example, that a scientist conducted an experiment to find out how many Calories people of different body masses burn while doing various activities. The data table shows the results.

Notice in this data table that the manipulated variable (body mass) is the heading of one column. The responding variable (for Experiment 1, the number of Calories burned while bicycling) is the heading of the next column. Additional columns were added for related experiments.

CALORIES BURNED IN 30 MINUTES OF ACTIVITY

Body Mass	Experiment 1 Bicycling	Experiment 2 Playing Basketball	Experiment 3 Watching Television
30 kg	60 Calories	120 Calories	21 Calories
40 kg	77 Calories	164 Calories	27 Calories
50 kg	95 Calories	206 Calories	33 Calories
60 kg	114 Calories	248 Calories	38 Calories

Bar Graphs

To compare how many Calories a person burns doing various activities, you could create a bar graph. A bar graph is used to display data in a number of separate, or distinct, categories. In this example, bicycling, playing basketball, and watching television are three separate categories.

To create a bar graph, follow these steps.

1. On graph paper, draw a horizontal, or *x*-, axis and a vertical, or *y*-, axis.
2. Write the names of the categories to be graphed along the horizontal axis. Include an overall label for the axis as well.
3. Label the vertical axis with the name of the responding variable. Include units of measurement. Then create a scale along the axis by marking off equally spaced numbers that cover the range of the data collected.
4. For each category, draw a solid bar using the scale on the vertical axis to determine the

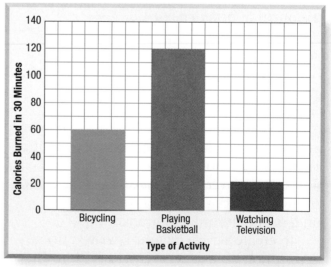

Calories Burned by a 30-kilogram Person in Various Activities

appropriate height. For example, for bicycling, draw the bar as high as the 60 mark on the vertical axis. Make all the bars the same width and leave equal spaces between them.
5. Add a title that describes the graph.

Line Graphs

To see whether a relationship exists between body mass and the number of Calories burned while bicycling, you could create a line graph. A line graph is used to display data that show how one variable (the responding variable) changes in response to another variable (the manipulated variable). You can use a line graph when your manipulated variable is *continuous*, that is, when there are other points between the ones that you tested. In this example, body mass is a continuous variable because there are other body masses between 30 and 40 kilograms (for example, 31 kilograms). Time is another example of a continuous variable.

Line graphs are powerful tools because they allow you to estimate values for conditions that you did not test in the experiment. For example, you can use the line graph to estimate that a 35-kilogram person would burn 68 Calories while bicycling.

To create a line graph, follow these steps.

1. On graph paper, draw a horizontal, or *x*-, axis and a vertical, or *y*-, axis.

2. Label the horizontal axis with the name of the manipulated variable. Label the vertical axis with the name of the responding variable. Include units of measurement.

3. Create a scale on each axis by marking off equally spaced numbers that cover the range of the data collected.

4. Plot a point on the graph for each piece of data. In the line graph above, the dotted lines show how to plot the first data point (30 kilograms and 60 Calories). Draw an imaginary vertical line extending up from the horizontal axis at the 30-kilogram mark. Then draw an imaginary horizontal line extending across from the vertical axis at the 60-Calorie mark. Plot the point where the two lines intersect.

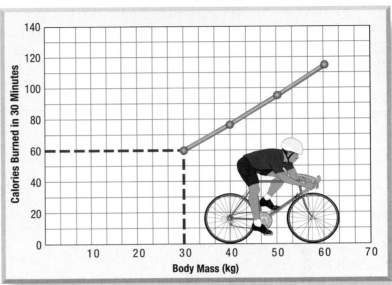

Effect of Body Mass on Calories Burned While Bicycling

5. Connect the plotted points with a solid line. (In some cases, it may be more appropriate to draw a line that shows the general trend of the plotted points. In those cases, some of the points may fall above or below the line. Also, not all graphs are linear. It may be more appropriate to draw a curve to connect the points.)

6. Add a title that identifies the variables or relationship in the graph.

Create line graphs to display the data from Experiment 2 and Experiment 3 in the data table.

ACTIVITY

You read in the newspaper that a total of 4 centimeters of rain fell in your area in June, 2.5 centimeters fell in July, and 1.5 centimeters fell in August. What type of graph would you use to display these data? Use graph paper to create the graph.

ACTIVITY

Circle Graphs

Like bar graphs, circle graphs can be used to display data in a number of separate categories. Unlike bar graphs, however, circle graphs can only be used when you have data for *all* the categories that make up a given topic. A circle graph is sometimes called a pie chart because it resembles a pie cut into slices. The pie represents the entire topic, while the slices represent the individual categories. The size of a slice indicates what percentage of the whole a particular category makes up.

The data table below shows the results of a survey in which 24 teenagers were asked to identify their favorite sport. The data were then used to create the circle graph at the right.

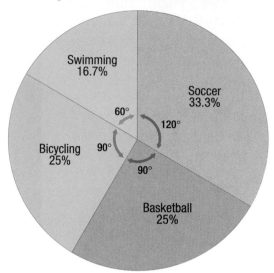

Sports That Teens Prefer

FAVORITE SPORTS

Sport	Number of Students
Soccer	8
Basketball	6
Bicycling	6
Swimming	4

To create a circle graph, follow these steps.

1. Use a compass to draw a circle. Mark the center of the circle with a point. Then draw a line from the center point to the top of the circle.
2. Determine the size of each "slice" by setting up a proportion where x equals the number of degrees in a slice. (NOTE: A circle contains 360 degrees.) For example, to find the number of degrees in the "soccer" slice, set up the following proportion:

$$\frac{\text{students who prefer soccer}}{\text{total number of students}} = \frac{x}{\text{total number of degrees in a circle}}$$

$$\frac{8}{24} = \frac{x}{360}$$

Cross-multiply and solve for x.

$$24x = 8 \times 360$$
$$x = 120$$

The "soccer" slice should contain 120 degrees.

3. Use a protractor to measure the angle of the first slice, using the line you drew to the top of the circle as the 0° line. Draw a line from the center of the circle to the edge for the angle you measured.
4. Continue around the circle by measuring the size of each slice with the protractor. Start measuring from the edge of the previous slice so the wedges do not overlap. When you are done, the entire circle should be filled in.
5. Determine the percentage of the whole circle that each slice represents. To do this, divide the number of degrees in a slice by the total number of degrees in a circle (360), and multiply by 100%. For the "soccer" slice, you can find the percentage as follows:

$$\frac{120}{360} \times 100\% = 33.3\%$$

6. Use a different color to shade in each slice. Label each slice with the name of the category and with the percentage of the whole it represents.
7. Add a title to the circle graph.

ACTIVITY

In a class of 28 students, 12 students take the bus to school, 10 students walk, and 6 students ride their bicycles. Create a circle graph to display these data.

Laboratory Safety

Safety Symbols

These symbols alert you to possible dangers in the laboratory and remind you to work carefully.

Safety Goggles Always wear safety goggles to protect your eyes in any activity involving chemicals, flames or heating, or the possibility of broken glassware.

Lab Apron Wear a laboratory apron to protect your skin and clothing from damage.

Breakage You are working with materials that may be breakable, such as glass containers, glass tubing, thermometers, or funnels. Handle breakable materials with care. Do not touch broken glassware.

Heat-resistant Gloves Use an oven mitt or other hand protection when handling hot materials. Hot plates, hot glassware, or hot water can cause burns. Do not touch hot objects with your bare hands.

Heating Use a clamp or tongs to pick up hot glassware. Do not touch hot objects with your bare hands.

Sharp Object Pointed-tip scissors, scalpels, knives, needles, pins, or tacks are sharp. They can cut or puncture your skin. Always direct a sharp edge or point away from yourself and others. Use sharp instruments only as instructed.

Electric Shock Avoid the possibility of electric shock. Never use electrical equipment around water, or when the equipment is wet or your hands are wet. Be sure cords are untangled and cannot trip anyone. Disconnect the equipment when it is not in use.

Corrosive Chemical You are working with an acid or another corrosive chemical. Avoid getting it on your skin or clothing, or in your eyes. Do not inhale the vapors. Wash your hands when you are finished with the activity.

Poison Do not let any poisonous chemical come in contact with your skin, and do not inhale its vapors. Wash your hands when you are finished with the activity.

Physical Safety When an experiment involves physical activity, take precautions to avoid injuring yourself or others. Follow instructions from your teacher. Alert your teacher if there is any reason you should not participate in the activity.

Animal Safety Treat live animals with care to avoid harming the animals or yourself. Working with animal parts or preserved animals also may require caution. Wash your hands when you are finished with the activity.

Plant Safety Handle plants in the laboratory or during field work only as directed by your teacher. If you are allergic to certain plants, tell your teacher before doing an activity in which those plants are used. Avoid touching harmful plants such as poison ivy, poison oak, or poison sumac, or plants with thorns. Wash your hands when you are finished with the activity.

Flames You may be working with flames from a lab burner, candle, or matches. Tie back loose hair and clothing. Follow instructions from your teacher about lighting and extinguishing flames.

No Flames Flammable materials may be present. Make sure there are no flames, sparks, or other exposed heat sources present.

Fumes When poisonous or unpleasant vapors may be involved, work in a ventilated area. Avoid inhaling vapors directly. Only test an odor when directed to do so by your teacher, and use a wafting motion to direct the vapor toward your nose.

Disposal Chemicals and other laboratory materials used in the activity must be disposed of safely. Follow the instructions from your teacher.

Hand Washing Wash your hands thoroughly when finished with the activity. Use antibacterial soap and warm water. Lather both sides of your hands and between your fingers. Rinse well.

General Safety Awareness You may see this symbol when none of the symbols described earlier appears. In this case, follow the specific instructions provided. You may also see this symbol when you are asked to develop your own procedure in a lab. Have your teacher approve your plan before you go further.

Science Safety Rules

To prepare yourself to work safely in the laboratory, read over the following safety rules. Then read them a second time. Make sure you understand and follow each rule. Ask your teacher to explain any rules you do not understand.

Dress Code

1. To protect yourself from injuring your eyes, wear safety goggles whenever you work with chemicals, burners, glassware, or any substance that might get into your eyes. If you wear contact lenses, notify your teacher.
2. Wear a lab apron or coat whenever you work with corrosive chemicals or substances that can stain.
3. Tie back long hair to keep it away from any chemicals, flames, or equipment.
4. Remove or tie back any article of clothing or jewelry that can hang down and touch chemicals, flames, or equipment. Roll up or secure long sleeves.
5. Never wear open shoes or sandals.

General Precautions

6. Read all directions for an experiment several times before beginning the activity. Carefully follow all written and oral instructions. If you are in doubt about any part of the experiment, ask your teacher for assistance.
7. Never perform activities that are not assigned or authorized by your teacher. Obtain permission before "experimenting" on your own. Never handle any equipment unless you have specific permission.
8. Never perform lab activities without direct supervision.
9. Never eat or drink in the laboratory.
10. Keep work areas clean and tidy at all times. Bring only notebooks and lab manuals or written lab procedures to the work area. All other items, such as purses and backpacks, should be left in a designated area.
11. Do not engage in horseplay.

First Aid

12. Always report all accidents or injuries to your teacher, no matter how minor. Notify your teacher immediately about any fires.
13. Learn what to do in case of specific accidents, such as getting acid in your eyes or on your skin. (Rinse acids from your body with lots of water.)
14. Be aware of the location of the first-aid kit, but do not use it unless instructed by your teacher. In case of injury, your teacher should administer first aid. Your teacher may also send you to the school nurse or call a physician.
15. Know the location of emergency equipment, such as the fire extinguisher and fire blanket, and know how to use it.
16. Know the location of the nearest telephone and whom to contact in an emergency.

Heating and Fire Safety

17. Never use a heat source, such as a candle, burner, or hot plate, without wearing safety goggles.
18. Never heat anything unless instructed to do so. A chemical that is harmless when cool may be dangerous when heated.
19. Keep all combustible materials away from flames. Never use a flame or spark near a combustible chemical.
20. Never reach across a flame.
21. Before using a laboratory burner, make sure you know proper procedures for lighting and adjusting the burner, as demonstrated by your teacher. Do not touch the burner. It may be hot. And never leave a lighted burner unattended!
22. Chemicals can splash or boil out of a heated test tube. When heating a substance in a test tube, make sure that the mouth of the tube is not pointed at you or anyone else.
23. Never heat a liquid in a closed container. The expanding gases produced may blow the container apart.
24. Before picking up a container that has been heated, hold the back of your hand near it. If you can feel heat on the back of your hand, the container is too hot to handle. Use an oven mitt to pick up a container that has been heated.

Using Chemicals Safely

25. Never mix chemicals "for the fun of it." You might produce a dangerous, possibly explosive substance.

26. Never put your face near the mouth of a container that holds chemicals. Many chemicals are poisonous. Never touch, taste, or smell a chemical unless you are instructed by your teacher to do so.

27. Use only those chemicals needed in the activity. Read and double-check labels on supply bottles before removing any chemicals. Take only as much as you need. Keep all containers closed when chemicals are not being used.

28. Dispose of all chemicals as instructed by your teacher. To avoid contamination, never return chemicals to their original containers. Never simply pour chemicals or other substances into the sink or trash containers.

29. Be extra careful when working with acids or bases. Pour all chemicals over the sink or a container, not over your work surface.

30. If you are instructed to test for odors, use a wafting motion to direct the odors to your nose. Do not inhale the fumes directly from the container.

31. When mixing an acid and water, always pour the water into the container first and then add the acid to the water. Never pour water into an acid.

32. Take extreme care not to spill any material in the laboratory. Wash chemical spills and splashes immediately with plenty of water. Immediately begin rinsing with water any acids that get on your skin or clothing, and notify your teacher of any acid spill at the same time.

Using Glassware Safely

33. Never force glass tubing or thermometers into a rubber stopper or rubber tubing. Have your teacher insert the glass tubing or thermometer if required for an activity.

34. If you are using a laboratory burner, use a wire screen to protect glassware from any flame. Never heat glassware that is not thoroughly dry on the outside.

35. Keep in mind that hot glassware looks cool. Never pick up glassware without first checking to see if it is hot. Use an oven mitt. See rule 24.

36. Never use broken or chipped glassware. If glassware breaks, notify your teacher and dispose of the glassware in the proper broken-glassware container. Never handle broken glass with your bare hands.

37. Never eat or drink from lab glassware.

38. Thoroughly clean glassware before putting it away.

Using Sharp Instruments

39. Handle scalpels or other sharp instruments with extreme care. Never cut material toward you; cut away from you.

40. Immediately notify your teacher if you cut your skin when working in the laboratory.

Animal and Plant Safety

41. Never perform experiments that cause pain, discomfort, or harm to animals. This rule applies at home as well as in the classroom.

42. Animals should be handled only if absolutely necessary. Your teacher will instruct you as to how to handle each animal species brought into the classroom.

43. If you know that you are allergic to certain plants, molds, or animals, tell your teacher before doing an activity in which these are used.

44. During field work, protect your skin by wearing long pants, long sleeves, socks, and closed shoes. Know how to recognize the poisonous plants and fungi in your area, as well as plants with thorns, and avoid contact with them. Never eat any part of a plant or fungus.

45. Wash your hands thoroughly after handling animals or a cage containing animals. Wash your hands when you are finished with any activity involving animal parts, plants, or soil.

End-of-Experiment Rules

46. After an experiment has been completed, turn off all burners or hot plates. If you used a gas burner, check that the gas-line valve to the burner is off. Unplug hot plates.

47. Turn off and unplug any other electrical equipment that you used.

48. Clean up your work area and return all equipment to its proper place.

49. Dispose of waste materials as instructed by your teacher.

50. Wash your hands after every experiment.

Identifying Common Minerals

GROUP 1
Metallic Luster, Mostly Dark-Colored

Mineral/ Formula	Hardness	Density (g/cm³)	Luster	Streak	Color	Other Properties/Remarks
Pyrite FeS₂	6–6.5	5.0	Metallic	Greenish, brownish black	Light yellow	Harder than chalcopyrite and pyrrhotite; called "fool's gold," but harder than gold and very brittle
Magnetite Fe₃O₄	6	5.2	Metallic	Black	Iron black	Very magnetic; important iron ore; some varieties known as "lodestone"
Hematite Fe₂O₃	5.5–6.5	4.9–5.3	Metallic or earthy	Red or red brown	Reddish brown to black; also steel gray crystals	Most important ore of iron; known as "red ocher"; often used as red pigment in paint.
Pyrrhotite FeS	4	4.6	Metallic	Gray black	Brownish bronze	Less hard than pyrite: slightly magnetic
Sphalerite ZnS	3.5–4	3.9–4.1	Resinous	Brown to light yellow	Brown to yellow	Most important zinc ore
Chalcopyrite CuFeS₂	3.5–4	4.1–4.3	Metallic	Greenish black	Golden yellow, often tarnished	Most important copper ore; softer than pyrite and more yellow; more brittle than gold
Bornite Cu₅FeS₄	3	4.9–5.4	Metallic	Gray black	Copper, brown; turns to purple and black	Important copper ore; known as "peacock ore" because of iridescent purple color when exposed to air for a time
Copper Cu	2.5–3	8.9	Metallic	Copper red	Copper red to black	Can be pounded into various shapes and drawn into wires; used in making electrical wires, coins, pipes
Gold Au	2.5–3	19.3	Metallic	Yellow	Rich yellow	Can be pounded into various shapes and drawn into wires; does not tarnish; used in jewelry, coins, dental fillings
Silver Ag	2.5–3	10.0–11.0	Metallic	Silver to light gray	Silver white, tarnishes to black	Can be pounded into various shapes and drawn into wires; used in jewelry, coins, electrical wire
Galena PbS	2.5	7.4–7.6	Metallic	Lead gray	Lead gray	Main ore of lead; used in shields against radiation
Graphite C	1–2	2.3	Metallic to dull	Black	Black	Feels greasy; very soft; used as pencil "lead" and as a lubricant

GROUP 2
Nonmetallic Luster, Mostly Dark-Colored

Mineral/Formula	Hardness	Density (g/cm³)	Luster	Streak	Color	Other Properties/Remarks
Corundum Al_2O_3	9	3.9–4.1	Brilliant to glassy	White	Usually brown	Very hard; used as an abrasive; transparent crystals used as gems called "ruby" (red) and "sapphire" (blue and other colors)
Garnet $(Ca,Mg,Fe)_3$ $(Al,Fe,Cr)_2(SiO_4)_3$	7–7.5	3.5–4.3	Glassy to resinous	White, light brown	Red, brown, black, green	A group of minerals used in jewelry, as a birthstone, and as an abrasive
Olivine $(Mg,Fe)_2SiO_4$	6.5–7	3.3–3.4	Glassy	White or gray	Olive green	Found in igneous rocks; sometimes used as a gem
Augite $Ca(Mg,Fe,Al)$ $(AlSi)_2O_6$	5–6	3.2–3.4	Glassy	Greenish gray	Dark green to black	Found in igneous rocks
Hornblende $NaCa_2(Mg,Fe,Al)_5$ $(Si,Al)_8O_{22}(OH)_2$	5–6	3.0–3.4	Glassy, silky	White to gray	Dark green to brown, black	Found in igneous and metamorphic rocks
Apatite $Ca_5(PO_4)_3F$	5	3.1–3.2	Glassy	White	Green, brown, red, blue, violet, yellow	Sometimes used as a gem; source of the phosphorus needed by plants
Azurite $Cu_3(CO_3)_2(OH)_2$	3.5–4	3.8	Glassy to dull	Pale blue	Intense blue	Ore of copper; used as a gem
Biotite $K(Mg,Fe)_3AlSiO_{10}$ $(OH)_2$	2.5–3	2.8–3.4	Glassy or pearly	White to gray	Dark green, brown, or black	A type of mica, sometimes used as a lubricant
Serpentine $Mg_6Si_4O_{10}(OH)_8$	2–5	2.2–2.6	Greasy, waxy, silky	White	Usually green	Once used in insulation but found to cause cancer; used in fireproofing; can be in the form of asbestos
Limonite Mixture of hydrous iron oxides	1–5.5	2.8–4.3	Glassy to dull	Yellow brown	Brown black to brownish yellow	Ore of iron, also known as "yellow ocher," a pigment; a mixture that is not strictly a mineral
Bauxite Mixture of hydrous aluminum oxides	1–3	2.0–2.5	Dull to earthy	Colorless to gray	Brown, yellow, gray, white	Ore of aluminum, smells like clay when wet; a mixture that is not strictly a mineral

GROUP 3
Nonmetallic Luster, Mostly Light-Colored

Mineral/ Formula	Hardness	Density (g/cm^3)	Luster	Streak	Color	Other Properties/Remarks
Diamond C	10	3.5	Brilliant	White	Colorless and varied	Hardest known substance; used in jewelry, as an abrasive, in cutting instruments
Topaz $Al_2SiO_4(F,OH)_2$	8	3.5–3.6	Glassy	White	Straw yellow, pink, bluish, greenish	Valuable gem
Quartz SiO_2	7	2.6	Glassy, greasy	White	Colorless, white; any color when not pure	The second most abundant mineral; many varieties are gems (amethyst, cat's-eye, bloodstone, agate, jasper, onyx); used in making glass
Feldspar (K,Na,Ca) $(AlSi_3O_8)$	6	2.6	Glassy	Colorless, white	Colorless, white, various colors	As a family, the most abundant of all minerals; the different types of feldspar make up over 60 percent of Earth's crust
Fluorite CaF_2	4	3.0–3.3	Glassy	Colorless	Purple, light, green, yellow, bluish green, other colors	Some types are fluorescent (glow when exposed to ultraviolet light); used in making steel
Dolomite $CaMg(CO_3)_2$	3.5–4	2.8	Glassy or pearly	White	Colorless, white, pinkish, or light tints	Used in making concrete and cement; fizzes slowly in dilute hydrochloric acid
Calcite $CaCO_3$	3	2.7	Glassy	White to grayish	Colorless, white, pale tints	Easily scratched; bubbles in dilute hydrochloric acid; frequently fluorescent
Halite $NaCl$	2.5	2.1–2.6	Glassy	White	Colorless or white	Occurs as perfect cubic crystals; has salty taste
Gypsum $CaSO_4 \cdot 2H_2O$	2	2.3	Glassy, pearly, silky	White	Colorless, white, light tints	Very soft; used in manufacture of plaster of Paris; form known as alabaster used for statues
Sulfur S	2	2.0–2.1	Resinous to greasy	White	Yellow to yellowish brown	Used in making many medicines, in production of sulfuric acid, and in vulcanizing rubber
Talc $Mg_3Si_4O_{10}(OH)_2$	1	2.7–2.8	Pearly to greasy	White	Gray, white, greenish	Very soft; used in talcum powder; found mostly in metamorphic rocks; also called "soapstone"

Glossary

aa A slow-moving type of lava that hardens to form rough chunks; cooler than pahoehoe. (p. 97)

active Said of a volcano that is erupting or has shown signs of erupting in the near future. (p. 98)

aftershock An earthquake that occurs after a larger earthquake in the same area. (p. 73)

alloy A solid mixture of two or more metals. (p. 138)

anticline An upward fold in rock formed by compression of Earth's crust. (p. 60)

asthenosphere The soft layer of the mantle on which the lithosphere floats. (p. 21)

atoll A ring-shaped coral island found far from land. (p. 161)

atom The smallest unit of an element that retains the properties of that element. (p. 120)

basalt A dark, dense, igneous rock with a fine texture, found in oceanic crust. (p. 20)

base-isolated building A building mounted on bearings designed to absorb the energy of an earthquake. (p. 76)

batholith A mass of rock formed when a large body of magma cooled inside the crust. (p. 107)

C

caldera The large hole at the top of a volcano formed when the roof of a volcano's magma chamber collapses. (p. 104)

cementation The process by which dissolved minerals crystallize and glue particles of sediment together into one mass. (p. 155)

chemical rock Sedimentary rock that forms when minerals crystallize from a solution. (p. 158)

cinder cone A steep, cone-shaped hill or mountain made of volcanic ash, cinders, and bombs piled up around a volcano's opening. (p. 104)

clastic rock Sedimentary rock that forms when rock fragments are squeezed together under high pressure. (p. 156)

cleavage A mineral's ability to split easily along flat surfaces. (p. 125)

compaction The process by which sediments are pressed together under their own weight. (p. 155)

composite volcano A tall, cone-shaped mountain in which layers of lava alternate with layers of ash and other volcanic materials. (p. 104)

compound A substance in which two or more elements are chemically joined. (p. 120)

compression Stress that squeezes rock until it folds or breaks. (p. 55)

conduction The transfer of heat by direct contact of particles of matter. (p. 26)

constructive force A force that builds up mountains and landmasses on Earth's surface. (p. 17)

continent A great landmass surrounded by oceans. (p. 17)

continental drift The hypothesis that the continents slowly move across Earth's surface. (p. 29)

controlled experiment An experiment in which all factors except one are kept constant. (p. 185)

convection The transfer of heat by movements of a heated fluid. (p. 26)

convection current The movement of a fluid, caused by differences in temperature, that transfers heat from one part of the fluid to another. (p. 26)

convergent boundary A plate boundary where two plates move toward each other. (p. 46)

coral reef A structure of calcite skeletons built up by coral animals in warm, shallow ocean water. (p. 160)

crater A bowl-shaped area that forms around a volcano's central opening. (p. 94)

crust The layer of rock that forms Earth's outer surface. (p. 20)

crystal A solid in which the atoms are arranged in a pattern that repeats again and again. (p. 120)

deep-ocean trench A deep valley along the ocean floor through which oceanic crust slowly sinks towards the mantle. (p. 38)

deformation A change in the volume or shape of Earth's crust. (p. 55)

density The amount of mass in a given space; mass per unit volume. (p. 26)

deposition The process by which sediment settles out of the water or wind that is carrying it. (p. 155)

destructive force A force that slowly wears away mountains and other features on the surface of Earth. (p. 17)

dike A slab of volcanic rock formed when magma forces itself across rock layers. (p. 106)

divergent boundary A plate boundary where two plates move away from each other. (p. 45)

dormant Said of a volcano that does not show signs of erupting in the near future. (p. 98)

earthquake The shaking that results from the movement of rock beneath Earth's surface. (p. 54)

element A substance composed of a single kind of atom. (p. 120)

epicenter The point on Earth's surface directly above an earthquake's focus. (p. 64)

erosion The destructive process in which water or wind loosen and carry away fragments of rock. (p. 155)

extinct Said of a volcano that is unlikely to erupt again. (p. 98)

extrusive rock Igneous rock that forms from lava on Earth's surface. (p. 151)

.... **F** ....

fault A break in Earth's crust where slabs of rock slip past each other. (pp. 44, 56)

fault-block mountain A mountain that forms where a normal fault uplifts a block of rock. (p. 58)

fluorescence The property of a mineral in which the mineral glows under ultraviolet light. (p. 126)

focus The point beneath Earth's surface where rock breaks under stress and causes an earthquake. (p. 64)

fold A bend in rock that forms where part of Earth's crust is compressed. (p. 59)

foliated Term used to describe metamorphic rocks whose grains are arranged in parallel layers or bands. (p. 163)

footwall The block of rock that forms the lower half of a fault. (p. 56)

fossil A trace of an ancient organism that has been preserved in rock. (p. 30)

fracture The way a mineral looks when it breaks apart in an irregular way. (p. 125)

.... **G** ....

gemstone A hard, colorful mineral that has a brilliant or glassy luster. (p. 135)

geologist A scientist who studies the forces that make and shape planet Earth. (p. 17)

geology The study of planet Earth. (p. 17)

geothermal energy Energy from water or steam that has been heated by magma. (p. 99)

geyser A fountain of water and steam that builds up pressure underground and erupts at regular intervals. (p. 99)

grain A particle of mineral or other rock that gives a rock its texture. (p. 147)

granite A usually light-colored rock that is found in continental crust. (p. 20)

.... **H** ....

hanging wall The block of rock that forms the upper half of a fault. (p. 56)

heat transfer The movement of energy from a warmer object to a cooler object. (p. 25)

hot spot An area where magma from deep within the mantle melts through the crust above it. (p. 91)

hot spring A pool formed by groundwater that has risen to the surface after being heated by a nearby body of magma. (p. 99)

hypothesis A possible explanation for a set of observations or answer to a scientific question; must be testable. (p. 184)

.... **I** ....

igneous rock A type of rock that forms from the cooling of molten rock at or below the surface. (p. 149)

inner core A dense sphere of solid iron and nickel in the center of Earth. (p. 21)

inorganic Not formed from living things or the remains of living things. (p. 119)

intrusive rock Igneous rock that forms when magma hardens beneath Earth's surface. (p. 151)

island arc A string of islands formed by the volcanoes along a deep ocean trench. (p. 90)

.... **L** ....

lava Liquid magma that reaches the surface; also the rock formed when liquid lava hardens. (p. 88)

lava flow The area covered by lava as it pours out of a volcano's vent. (p. 94)

liquefaction The process by which an earthquake's violent movement suddenly turns loose soil into liquid mud. (p. 73)

lithosphere A rigid layer made up of the uppermost part of the mantle and the crust. (p. 20)

luster The way a mineral reflects light from its surface. (p. 123)

.... **M** ....

magma The molten mixture of rock-forming substances, gases, and water from the mantle. (p. 88)

magma chamber The pocket beneath a volcano where magma collects. (p. 94)

magnitude The measurement of an earthquake's strength based on seismic waves and movement along faults. (p. 67)

manipulated variable The one factor that a scientist changes during an experiment. (p. 185)

mantle The layer of hot, solid material between Earth's crust and core. (p. 20)

Mercalli scale A scale that rates earthquakes according to their intensity and how much damage they cause. (p. 67)

metamorphic rock A type of rock that forms from an existing rock that is changed by heat, pressure, or chemical reactions. (p. 149)

mid-ocean ridge The undersea mountain chain where new ocean floor is produced; a divergent plate boundary. (p. 34)

mineral A naturally-occurring, inorganic solid that has a crystal structure and a definite chemical composition. (p. 119)

Mohs hardness scale A scale ranking ten minerals from softest to hardest; used in testing the hardness of minerals. (p. 121)

moment magnitude scale A scale that rates earthquakes by estimating the total energy released by an earthquake. (p. 68)

normal fault A type of fault where the hanging wall slides downward; caused by tension in the crust. (p. 56)

operational definition A statement that describes how a particular variable is to be measured or a term is to be defined. (p. 185)

ore Rock that contains a metal or economically useful mineral. (p. 135)

organic rock Sedimentary rock that forms where remains of organisms are deposited in thick layers. (p. 157)

outer core A layer of molten iron and nickel that surrounds the inner core of Earth. (p. 21)

P wave A type of seismic wave that compresses and expands the ground. (p. 65)

pahoehoe A hot, fast-moving type of lava that hardens to form smooth, ropelike coils. (p. 97)

Pangaea The name of the single landmass that broke apart 200 million years ago and gave rise to today's continents. (p. 29)

pipe A long tube through which magma moves from the magma chamber to Earth's surface. (p. 94)

plate A section of the lithosphere that slowly moves over the asthenosphere, carrying pieces of continental and oceanic crust. (p. 42)

plate tectonics The theory that pieces of Earth's lithosphere are in constant motion, driven by convection currents in the mantle. (p. 43)

plateau A large area of flat land elevated high above sea level. (p. 61)

porphyritic texture An igneous rock texture in which large crystals are scattered on a background of much smaller crystals. (p. 151)

pressure The amount of force pushing on a surface or area. (p. 19)

pyroclastic flow The expulsion of ash, cinders, bombs, and gases during an explosive volcanic eruption. (p. 98)

radiation The transfer of energy through empty space. (p. 25)

responding variable The factor that changes as a result of changes to the manipulated variable in an experiment. (p. 185)

reverse fault A type of fault where the hanging wall slides upward. (p. 57)

Richter scale A scale that rates seismic waves as measured by a particular type of mechanical seismograph. (p. 67)

rift valley A deep valley that forms where two plates move apart. (p. 45)

Ring of Fire A major belt of volcanoes that rims the Pacific Ocean. (p. 89)

rock The material that forms Earth's hard surface. (p. 17)

rock cycle A series of processes on the surface and inside Earth that slowly change rocks from one kind to another. (p. 166)

S wave A type of seismic wave that moves the ground up and down or side to side. (p. 65)

scientific theory A well-tested concept that explains a wide range of observations. (p. 43)

sea-floor spreading The process by which molten material adds new oceanic crust to the ocean floor. (p. 35)

sediment Small, solid pieces of material that comes from rocks or organisms. (p. 154)

sedimentary rock A type of rock that forms when particles from other rocks or the remains of plants and animals are pressed and cemented together. (p. 149)

seismic wave A vibration that travels through Earth carrying the energy released during an earthquake. (pp. 18, 64)

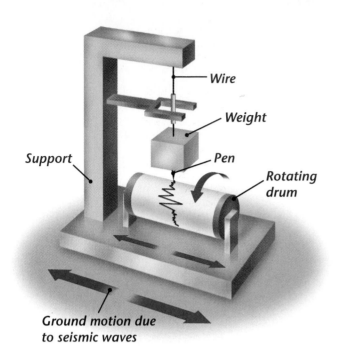

Wire
Weight
Pen
Rotating drum
Support

Ground motion due to seismic waves

seismograph A device that records ground movements caused by seismic waves as they move through Earth. (p. 66)

shearing Stress that pushes a mass of rock in opposite directions. (p. 55)

shield volcano A wide, gently sloping mountain made of layers of lava and formed by quiet eruptions. (p. 104)

silica A material that is formed from the elements oxygen and silicon; silica is found in magma. (p. 96)

sill A slab of volcanic rock formed when magma squeezes between layers of rock. (p. 106)

smelting The process by which ore is melted to separate the useful metal from other elements. (p. 138)

solution A mixture in which one substance is dissolved in another. (p. 130)

sonar A device that determines the distance of an object under water by recording echoes of sound waves. (p. 34)

streak The color of a mineral's powder. (p. 122)

stress A force that acts on rock to change its shape or volume. (p. 54)

strike-slip fault A type of fault where rocks on either side move past each other sideways with little up-or-down motion. (p. 56)

subduction The process by which oceanic crust sinks beneath a deep-ocean trench and back into the mantle at a convergent plate boundary. (p. 38)

surface wave A type of seismic wave that forms when P waves and S waves reach Earth's surface. (p. 66)

syncline A downward fold in rock formed by compression in Earth's crust. (p. 60)

tension Stress that stretches rock so that it becomes thinner in the middle. (p. 55)

texture The look and feel of a rock's surface, determined by the size, shape, and pattern of a rock's grains. (p. 147)

transform boundary A plate boundary where two plates move past each other in opposite directions. (p. 44)

tsunami A large wave produced by an earthquake on the ocean floor. (p. 74)

variable Any factor that can change in an experiment. (p. 185)

vein A narrow slab of a mineral that is sharply different from the surrounding rock. (p. 130)

vent The opening through which molten rock and gas leave a volcano. (p. 94)

volcanic neck A deposit of hardened magma in a volcano's pipe. (p. 106)

volcano A weak spot in the crust where magma has come to the surface. (p. 88)

Index

Acknowledgments

Staff Credits

The people who made up the **Science Explorer** team—representing design services, editorial, editorial services, electronic publishing technology, manufacturing & inventory planning, marketing, marketing services, market research, online services & multimedia development, production services, product planning, project office, and publishing processes—are listed below.

Carolyn Belanger, Barbara A. Bertell, Suzanne Biron, Peggy Bliss, Peter W. Brooks, Christopher R. Brown, Greg Cantone, Jonathan Cheney, Todd Christy, Lisa J. Clark, Patrick Finbarr Connolly, Edward Cordero, Robert Craton, Patricia Cully, Patricia M. Dambry, Kathleen J. Dempsey, Judy Elgin, Gayle Connolly Fedele, Frederick Fellows, Barbara Foster, Paula Foye, Loree Franz, Donald P. Gagnon Jr., Paul J. Gagnon, Joel Gendler, Elizabeth Good, Robert M. Graham, Kerri Hoar, Joanne Hudson, Linda D. Johnson, Anne Jones, Toby Klang, Carolyn Langley, Russ Lappa, Carolyn Lock, Cheryl Mahan, Dotti Marshall, Meredith Mascola, Jeanne Y. Maurand, Karen McHugh, Eve Melnechuk, Natania Mlawer, Paul W. Murphy, Cindy A. Noftle, Julia F. Osborne, Judi Pinkham, Caroline M. Power, Robin L. Santel, Suzanne J. Schineller, Emily Soltanoff, Kira Thaler-Marbit, Mark Tricca, Diane Walsh, Pearl Weinstein, Merce Wilczek, Helen Young.

Illustration

Carol Barber: 26
Kathleen Dempsey: 40, 48, 62, 70, 92, 108, 127, 140, 165, 170
John Edwards: 74
Chris Forsey: 13r, 27, 34t, 35, 38, 44, 45, 91
Geo Systems: 11m, 29, 30, 34b, 43, 51, 58t, 69, 70b, 81, 82, 89, 132
Jared D. Lee: 178–179t,
Martucci Design: 71b, 85, 115,
Morgan Cain & Associates: 22, 23, 24, 36, 37, 51, 55, 60, 65tl, 66, 76, 77, 79, 80, 95, 105, 106, 152, 155, 173
Matt Mayerchak: 49, 83, 113, 124, 142, 171
Ortelius Design Inc.: 11m, 46, 47, 100, 101, 136, 137, 176
Matthew Pippin: 65br, 75, 90, 130, 138
J/B Woolsey Associates: 44, 56, 57, 58b, 59, 85

Photography

Photo Research Paula Wehde
Cover Image Paul Chesley/TSI

Nature of Science
Page 10, 12, Paul Mann; 11, Carol Prentice/US Geological Survey.

Chapter 1
Pages 14–15, Earth Satellite Corporation/Science Photo Library/Photo Researchers; 16, Gardar Palsson/Mats Wibe Lund; 17t,b, M. W. Franke/Peter Arnold; 18, Michael Nichols/Magnum; 19, Tracy Frankel/The Image Bank; 20–21t, Linde Waidhofer/Liaison International; 20m, E. R. Degginger; 20b, Breck P. Kent; 24, Runk/Schoenberger/Grant Heilman; 25, Richard Haynes; 28t, Russ Lappa; 28b, The Granger Collection, NY; 31, Breck P. Kent; 32, Bildarchiv Preussischer Kulturbesitz; 33, Emory Kristof/National Geographic Image Collection; 36tl, Woods Hole Oceanographic Institute/Sygma; 36tr, USGS/HVO 3cp/U. S. Geological Survey; 37, SCRIPPS Oceanographic Institute; 39, Norbert Wu; 40 all, Richard Haynes; 41t, Richard Haynes; 42t, Russ Lappa.

Chapter 2
Pages 52–53, Science Museum/Michael Holford; 54, Ben S. Kwiatkowski/Fundamental Photographs; 56t, David Parker/Science Photo Library/Photo Researchers; 56b, David Muench Photography; 57, Sharon Gerig/Tom Stack & Associates; 58, Stan Osolinski/TSI; 59, Phillips Petroleum; 60–61,Tom Bean; 63b, inset, Richard Haynes; 64, 66t, Richard Haynes; 66b, Russell D. Curtis/Photo Researchers; 67, Leonetto Medici/AP Photo; 68, EERC/Berkeley; 72t, Richard Haynes; 72b, Natsuko Utsumi/Gamma Liaison; 73, EERC/Berkeley; 76, Esbin-Anderson/The Image Works; 78, Terraphotographics/BPS.

Chapter 3
Pages 86–87, Soames Summerhays/Photo Researchers; 88, Savino/Sipa Press; 93 all, Breck P. Kent; 94, E. R. Degginger; 95, B. Ingalls/NASA/Liaison International; 96t, Ed Reschke/Peter Arnold; 96b, E. R. Degginger; 97l, Dave B. Fleetham/Tom Stack & Associates; 97r, William Felger/Grant Heilman Photography; 98l, r, Alberto Garcia/Saba Press; 99l, r, Alberto Garcia/Saba Press; 99b, Norbert Rosing/Animals Animals/Earth Scenes; 100tl, North Wind; 100tr, Kim Heacox/Peter Arnold; 100b, Robert Fried Photography; 101, Alberto Garcia/Saba Press; 102l, Pat Roqua/AP/Wide World; 102r, Antonio Emerito/Sipa Press; 103t, Richard Haynes; 103b, Hela Lade/Peter Arnold; 104, Greg Vaughn/Tom Stack & Associates; 105t, Picture Perfect; 105b, Manfred Gottschalk/Tom Stack & Associates; 106tl, Brownie Harris/The Stock Market; 106bl, Tom Bean/DRK Photo; 106br, David Hosking/Photo Researchers; 107, Bob Newman/Visual Unlimited; 109, Richard Haynes; 110t, m, NASA; 110b, Chris Bjornberg/Photo Researchers; 111t, b, 112, NASA.

Chapter 4
Pages 116–117, Thomas R. Taylor/Photo Researchers; 118t, Richard Haynes; 118b, Richard B. Levine; 119t, Mark A. Schneider/Visuals Unlimited; 119m, Ben Johnson/Science Photo Library/Photo Researchers; 119b, E. R. Degginger; 120l, Richard Treptow/Visuals Unlimited; 120r, Gregory G. Dimijian/Photo Researchers; 120m, McCutcheon/Visuals Unlimited; 121l, Arne Hodalic/Corbis; 121r, Breck P. Kent; 122, Paul Silverman/Fundamental Photographs; 123l, r, Breck P. Kent; 124 sulfur, E. R. Degginger; 124 all others, Breck P. Kent; 125l, A. J. Copley/Visuals Unlimited; 125tr, Paul Silverman/Fundamental Photographs; 126l, r, E. R. Degginger; 128t, Richard Haynes; 128b, Gerhard Gscheidle/Peter Arnold; 129, Jeffrey Scovil; 130l, Ken Lucas/Visuals Unlimited; 130r, Ted Clutter/Photo Researchers; 131, Jay Syverson/Stock Boston; 133, Nautilus Minerals Corp.; 134, C. M. Dixon; 135t, Runk/Schoenberger from Grant Heilman; 135b, Mike Husar/DRK photo; 136t, C. M. Dixon; 136bl, Scala/Art Resource, NY; 136br, C. M. Dixon; 137, The Granger Collection, NY; 138t, Charles D. Winters/Photo Researchers; 138b, Russ Lappa; 139, Visuals Unlimited; 140, Richard Haynes; 141t, b, 143, Breck P. Kent.

Chapter 5
Pages 144–145, Jim Nelson/Adventure Photo; 146t, m, Breck P. Kent; 146b, Jeff Zaroda/The Stock Market; 147tl, bl, E. R. Degginger; 147tr, m, Breck P. Kent; 147br, Barry L. Runk/Grant Heilman; 148 slate, gneiss, E. R. Degginger; 148 quartzite, Jeff Scovil; 148 all others, Breck P. Kent; 149, Martin Rogers/Stock Boston; 150tl, Breck P. Kent; 150tr, Doug Martin/Photo Researchers; 150b, Greg Vaughn/Tom Stack & Associates; 151tl, tm, Breck P. Kent; 151tr, E. R. Degginger; 152, Alfred Pasieka/Science Photo Library/Photo Researchers; 153, Michele & Tom Grimm/TSI; 154, Clyde H. Smith/Peter Arnold; 156, Specimen from North Museum/Franklin and Marshall College/Grant Heilman Photography; 157t, E. R. Degginger; 157b, Kevin Sink/Midwestock; 158, Grant Heilman/Grant Heilman Photography; 159t, Ted Clutter/Photo Researchers; 159b, Stephen Frink/Waterhouse; 160, Norbert Wu/The Stock Market; 160b, Jean-Marc Truchet/TSI; 161, Grant Heilman/Grant Heilman Photography; 162tl, E. R. Degginger; 162bl, Barry L. Runk/Grant Heilman Photography; 162br, 163bl, Andrew J. Martinez/Photo Researchers; 164, David Hosking/Photo Researchers; 166tl, tr, Jeff Scovil; 166tm, Breck P. Kent; 167, Corbis; 168tl, Tom Algire/Tom Stack & Associates; 168bl, Breck P. Kent; 168br, N.R.Rowan/Stock Boston; 169, Breck P. Kent; 170t, m, b, Russ Lappa; 173l, r, E. R. Degginger; 173m, Breck P. Kent.

Interdisciplinary Exploration
Page 174tl, Rosenfeld Imaged Ltd/Rainbow; 174br, Michael Holford; 174–175m, B. Daemmrich/The Image Works; 175 inset, NASA/The Image Works; 176 border, Marilyn "Angel" Wynn; 178b, John Coletti/Stock Boston.

Skills Handbook
Page 180, Mike Moreland/Photo Network; 181t, Foodpix; 181m, Richard Haynes; 181b, Russ Lappa; 184, Richard Haynes; 186, Ron Kimball; 187, Renee Lynn/Photo Researchers.